5-30-73

HOW

ADULTS LEARN

BY J. R. KIDD

ASSOCIATION PRESS *New York*

4th printing – 1965
5th printing – 1967
6th printing – 1968
7th printing – 1969
8th printing – 1971

Library of Congress catalog card number 59:12103

Printed in the United States of America

CONTENTS

INTRODUCTION

Homo sapiens is a strange being! Most of us, on the one hand, say that the thing which most distinguishes man from other animals is that he is able to learn, to profit from experience, to adapt, to innovate in a manner markedly different from other living inhabitants of our world. A chief attribute of the human being is *learning.* At the same time, when we speak of learning we do so as if it transpired only in a few brief years of life, something associated with childhood, that can be likened to childhood diseases, like measles.

Adults can learn! They continue to learn throughout life, right until the time when life itself is passing. Adults are, or can be, effective learners. Of course there are great differences between individuals; and the success of any learner, youth or adult, is bounded by his innate capacities. But few, if any, adults have ever approached their potential achievement in learning. We need to remember that the stoutest shackles binding an adult learner have little or nothing to do with age; they are self-imposed.

Adult learning has always gone on. But only in relatively recent times has effort been directed to systematized means for adult learning, or has there been any attention to the way adults learn. The self-learner, the man or woman who would continue to study and grow on his own, has always been known in history and literature. However, most organized efforts in adult education, in by far the majority of cases, were directed to *remedial* tasks, that is, helping an adult to gain the kind of education that he ought to have been able to have as a child.

But today learning for adults goes far beyond the remedial: it deals with all the intellectual and spiritual needs that a man or woman possesses at any time of life. Education conceived

9

as providing the adult with something he missed as a child might be planned as an adaptation of materials and methods designed for children, although this approach was rarely successful. But an education planned for free men and women, and for all their pursuits and interests, can never be designed on some childish model, or on any model other than what is suited to the learner himself.

Someone has said that the most important development of the nineteenth century, because of its influence on everything else, was the establishment of free and universal schooling for children. Of course the idea was never fully achieved anywhere and at best was limited in application to a few countries in the "Western world." A parallel phenomenon in the twentieth century is the recognition that all life is for learning, and the gradual *organization* of this idea, not just in a few countries, but in every part of the world. In some countries of the world, in the face of stark problems of ignorance, disease, and malnutrition, education has first been provided for parents, only later for children. In many countries—both those that are *developed* and those that are not—adult education is not considered a luxury or amenity, it is a social necessity. Indeed, one of the new problems respecting adult education is to balance the motives and goals of the individual who is learning with the demands and needs of society.

Adult education, then, has become an extensive activity, and it seems that we are just at the beginning. A great many people are engaged full time in work directly related to the learning of adults—for example, teachers in nightschools, librarians, managers, foremen, coaches, counselors, agricultural extension agents, trade union educational officers, program directors in social agencies. These practitioners have been trained usually in some field other than that of adult education but they are expected to display superior competence in many skills and fields of knowledge. Yet (with a few distinguished exceptions) few philosophers (even those who are identified as "educational philosophers") have paid much attention to adult learning although it is sometimes possible to make some application of general philosophical theories. There are, of course, many psychological theories about learning. Unfortunately, little has been done to bring them into any coherent *pattern* or *scheme*, and relatively little is directly applicable to adults. Of course we do not mean to argue that adults are of a different kind of species than are children, but simply to emphasize the obvious, that learning theory and practice should be concerned with the person *as he is*—not as he was, or may become. We need to give attention both to the quantitative and qualitative differences between children and adults as well as stress underlying continuities.

In a great many practical fields, such as industrial training or communications research, much is being learned *about* learning. In a very real sense, the laboratory for adult learning is not the classroom; it is found in these fields of practice. Yet seldom has application been made, beyond the immediate field itself, of what has been learned in these many promising experiments.

What is now needed is a large-minded synthesis of theory and experience regarding the learning of adults, the kind of synthesis that Plato and Thomas Aquinas provided in their respective ages. In all probability though, since so many fields of work are implicated, this synthesis may result only from the efforts of a *team* of workers. This is a very large order.

Yet in an elementary, exploratory way, something of the sort is being attempted in this book. *Why should anyone be so foolhardy?*

First of all, for at least ten years, the author has been attempting to persuade those more able than himself to undertake this assignment because he felt the need of it so keenly for his own teaching.

Second, until there is such a bringing together of theory and experience, every practitioner *has to do it anyway*. What is here being attempted is no more than every adult teacher must do, well or badly, for himself. This is a book not for theorists by a theorist, but for practitioners by a practitioner.

The book is modest enough in performance, if lofty in aim. It is conceived as an introduction, not as anything definitive. It is a *guidebook*, not a textbook. It is meant as an aid in an inquiry into what is known, what has been said, and what is being found out about adult learning. Through such a quest, it is hoped, the adult teacher or leader may be aided to build for himself a body of theory and experience to guide his practice.

Since the book is intended as an inquiry, the author will rarely impose his own opinions, notions, or theories. He is, of course, responsible for the selection and presentation of material and in this he reveals what he believes as well as some of his prejudices and limitations in understanding. On many points where there exist sharp differences of opinion he has tried to summarize the views in a fair and balanced way, believing that through further study, perhaps even through controversy, more common ground and consensus will be attained than has sometimes seemed possible. Where he may have given an improper emphasis, or has been obscure because of his efforts to be selective and to simplify, he wishes to apologize.

Because this book constitutes an inquiry, the writer has made extensive use of the experience and theories of others, including considerable direct quotation. He has also included many suggestions for further reading which are helpful, perhaps essential, if the search for understanding is to be pressed forward. The writer is indebted to many colleagues and scholars for their part in this common task.

An attempt has been made to organize the material in a fashion that is itself illustrative of good practice in adult education. Basic principles are considered and then appear and reappear, each time in a different setting, with additional illustrations. This means, of course, that there is considerable repetition of ideas and subject matter. We simply mention this as a fact, not as an apology. Some ideas can be absorbed at once, if they are presented lucidly and forcibly. Others need to be observed and tested in different contexts, over a full range of shapes and textures, before, as it has been said, "they get into the mind, the emotions, and the muscles."

The author writes about learning with a background of considerable personal observation of the remarkable achievements of people of all ages and occupations, in four different countries. He may be accused of overoptimism. But what he presents about the capacity of adults is neither sentimentality nor romanticism: it is based on observed performance under exacting conditions. More and more, as objective evidence comes in, it becomes clearer that man has only begun to use the resources of his mind and being. The author deeply believes that all human beings can be aided to become increasingly self-reliant and autonomous, that the most important single principle is that the learner be fully *engaged*, and that the main goal of adult learning is to develop men and women who are, at the same time, compassionately sensitive and tough-minded.

Chapter 1

LEARNING THROUGHOUT LIFE

It is usually considered that teaching-learning are two un-severable parts of the same process, opposite sides of the same coin. In this book, however, the emphasis is going to be placed firmly on learning. Perhaps the oldest joke about the classroom, one that was laughed at long before this century, has to do with the teacher whose sensibilities were disturbed by a boy pupil who was not given to frequent washing. A message was sent to the mother, suggesting the advisability of a bath, and back came the reply: "Tommy ain't no rose. Don't smell him, learn him." Tommy's mother may have had a naïve conception about the educational process, but her emphasis was one that we shall follow.

However, it is a fact that rarely has there been much attention given to *learning* though there has been an enormous amount of concern about *teaching*. Think of the millions of books and pamphlets in every language that have as their subject how to teach, how to train, how to instruct, how to propagandize. These books vary in quality and scope but, barring a few distinguished exceptions, by far the majority of them deal with the way one human being imposes his will, or knowledge, or skill, upon another. Consciously or unconsciously, most of them are about how a communication is shaped and directed, almost always from the point of view of the director or the fashioner or giver of that communication. In all ages, of course, wise men have recognized that learning is the active, not the passive, part of the process: the learner opens up himself, he stretches himself, he reaches out, he incorporates new experience, he relates it to his previous experience, he reorganizes this experience, he expresses or unfolds what is latent within him. The critical part of the process of teaching-learning is how the learner is aided to embark on this active, growing, changing, painful, or exhilarating experience we call learning.

We can put it another way. Most of what has been written about the practice of medicine describes how certain chemicals or herbs, and certain techniques, may be used to heal the body. Yet the most profound fact about the living body is that it is health seeking—that its forces reach out toward health and healing. The art of medicine is not so much doing things to the body but inhibiting destructive influences and enabling the body to achieve healing. It seems to be very much the same with learning. Human beings seem to seek after learning; learning seems to be a condition of a healthy organism. The objective is to provide the climate and atmosphere and freedom and self-discipline in which learning is promoted. It is not so much doing something to the body-mind-emotions but setting up the conditions whereby the person will behave in a learning way.

What a human being needs is a "fair field" for the kind of encounter that is learning. One of the best-known fables of the West is about the hardy pioneer who came face-to-muzzle, on a mountain pass, with a grizzly bear. His hasty prayer to the Almighty was that he needed no special aid—"but please don't help that bear!" Given suitable conditions men and women can be counted on to demonstrate capacity for learning. And, as we shall see in a later chapter, whether an activity is "teacher-centered" or "learner-centered" influences considerably how many facts or skills or attitudes are learned and retained.

To be sure, the dictionary definitions of learning have not always emphasized this active principle. One common definition is "to receive instruction." However, most of the other meanings offered are much more active:

> "to ascertain"
> "to find out"
> "to come to know"
> "to come to know how"
> "to acquire knowledge or skill"

"to fix in mind"
"to acquire a habit"

The dictionaries go on to note that learning happens as the result of observation, study, experience, or instruction. That is, learning may go on with or without conscious plan or direction. It is thus most easily distinguished from education by the fact that the latter word suggests conscious plan or organization of experience. Education is planned learning. Some definitions emphasize the lifelong aspect of education: "It is the systematic development and cultivation of the mind and natural powers. It begins in the nursery, continues through school, and also through life."

There is a corresponding close relationship between *learning* and intelligence. The latter word has often been defined in practice as the "capacity for learning," or "intelligence is the power to learn," particularly learning academic things, utilizing verbal and mathematical symbols. This subject will be dealt with much more thoroughly in Chapter 4.

Learning Means Change

One of the most useful descriptions of a learner was once put forward by John Dollard: "The learner is a person who wants something; the learner is a person who notices something; the learner is a person who does something; the learner is a person who gets something." Notice that these are all active verbs. Learning means change. It is not simply a matter of accretion—of adding something. There is always reorganization or restructuring. There may be *un*learning. Indeed, as we shall see, this may be the most difficult part. What there is of pain in learning is not so much coming to terms with what is new, but reorganizing what has been learned.

Usually when we speak of learning we are thinking about changes which we anticipate will occur in the learner. These may be primarily "intellectual" changes—acquiring new ideas or some reorganization of presently held ideas. The changes may be in attitude where we hope that people will come to a different appreciation and more positive feelings about a subject, not simply have more information. Or they may be changes in skill where we expect the learner to become more efficient in performing certain acts—such as operating a machine, maintaining records, submitting reports, counseling others, leading a discussion. Sometimes we hope for changes in many ways—in some combination which we may express as "better citizens," or "mature."

Recently the president of a great corporation was asked why his company spent large sums of money on the education of its executives and what outcomes had been found. Notice how, in his summary, changes of several kinds are reported:

1. There was tremendous enthusiasm on the part of each year's participants. They tell us they have increased personal identification and self-realization. In other words, this means that the men know where they are going and why, and they also know why they have chosen the path they have.
2. The changes in the men were apparent to those watching them. They have greater intellectual curiosity and self-confidence and are better able to express their ideas.
3. They tell us it has made them better family men, better citizens in their communities, and better individuals.[*1]

Learning Is Learning

This book is about the ways in which adults learn. That is its focus, and most of the examples used will be drawn from the experience of adults. We have already pointed out that what we describe as adult learning is not a different kind or order from child learning. Indeed, our main point is that man must be seen as a whole, in his lifelong development. Principles of learning will apply, in ways that we shall suggest, to all stages in life. The reason that we specify adults throughout is obvious. This is the field that has been neglected, not that of childhood.

Not only has there been neglect, but usually, except in novels and plays, adulthood is referred to as one long endless plain or desert. With such a view it doesn't much matter if adults

---

[*] Numbered footnotes are found under "References" at the end of each chapter.

can learn or not. But, seen as Havighurst sees it, adult learning becomes crucial, for the community and the race, but not less for the individual human being.

> Adulthood is not all smooth sailing across a well-charted sea with no adventures or mishaps. People do not launch themselves into adulthood with the momentum of their childhood and youth and simply coast along to old age. There are fully as many new problems to solve and new situations to grasp during the adult years as there are during the earlier periods of life. Adulthood has its transition points and its crises. It is a *developmental period* in almost as completely a sense as childhood and adolescence are developmental periods.[2]

Some Myths of Learning

Before proceeding very far it may be well to face squarely one of the most difficult obstacles to effective learning for adults. When we begin to review the data about how adults learn, we are going to note a very curious fact. We shall see that there are two main limits to human growth and development. There is the real, practical limit of one's maximum ability or potential capacity. And there is the *no less real* psychological limit which each man places upon himself. Unfortunately, it would seem that the barriers that most restrict and hobble us, the chains that bind most severely, are those which we fashion for ourselves.

Why is this? Why do we limit ourselves? Why, despite evidence to the contrary, are we so unready, so fearful of trying out and extending our powers?

This is a difficult question to which we shall return from time to time. But a part of the explanation is that much of our tradition is negative and pessimistic about human progress and growth. Myths and fables, religious literature and secular admonitions, learned histories and old wives' tales, are full of references to human inadequacy to learn. Our books, and those parts of our culture which continue to be transmitted orally, abound in myths about learning. Some are as old as the race; some we have created in our own generation. Ancient and superstition-laden or modern and pseudoscientific, these myths and lies affect all of us; for even if we do not bear their imprint, they affect those with whom we work. Part of the task for all of us is the eradication of such falsehoods and half-truths, by replacing them with sound ideas.

Of course there may be some slight aspect of truth to each. Myths or distortions of fact rarely survive unless they contain at least a vestige of truth, enough to make the barb stick. One could compile a sizable array of these myths, but we shall note only some of those which have had the most pernicious influence.

1. *You can't change human nature.* This assertion, delivered with profound confidence from the earliest of times, and often held with the deepest conviction, has been used to show how futile any attempt would be to try to do anything about slavery, or slums, or war, or child labor, or inequality of opportunity for women, or discrimination based on color or creed. Man is what he is: there is something unalterable in his nature and make-up; or so it is claimed. Of course, the truth is that human behavior, in very fundamental ways, is being changed every day, and human nature and human personality can be profoundly reshaped. Consider what was *natural* for our fathers to think and do, and compare this with how we live. Consider what was natural for millions of Asians and Africans well into this century, and what is now natural. Canadian Eskimos continue in a stone-age existence and yet are beginning to take part in the complexities of life in the twentieth century. One of the miracles of humankind is the extraordinary capacity of men and women for change and growth. In the past fifty years our notions about what is specifically human nature have been radically altered, due in part to the evidence about different cultures, supplied by the anthropologists.

2. *You can't teach an old dog new tricks.* Our canine-loving friends have been quick to point out that this is a vile lie, perpetrated and repeated by those who are ignorant about dogs. But of course the charge has been employed for centuries to describe men and women. That it is equally wide of the mark when applied to them will be the main subject of

Chapters 3 and 4. Still, it is an observation you will hear again and again. But before you accept any part of the slander, read carefully the evidence about the capacity of adults to learn found in this book and in the suggested readings.

3. *The "hole in the head" theory of learning.* Many people, some of them quite sensible in other respects, talk about learning as if it were some process by which an entrance is somehow forced into the brain and facts are poured in, or pressed in, or stamped in. The process is seen as a simple one. Organize your facts carefully; use repetition and other devices to be sure that they are properly injected into the mind. One concomitant of this notion is that the heads and minds of children are regarded as being easier to penetrate, as less cluttered than those of adults. The attic isn't yet stuffed with the accumulation of the years and something more may be put in. This is a fantastic theory, much too silly to be dignified by a refutation. It had the appearance of truth only in such eras when there was little social change. But if you will listen and look carefully during any Education Week you are almost certain to hear sermons or speeches, or to read articles in reputable newspapers and magazines in which these conceptions are developed with authority and rhetoric.

4. *The all-head notion of learning.* Many people think about and talk about learning as if it were completely an affair of the mind. They claim that it is entirely a rational, intellectual process. According to this theory learning is not particularly difficult to understand. You simply select and arrange the content of your subject in a rigorously rational way, and present it to the student. However, unfortunately for this notion, man is actually much more than mind and intellect. Most of us have become increasingly aware that man is a creature of emotions and feelings, and that these have an important part in learning, It has long been recognized that in childhood, emotion is a dominant influence and that one must understand this fact when dealing with the young. But some have assumed that for the mature an intellectual approach is all that is needed. Worse still, *intellectual* has often been an euphemism for *dull.*

5. *The "bitter-sweet" notions.* These are two equally fallacious and contradictory views. The first is that learning cannot happen at all unless it is exciting and exhilarating. Unless it is easy and delightful, no learning. Now most of us know from our own experience that much of learning is difficult, wearing, repetitive—the hardest kind of hard work, which we accept only because of the importance of objectives we seek and the satisfactions we shall earn. Yet, we are told by the advocates of the "fun and games" approach that drudgery and effort can be eliminated, that rich, insightful learning can be painless. Of course, some who are attracted by these claims may become quickly disillusioned.

Just as dishonest, and perhaps even more baleful in result, are the views of those who proclaim that there is no learning except when accompanied by harsh unpleasantness. If you will listen to some convocation addresses, or the talk of elderly educational administrators, you will find that it is not uncommon to hear one state, "It doesn't much matter what one studies so long as one detests or hates it sufficiently." It has frequently been claimed that the worth of learning lies in the transformation of the human personality through stern, disagreeable, painful discipline. This perversion of the Puritan ethic is surprisingly widespread. Unfortunately, the effect is to cause most normal human beings to recoil in disgust.

6. *The mental age of the average adult is twelve years.* One of the characteristics of our times is that we pretend to be a little scornful of the fables, superstitions, and myths of previous ages. But that has not prevented us from creating some of our own. A successful myth must always have the appearance of reality and wear some of the coloration of its time of origin. Myths, to be accepted in our era, are all likely to have some appearance of science, to seem to depend upon scientific inquiry for justification. An excellent example of such a myth is, "The mental age of the average adult is twelve years." This is such a perversion, such a misinterpretation of psychological research data, that if its effects were not so serious it could be dismissed as a schoolboy howler, in the same class as "Geometry teaches us to prove what we already

know to be true" and "Ambiguity means telling the truth without intending to." This myth, like Minerva, sprang up full-armed.

In the American army during World War I there was, for the first time, an opportunity to give thousands of men "intelligence" tests. The tests used were mostly based on academic materials, employed "norms" based on the performance of children, had rigid time limits, and were given to men who, on the average, had had only a few years of schooling. Men tested in this way made average scores which corresponded to the average scores of school children of the years twelve, thirteen, and fourteen. Most of the psychologists understood these results and treated them for what they were. However, some people compared the scores of men and children in school in a way that was completely unwarranted and which led to the foolish assertion that the mental age of service men (and therefore presumably of adults generally) was twelve years. (Sometimes this has been stated as thirteen, sometimes as fourteen.) One might have expected that such a palpable blunder would have been washed away in gales of laughter. Unfortunately it stuck; it has been repeated thousands of times; and, despite the vast amount of evidence to the contrary, it continues to be repeated. If, for example, you ask those responsible for some of the most inane, repetitive film, radio, or television shows, why they choose the content and style that they do, they are quite likely to tell you seriously that their show is aimed at the "average adult who has a twelve-year-old intelligence." This notion has been used with such destructive consequences that we shall return to its discussion in Chapter 4. One aspect of this may need a special footnote—the frequency with which the results of observations of animals or children are applied to adults, as if a man were only a "great big boy." The adult is *not* just a larger child: the cells of his body are different, his experiences are vastly different. Data derived from research with children are only useful if applied with care and if rigorously checked against adult experience as well as with data collected from systematic observation of adults. This is elementary enough, but it is a point that is frequently overlooked.

7. *Unless you have a high IQ, all hope abandon.* This is a strange notion that also has achieved widespread circulation. No sensible person would ever deny the importance of intellectual capacity. We shall all want to cherish every vestige of intellect that can be mustered and seek to encourage its unfolding and development in every child and adult. But there is a great part of human life, human achievement, and human dignity, that is not at all comprehended by even the best intellectual standards. There are other kinds of worthiness to be sought after and nourished. Concentrating all attention on what is measured by rather imperfect instruments (the "intelligence tests") is to omit much of what is richest in life.

Growing Acceptance

But enough of these myths, for, although the continued repetition of error is harmful in its effect, perhaps beyond what we can estimate, there has been at the same time an increasing acceptance of a contrary view, *that adults can learn effectively.* It would be wrong to suggest that such an idea attained recognition only during our own time. The achievements of some older men and women (such as Goethe's writing great literature when over eighty), and the success of older people's learning new skills or knowledge, have always been known about. But for the most part these were considered exceptions to the general rule.

Teachers of adults, as far as they were able, strove to correct false claims. "We have known," wrote Robert Peers, "each in his own experience, hundreds of cases of men and women for whom, at the beginning, serious reading was an effort and the putting together of a few sentences in writing a terrifying task, who have overcome these difficulties in their tutorial classes and, by the end of their courses, have acquired new intellectual interests and new powers of expression in speech and writing."[3]

One of the most decisive checks to outworn notions came

with the printing of E. L. Thorndike's book, *Adult Learning*[4] in 1928. Upon its publication the book was hailed as a foundation stone for adult education and was widely quoted. Thorndike bluntly asserted that all adults can learn, that in all probability they can learn all they need to learn, and that the quality of adult learning is substantial. He was able to marshal considerable evidence from his studies to support these contentions. One hears less of *Adult Learning* these days but in all probability it will always be regarded as a landmark effort in the long uphill struggle to provide education for everyone.

In previous centuries learning was rarely considered a field for psychological or sociological inquiry. Views about learning were much more likely to be associated with philosophy or theology. The conception of how a man learned was intimately tied up with one's general view of man. If one believed, for example, that man was sinful and lost, then it might also be concluded that learning must always be accompanied by pain, hardships, and chastisement.

However, with the systematic development of the social sciences during the nineteenth century, first in Germany and then elsewhere, speculation began to be replaced by direct observation of behavior and by theories deduced from this observation. Experimental psychologists were quite early attracted to the study of learning. Initially they began to watch the behavior of animals, later of children, still later of adults who were living in various kinds of institutions such as sanitariums or reformatories. Only recently has there been much attention given to those of older age, and observations and study of the "normal" adult in the middle years have hardly happened yet, although in the work of Havighurst and others there are promising beginnings. As we shall see, there has always been some application of learning theory to adults, but this has been sporadic.

In the past two decades in particular there have been a number of developments which when brought together may provide considerable information about adult learning. This has come about in many ways: through the work of anthropologists, social psychologists, psychiatrists, and counselors;

from such fields as linguistics (how a man may learn and begin to think with new symbols), gerontological research, training programs in industry and in various military services; from communication research and theory, to mention only some of the fields. In Chapter 8 an attempt will be made to review a few of these developments and make a rough assessment of their importance. It is heartening that the Fund for Adult Education has recently commissioned the Bureau of Applied Social Sciences at Columbia University to bring together results of research from many fields that have a bearing on this subject.[5]

What Is Learning?

The title of this book is *How Adults Learn*. In one sense there is no answer to this question, just as there is no answer to the question, "What is electricity?" Once a student was asked that question and, very puzzled, he replied, "I did know, but I forgot." The professor smote his brow. "My God! The only man who ever knew what electricity is has forgotten!"

We know how to make electricity, or at least how to induce it, but it still defies definition. Augustine once said, "I understand what time is, but don't ask me." Similarly, though we cannot pin down anything as dynamic as learning in any way that is thoroughly satisfying, we can observe it, note its course and its character.

Part of the problem comes about because of the various uses to which the term *learning* is put. Kenneth Benne identifies three of the main uses:

- Learning may be thought of as acquisition and mastery by a person of what is already known on some subject.
- Learning may also be thought of as the extension and clarification of meanings of one's own individual experience.
- Learning is a process (in which) one tests ideas and generalizations relevant to some delimitable problems, and tests them in some more or less objectified and controlled experiences designed for the purpose.[6]

We have already stated that learning results in certain kinds of changes, the most common being the committing to memory of facts, the acquiring or improvement of a skill or process, the development of a changed attitude. Does the process of change in each case have enough similarity so that each can be termed learning without ambiguity? That is, is learning always the same thing? Let us suppose, for a moment, that in some foreign language separate words were used to denote each of these processes, for example:

- *Xing*   facts and information
- *Ying*   the forehand drive in tennis
- *Zing*   to live and work with people of another color

This might lead to clearer understanding. But then, of course, we should be obliged to seek relationships between the three notions and words. So we might as well stick to English!

But we need to pay attention to the entire process of learning, including the establishment of goals and objectives, the development of a curriculum or program, establishing the requirements and conditions of learning, and evaluating the changes in behavior that constitute learning.

The Development of Learning Objectives

There are at least three main sources of educational goals—(1) what a person is like and what are his needs, (2) the opportunities and demands of contemporary society, and (3) the main fields of knowledge. We shall deal more fully with this subject in Chapter 10.

Having identified a great number of possible learning objectives in these three ways, we must employ some means of selecting those objectives which are of greatest relevance. There are again three main ways of doing this, as it were, three *screens* through which these many objectives may be filtered, so that only the most significant remain. One such screen is made up of the nature and character of the organization or community in which we work. A second major screen comes from our understanding of the learning process itself, with which much of this book will deal directly. And the third, and very important, is our educational philosophy.

This is not a book about educational philosophy except that every word in it is marked or marred by the author's understanding and beliefs about the nature and purpose of education. Long ago a well-known teacher was asked, "Where in your timetable do you teach religion?" "We teach it all day long," he answered. "We teach it in Arithmetic by accuracy. We teach it in Geography by breadth of mind. We teach it in Astronomy by reverence. We teach it in the playground by fair play. We teach it by kindness to animals, by good manners to one another, by truthfulness in all things." Just as one's philosophy is expressed, is worked out in every educational activity, so one cannot consider any aspect of learning without considering the ends of learning.

However, as indicated earlier, the purpose of this book is a *quest,* a *search* for a body of ideas, theories, and experience which will guide practical workers in many fields of adult learning. It is probably no longer necessary to justify the importance of theory. Theory is usually the result of the distillation of practice. Nothing is so practical as good theory. Put in the words of the old saw—theory without practice is empty, and practice without theory is blind. What we shall try to do constantly is to show the balanced relationship between learning practice and learning theory. Our effort will also be to discover agreement and integration of views wherever this exists or seems to be possible. We shall not evade or gloss over the real and important differences of view that exist. But all these issues we shall treat as questions for further speculation and investigation, rather than as matters of faith or ideology on which we must now take a stand or "break a lance."

One can identify at least a dozen distinct philosophical points of view held by practitioners in adult education. For our purposes though, we shall deal with three major tendencies or emphases. Note that they are just that, *points of emphasis;* they are not fully articulated philosophic schools or theories.

One such stress is upon the development of the *intelligent, rational, humane individual,* who becomes so in large measure through intensive study of certain forms and fields of knowledge. Some urge that this result is achieved through vigorous study of mathematics and sciences. For others, like Sir Richard Livingstone, the heart of the study is history and literature. For Mortimer Adler it is in the "Great Books."

> The program of adult learning must be something that will sustain learning through 20, 30, or 40 years; something that treats adults as adults, not as children in school, something they can do voluntarily; something that fits them as adults or mature persons. . . . The Great Books deal with the basic problems, both theoretical and practical, of yesterday and today and tomorrow, the basic issues that always have and always will confront mankind. The ideas they contain are the ideas all of us have to think about. The Great Books represent the fund of human wisdom, at least so far as our culture is concerned, and it is this reservoir that we must draw upon to sustain our learning for a lifetime.[7]

Others would hasten to add, while possibly in agreement with the goal as stated, that *means* must be considered at the same time as goals. S. M. Corey once said, in an address:

> Students who spend a great deal of time reading and discussing Great Books are learning primarily how to read and discuss Great Books. They are not necessarily learning how to behave in harmony with the principles elucidated in the Great Books. . . . If students get a great deal of practice following directions which members of the faculty give them, these student primarily are learning better how to follow the directions given them by members of the faculty. They are not necessarily learning to be resourceful and to stand on their own feet and to identify problems as well as methods of solutions of these problems.

Another kind of emphasis is upon *effective functioning,* not just upon a man of ideas or knowledge or humane principles but one who is equipped and able to take his part as father, workman, voter, or, if necessary, soldier. He becomes this way, most would urge, through disciplined study and practice that is based upon his roles in the family and community. Some stress the community as a starting point for this development; others, as in the Antigonish Movement in Nova Scotia, start with his economic interests, and broaden out from there.

A third kind of emphasis is upon the special demands upon an adult *in a democracy*. Robert Hutchins once stated this notion in striking form: "The foundation of democracy is universal suffrage. Universal suffrage makes every man a ruler. If every man is a ruler, every man needs the education that rulers ought to have."[8] Here such characteristics are favored as concern about the common weal, ability to take self-initiated action, responsibility for choice and direction of action, ability for critical observation and thinking, capacity for adaptation and application of what has been learned.

Some Issues to Be Considered

A number of practical questions have arisen on which there are differences of opinion. These have sometimes grown out of philosophic inquiry or sometimes out of the practical day-to-day problems of those engaged in adult education. We shall state some of them here, without comment, simply to anticipate and open up some of the central problems affecting adult learning. In succeeding chapters considerable information about each of them will be presented. Here the extremes are stated in sharp contrast for the sake of clarity, but this does not necessarily represent positions that are actually held.

This list is not exhaustive. The reader will want to place some of his own queries here in this context:

The needs of the individual *contrasted with* the needs of society?

Is adult learning concerned primarily with the clarification of ideas and intellectual processes	or preparing the learner for action in community or society?
Emphasis upon the group:	does this pose any threat to the individual?
Should the curriculum satisfy what the adult says he wants	or what he ought to have?

Should the curriculum be selected, organized, and evaluated by a "teacher"	or by those taking part in the educational program?
Are the requirements of the *adult* learner significantly different	from those of the child?
Should stress be placed on the content and subject matter of adult education	or upon the methods of adult education?
Should the primary content of adult education be based on the humanities	or the social sciences?
Should the teacher of adults have a "permissive" philosophy	or seek to bring about changes in the adult student?
Does the investing of many social agencies and social processes with education	spoil spontaneity, destroy enthusiasm, and inhibit action?

The Plan of the Book

We have already stated that our purpose is to assist an inquiry by practitioners in adult education leading to the organization of a body of theory and experience to guide their practice.

First of all, we shall deal with the learner himself, his personality, his physical changes, intellectual development, and the role of motives and emotions in learning.

Next, we shall select from the wealth of theory some of those formulations which seem to help us understand the learner and learning.

We shall also sample a number of fields of practice, where learning *about* learning is taking place. Attention will also be given to the forms and arrangements for learning, how organization and administration may condition and modify learning. In summarizing, we shall review some of the main features of the teaching-learning transaction—and finally, the particular role of the teacher or practitioner.

REFERENCES

1. Wilfred D. Gillin, *Toward the Liberally Educated Executive* (White Plains, N. Y.: Fund for Adult Education, 1957).

2. Robert J. Havighurst, *Social Roles of the Middle-Aged Person* (Chicago: Center for the Study of Liberal Education for Adults, 1955).
3. Robert Peers, *Adult Education* (New York: Humanities Press, Inc., 1958).
4. E. L. Thorndike, *Adult Learning* (New York: The Macmillan Company, 1928). By permission of Teachers College, Columbia University, New York, copyright owners.
5. E. deS. Brunner and Others, *An Overview on Adult Education Research* (Chicago: Adult Education Association, 1959).
6. Kenneth D. Benne, "Some Philosophic Issues in Adult Education," *Adult Education* (Chicago: Adult Education Association, hereafter designated as AEA), Vol. 7, No. 2.
7. Mortimer Adler, *Adult Education*, a lecture reprinted by the Great Books Foundation, 1952, copyright owners.
8. Robert M. Hutchins, "Education and Democracy," *School and Society*, 1949, Vol. 69.

Suggested Reading

ADULT EDUCATION ASSOCIATION, *Seeking Common Ground in Adult Education* (Chicago: AEA, 1959).
ADULT EDUCATION ASSOCIATION, "Workshop—Special Problems in Adult Education," *Adult Leadership* (Chicago: AEA), Vol. 5, No. 10.
BLAKELY, R. J., *Adult Education for a Free Society* (Toronto: Guardian Bird Publications, 1958).
BODE, BOYD H., *How We Learn* (New York: D. C. Heath and Company, 1940).
GETZELS, J. W., *Learning Theory and Classroom Practice in Adult Education* (Syracuse: Syracuse University, 1959).
MURPHY, GARDNER, and KUHLEN, RAYMOND, *Psychological Needs of Adults* (Chicago: Center for the Study of Liberal Education for Adults, 1955).
SCHWARTZ, MILTON M., and HARRISON, IRVINE L., *The Learning Process* (New Brunswick, N. J.: Institute of Management and Labor Relations, Rutgers University, 1956).

Chapter 2

THE ADULT LEARNER

We have already discovered that the term *learning* is used in several different ways and that our central question, *"How do adults learn?"* is not one that can be answered directly. We shall now begin to get further understanding of the term by paying particular attention to the *learner*.

In Chapter 3 we shall consider changes in the learner's physical and sensory capacity and ways in which this may affect his capacity for learning. In Chapter 4 we shall deal with intellectual changes; in Chapter 5, with the effect of emotions; in Chapter 6, with motivation. But before considering these aspects of the learner we need to think of him as a *whole*, as a person. We don't want to fall into such a trap as to consider body or mind or emotions as separate entities.

What do we know about the adult learner that helps us to understand him?

At first glance it seems not very much. We noted in Chapter 1 that the middle years of adulthood are *terra incognita*, that they have rarely been studied systematically. Any chart of the middle years is likely to be somewhat like that described in a verse by Lewis Carroll:

He had bought a large map representing the sea
Without the least vestige of land
And the crew were much pleased when they found it to be
A map they could all understand.

And about as useful, for predicting the shoals and hazards, or safe passages of life.

However, we need not be too pessimistic. A good deal is known even though it has not all been brought together. For example, a growing number of studies[1] have come out in the past few years about the adult student.

33

Studies About the Adult as a Student

University extension departments and boards of education have begun to collect information much more systematically about the age, sex, occupation, previous educational experience, and achievements of their adult students. Until recently these facts were not obtained in any uniform way and rarely, if ever, were efforts made to find out much about such important matters as the previous educational experience of the students. Even now "follow-up" studies are relatively rare, and so it has been difficult to trace the record of progress of many students. However, more information is becoming available. The number of adult students in the United States is very high indeed and growing rapidly, although differences of opinion exist about the totals. One observer reports 15 million in 1924 and an estimated 22 million in 1934, 30 million in 1950, and 50 million in 1955, with marked growth since 1955.[2] This huge estimate includes many informal activities as well as formal. A recent census study placed the number of participants in formal classes at 8,270,000, or about 7.8 per cent of the out-of-school population above the age of 14.[3] Even if we accept the most conservative figure, there is still a very sizable "student body."

Moreover, the average age for leaving school is still rising. We shall see in Chapter 4 what an important effect this has upon the ability of the adult to perform academic kinds of tasks, the kind measured on an "intelligence" test. Adults of all ages are "going back to school," the increase in all ages is more noticeable than that in any particular age group. Of course, at any particular time this distribution may be affected by a special event. For example, provision of education of all kinds for veterans raised appreciably the number of men and women in their twenties and thirties taking full-time or part-time studies. Over the next two decades it is certain that the percentage of older people enrolling will markedly increase, due both to the increasing proportion of older people in the total population and to the number of new opportunities for education and recreation being planned specially for older people.

In a recent book entitled *Classrooms in the Factories*[4] the authors pointed out that corporations have educational programs for workmen and executives that in many ways rival those in colleges and universities. Thousands of men and women are enrolled in technical and academic classes and, in many cases, undertake advanced work in the natural sciences and sometimes in the social sciences and humanities.

Studies are beginning to appear which deal with the motives with which adult students enter upon a course of study. Robert Love[5] found that these are often highly complex. Two factors, at least, were present before adults enrolled in his institution: the student had an awareness of education as a positive value in solving problems and, at the same time, a belief that education is somehow equated with happiness and success. This and similar studies begin to explain some of the mistakes and failures that can occur, where the student may have an unrealistic view of the possibilities and values of his planned course of learning. Bernard James[6] has written that adult students who came to his class in "creative writing," ostensibly to learn how to write, in reality felt that they already knew how, but hoped to obtain some gimmick or acquire a slick style so that they could sell their wares.

The author once was interviewing a student who was registering for a course in calculus. In the conversation that ensued, the prospective student reported that he had gone only as far as the third grade in public school. When asked why he was enrolling for a course in higher mathematics he said, "You see, I used to work in the fifteen-cent store. I could figure prices and things pretty well. But now I am in a wholesale grocery and I have to multiply things like $37\frac{1}{2}$ dozen eggs times $57\frac{1}{2}$ cents. Hell, that's higher mathematics, ain't it?"

What about achievement of the adult student? Knowing as we do that there is a widespread belief that adults do not learn well, one might expect that this belief would have been based, in part at least, on poor class performance. One might even have assumed that in comparison with daytime college students, adult students would not show up well when tested on the same examinations. However, *such is not the case*. In almost every single example where comparative results have been obtained, the adult student has obtained equal or better results than the daytime student.

In 1933 Herbert Sorenson made a thorough study of adult ability, and reports as one of his main conclusions:

> The evidence indicates that the measured abilities of extension and nonextension students are essentially equal. In some universities the extension students have higher abilities and in others the full-time students are slightly superior; but the differences are not very large at any university. They do indicate, however, that any existing superiority is found within the adult group.[7]

Nearly twenty years later John Dyer[8] reported that the superior adult student is as good as, or better than, the superior day student, and the average students in both classifications are about equal.

As we shall see later, the adult student tends to do better in some subjects like history or literature than he does in subjects like mathematics or physics. Although studies of this sort are limited to university and nightschool fields it is already clear, however, that adult performance on academic tests warrants the fullest opportunity for adults to enter any field of scholarship.

As far as the evidence goes there do not appear to be significant differences between the sexes at any time during adulthood, either in achievement on tests or in learning capacity.

It has long been known that adults will read books that are accessible to them much more often than those which they claim that they want to read. Similarly, some studies have indicated that adults seem to take part in educational activities that are close at hand more often than those in which they claim to be interested but which are more remote in time or place.

There is now appearing evidence from research to support the contentions by sociologists such as Hallenbeck[9] that adults will readily engage in learning activities associated with certain major social goals, such as obtaining improved housing. As we have noted in another context, this is the basis for much adult education associated with "community development" all over the world.

One kind of evidence shows up both with remarkable clarity and consistency: that is, that social attitudes vary directly with the *amount* of education. Adults with less education tend to have less regard for civil liberties, less tolerance for groups other than their own, and to hold more authoritarian attitudes.

The Adult—in What Ways Different from the Child?

People in adult education have always faced a dilemma. They were obliged to show a difference between children and adults that would justify special planning and yet do no violence to their understanding of the continuity of life, or their belief that the learner can and must be seen as one developing personality all through life.

Schools and colleges have traditionally planned with needs of children or youths in mind. Accordingly, if it was assumed that what was being offered was *education,* then if an adult wanted education he ought to take what was offered. It actually happened for many years that many adults seeking an education not only took a curriculum designed for children, were taught by teachers whose only experience was with children, but were obliged to sit at desks built for children.

Now most educationalists agree that curriculum and methods should be related both to the goals of education and to the needs of the student.

Are adults different only in that their bodies cannot easily be crammed into children's desks? Or are their needs and their experience so varied that there should be special provision of facilities, curricula, teaching style, texts and study materials, methods of instruction?

More and more evidence has been accumulating that justifies a special attack on adult learning. We shall not present this evidence here because much of it will come out in the subsequent chapters. Instead, we shall simply illustrate this whole problem by selecting four of many ways in which an adult learner may perceive, or understand, or feel differently than a youth does about what he is learning.

No "correct" answer. Most of the significant problems faced by an adult do not have a "correct" answer in the sense that the answer can be verified to the point that doubt or uncertainty is removed. This uncertainty usually characterizes problems in business, or marital relations, or politics. On the other hand, for most classroom problems of young people there is a "correct" answer, in the back of the book or elsewhere.

"Correctness" associated with traditions or religion. The situation for the adult learner may be further complicated because for many problems, though there may be no answer that will stand up to rigorous rational tests, some answers are regarded as being "correct" in terms of tradition, or cultural habits, or religion, or an institution. The adult, more than the child, is bound by these stereotypes of what is "correct" and though modification is always possible, such modifications may have to run the gauntlet of rigid internal and external pressures to the contrary.

Solutions have effects! Any solution that an adult gives to a problem is likely to have its immediate effects upon other individuals. In regard to personal problems or labor-management discussions, what he decides to do will implicate others and he must take these possible implications into account. Many social problems might be "solved" theoretically, but a real-life solution may not seem immediately possible because of the human personalities involved. However, it should not be forgotten that one of the most important purposes of adult education is to give adults the opportunity to work out solutions free from the high, perhaps dangerously high, cost of error. By using role playing, for example, the learner may investigate the kinds of feelings that are associated with deeply disturbing emotional or social conflicts such as the "integration of a school" and try out actual solutions of these conflicts under conditions in which real life is simulated, but where the effects of a "mistake" are not disastrous.

Expectations of the "student" and "teacher" may be different. The child comes to school more or less to learn what the school is teaching. The adult may and often does bring quite different views to the classroom from those held by the teacher. This may result in conflict. The teacher may perceive this difference as undesirable: for example, as a failure by the adult to appreciate the subject or the worth of high standards. The adult learner may even feel guilty about his expectations. But the tension set up between the expectations of the teacher and learner is not necessarily undesirable; it can be the basis for effective learning by *both.*

Exploring Useful Hypotheses About Adult Learning

Any search or inquiry must proceed in part through the examination of certain hunches, guesses, notions, or hypotheses. Since, by many, adult learning was considered only as *remedial,* the number of conceptions designed to guide or challenge observation and reflection have not been plentiful. However, a change is also coming in this respect. We shall now summarize a few of these notions simply to note the light they cast upon learning, the objectives they raise to be tested or evaluated, and the critical questions they suggest. Again we have not included here all the notions worthy of attention but have selected a few for illustrative purposes.

The usefulness of such concepts can be illustrated negatively as well as positively. For example, take a trait such as intellectual curiosity. It is often said that every child is born with curiosity and that it is basic to much of learning, to man's intellectual progress, and to the advancement of science. Ordway Tead once wrote that a central purpose of college is to encourage "the student's sense of the wonder and mystery of life and reverence for living it. . . . His sense of curiosity and his grasp of the operating meaning of rationality should be fostered in every course."[10] But some people charge that the schools damage or destroy this priceless gift. Adult education is supposed to rekindle the fires of curiosity which somehow have been quenched. Now if we knew what curiosity is, or how it manifests itself, how it is cultivated or stunted, it might be of great value. But there has not yet been much careful work defining what curiosity is *in terms of behavior,* or establishing hypotheses for testing; to the point that the notion of curiosity is of much practical use for experiment.

These are some of the concepts that have yielded useful hypotheses for investigation:

- the life span
- maturation
- adult experience
- the self-educating adult
- the significance of "time"

THE LIFE SPAN

It is not a strange or radical idea that if we are to have much understanding of the nature of human beings, we ought to consider the whole span of life, the growth or development of man through all his years. However, it is a surprising fact that except for a few life insurance tables, and some isolated research reports, there are scarcely any such studies or organized bodies of data.

We have hundreds of studies about the child; the child of one week, the child of two weeks, the child of six months. There are also innumerable books about personality changes in children, about health, intellectual development, and hundreds of other aspects. We also have scores of studies about various phases of adolescence. In recent years there have been an increasing number of studies of older people, particularly those of advanced years. For the middle years there is a handful of highly specialized reports. But there is practically nothing which deals with the full-life development of man in any comprehensive way, at least as it affects learning. It is almost as if we assumed that all of adulthood was identical; that it progressed at the same pace, in the same directions, on the same plane.

But what a denial this is of human experience! Every minister, historian, poet, or novelist knows better.

In the last decade or so, some scholarly texts have begun to deal with this fact with the same understanding that religion and literature have always had. The successive editions of a medical text entitled *Problems of Ageing*[11] have made a genuine contribution because much of the material is presented in developmental terms. More recent is the book of Sidney L. Pressey and Raymond G. Kuhlen, entitled *Psychological Development Through the Life Span*,[12] which is a reworking of a pioneer effort by the same authors, formerly entitled *Life, a Psychological Survey*.

The results of these development studies are certain to have their effect on the curriculum, the facilities planned for adults, and methods and techniques. As we shall see in Chapter 3 the variations in sensory capacity over the years are of surprising magnitude.

Recently a national conference was considering some of the tasks of middle age, all of which involve substantial changes and require considerable learning:

- setting adolescent children free and helping them to become responsible adults
- discovering new satisfactions in relations with one's spouse
- working out a satisfying relationship with aging parents
- creating a home which has a new focus as the children leave
- reaching the peak of one's work career
- achieving mature social and civic responsibility
- accepting and adjusting to psychological changes
- making an art of friendship
- making a satisfying and creative use of leisure time
- becoming or maintaining oneself as a member of an active organization or church member.

For each of the overlapping stages of life an equally formidable list of learning opportunities and obligations can be stated. Interest in the development of man through successive states is beginning to increase and in its train the kind of inquiries that will probably modify common views about adult learning.

MATURATION

A most useful conception in adult education is that of *maturity* or *maturation*. The word maturity has been used so often, so loosely, and to cover so many ideas, that for a while, it appeared that it might lose most of its meaning and usefulness and become a spineless synonym for "good." Fortunately, it now seems to be becoming invested with new meaning, giving forth a number of hypotheses which are being studied.

A number of writers such as Angyal[13] and Snygg,[14] have pointed out that the human organism develops in certain predictable ways. It seems to move toward greater independence and greater self-responsibility. The tendency is in the direction of increasing self-government, self-regulation and autonomy, and away from reliance upon control from external forces. This seems to be true equally when we are speaking of organic processes that are not conscious, such as the changing amount of water content in the body, or such intellectual functions as choosing what a person will do with his life. The human organism does not become highly specialized as most animals have done. It does not seem to exploit some possibilities open to it; for example, the capacity for enduring pain or enduring terror (although both might be necessary under some modern inhumane conditions). Becoming mature, for the human species, means a greater differentiation of organs and of function, through extending itself by the use of tools. It seems, also, that man develops in the direction of socialization. Robert Blakely has aptly described this human condition:

Man is the most highly adaptable form of life. . . .
Man makes the tools and machines that make further physical evolution unnecessary. Does he want to hunt like the bear? He invents the spear. Does he want to dive like the fish? He invents the submarine. Does he want to fly like the bird? He invents the airplane. There is no end in sight: yet he himself remains unspecialized. He takes on and puts off at will the

specialized organs and capacities that encumber the bear, the whale and the eagle.

To do all this man had to become social. This meant language and culture. Language and culture meant something astoundingly new—the transmission of experience and knowledge. What one man discovered, all men could learn. What one generation accomplished, the next could build upon.[15]

Many writers, such as Riesman, have been noting with concern the tendency for modern man to become "outer-directed," to conform, to lose his autonomy. *The Lonely Crowd*[16] describes in detail what pressures are exerted on all of us. The dangers are real enough. But what is equally real is the human tendency to resist, the will to grow. In a memorable sentence, Karen Horney writes: ". . . the ultimate driving force is the person's unrelenting will to come to grips with himself, a wish to grow and leave nothing untouched that prevents growth."[17] Carl Rogers has summarized the same tendencies, based on his practice:

> I find that the urge for a great degree of independence, the desire for a self-determined integration, the tendency to strive, even through much pain, toward a socialized maturity, is as strong as—no, is stronger than—the desire for a comfortable dependence, the need to rely upon external authority for assurance. . . . Clinically I find it to be true that though an individual may remain dependent because he has always been so, or may drift into dependence without realizing what he is doing, or may temporarily wish to be dependent because his situation seems to be desperate, I have yet to find the individual who, when he examines his situation deeply, and feels that he perceives it clearly, deliberately chooses dependence, deliberately chooses to have the integrated direction of himself undertaken by another. When all the elements are clearly perceived, the balance seems invariably in the direction of the painful but ultimately rewarding path of self-actualization or growth.[18]

These writers assert that it is part of the nature of man to grow toward self-direction, self-discipline, autonomy. Some call this tendency maturation.

One well-known statement of this view is that of Overstreet in *The Mature Mind*.[19] In this book the author brings together findings from psychology, sociology, anthropology, and psychiatry, attempting to fuse them into a harmonized view of what makes for maturity in human behavior. The mature person, he says, is one "whose linkages with life are constantly becoming stronger and richer because his attitudes are such as to encourage their growth rather than their stoppage." These attitudes are directed toward knowledge, social responsibility, vocational adjustment, skill in communicating, and social relationships. Overstreet believes that maturing in respect to any one of these has an influence on development over all the others.

Another useful formulation of maturity, applied to reading, has been developed by William S. Gray and Bernice Rogers. In their study, reported in the book *Maturity in Reading*,[20] the authors distinguished a number of characteristics of the mature reader:

- A genuine enthusiasm for reading
- Tendency to read (a) a wide variety of materials that contribute pleasure, widen horizons, and stimulate creative thinking; (b) serious materials which promote a growing understanding of one's self, of others, and of problems of a social, moral, and ethical nature; and (c) intensively in a particular field or materials relating to a central core
- Ability to translate words into meanings, to secure a clear grasp and understanding of the ideas presented, and to sense clearly the mood and feelings intended
- Capacity for and habit of making use of all that one knows or can find out in interpreting or construing the meaning of the ideas read
- Ability to perceive strengths and weaknesses in what is read and to detect bias and propaganda, and to think critically concerning the validity and values of the idea presented, and the adequacy or soundness of the author's presentation, views and conclusions
- Tendency to fuse the new ideas acquired through reading with previous experience, thus acquiring new or clearer understandings, broadened interests, rational attitudes, improved patterns of thinking and behaving, and richer and more stable personalities

- Capacity to adjust one's reading pace to the needs of the occasion and to the demands of adequate interpretation.

This list raises a number of questions which can be refined, tested, and evaluated.

It also suggests similar formulations which might be attempted; for example, what "mature" means in speech, or in writing, or in group discussion.

ADULT EXPERIENCE

We have already noted the danger of so emphasizing the differences associated with growing older that we lose sight of the underlying continuities in life.

Nevertheless, a principal factor—for some *the* principal factor[21]—in adult learning is the comparatively richer experience of the adult and what use is made of this in the learning transaction.

There are three related notions here:

- Adults have *more* experiences.
- Adults have different *kinds* of experiences.
- Adult experiences are *organized differently.*

These points seem self-evident. An adult's sexual or social experiences are of a kind that mark him off from the world of children. The same can be said of experiences of a job, or politics, or war. But this point has not always been understood or accepted. We have noted that it is forgotten or explicitly denied in the many cases where a curriculum for adults is simply something "warmed over" that had been designed for youth.

In the adult years, despite all tendencies to conformity, the range of experience from adult to adult is greater than among children. Moreover, adults generally have dealings with individuals of all ages; in some societies this used to be true of everyone, but at present children outside of their own family meet individuals of other ages in rather formal ways.

Inquiries are now going forward to examine these differences quantitatively, to discover their qualitative aspects, and to identify the kinds of experience that may dispose the adult toward effective and continuous learning. Past experience provides life examples for generalizing. Moreover, the *emotional tone* of these experiences may result in readiness for, or may increase resistance to, learning. Such hypotheses are being developed and tested; for example, that adults have an ability superior to young people in learning *relationally*. That is, they have more capacity, not just to memorize facts or understand ideas but to perceive how these facts affect themselves or others.[22]

In addition, there has been considerable research in regard to the effect of experience upon perception itself. This can be best illustrated from the results of a single ingenious experiment. The experimenter put a blob of red on a card and flashed it before the eyes of the adult students for a fraction of a second, and asked them what they saw. All of them said that they saw *red*. Next he took an identical card, with an area of red of the same number of square inches, but appearing in the shape of the ace of spades. After exposure of the card the subjects were again queried about what they saw. Now no subject reported that he saw red: some reported they saw *gray*, or *brown*, or *purple*, or nothing at all they could identify. Past experience in seeing a "spade" as black caused them to perceive any spade-like shape not as red, but as other colors; or the experience was so confusing that nothing identifiable was perceived. Past experience may block, modify, or enhance—it affects perception, as well as how we solve problems and make decisions.

Of course, the most important aspect about experience and learning is the way that the learner perceives his own experience as unique and private. This significant matter we shall consider in part in a later discussion of the self.

THE SELF-LEARNER

Throughout recorded history there have been men and women who continued to pursue learning with vigor until the end of their days. This was so in the Greek, Roman, and Renaissance periods in the Western world; Asian literature and history have many more examples. Henry Adams was far from being the most distinguished of these, but he will be remembered for suggesting that his education went on all through life and then for detailing in what manner this happened.

It has often been said that the purpose of adult education, or of any kind of education, is to make of the subject a continuing, "inner-directed," self-operating learner. "The primary task of an education," said Sir Arthur Currie, formerly principal of McGill University, "is to make men alive, to send them out alive at more points, alive on higher levels, alive in more effective ways. The purpose of an education is not the mere getting of the ability to sell your efforts at a higher figure than unlearned men do, but to make you a thinker, to make you a creator, with an enlarged capacity for life."

One can come upon the autonomous learner in novels, in plays, most often in memoirs, biographies, and autobiographies. Some systematic study of such learners has begun at the University of Chicago,[23] and in one or two other places.

What we need to know is, Does such a learner differ in any marked way from other people? Are his interests wider, or deeper, and are they found in certain fields, or well distributed? What about his motivation? Does he participate to a larger or to a lesser extent in group and community activities than is common? Is he more intelligent? Has he had more extensive formal education? Do his habits display more of persistence and sustained effort than is usual?

This inquiry may soon provide additional hypotheses about learning as well as considerable information about the conditions under which it takes place.

Relating the concept of self-learner to that of "social roles" may also have useful consequences. A number of studies have identified many social roles, such as parent, or spouse. With each such role there are associated tasks which the individual must learn to perform. At the point in his development when an individual must quickly be prepared within a limited time to fill such a role, occurs what Havighurst has called the "teachable moment."[24] Much of parent education is based

on the heightened motivation that occurs in the earliest months
and years of parenthood. How such "teachable moments" may
be utilized for other kinds of learning and how they may be
related to continuing self-learning are very important questions which have not yet been explored.

TIME

For an adult learner *time* is of very great consequence.
This is true in several different respects—physically, culturally,
emotionally.

We shall see in Chapters 3 and 4 that as one grows older he
takes longer to perform certain manual or intellectual tasks.

It has often been mentioned that in our culture we do not
have the same conception of history, the same feeling that
we are living in a great continuum with men and women who
went before, or those who will come after, as do some other
peoples. In general, our culture places more emphasis upon
youth than do others. This fact influences in important ways
what people will try to learn, or whether they will make the
effort. If they accept the notion that life is mostly over at 35
or 45, why bother to learn?

Adults tend to perceive time differently. The child or youth
lives not only in the present but in the future. Time seems
endless to the youth. To the old it may appear very short,
to be valued, perhaps even to be hoarded, rather than spent.
Howard McClusky[25] has pointed out that the adult's view of
himself—his self-adequacy is very closely linked with his view
about time. "I am too old," "If I were twenty years younger,"
may be ways in which the adult is not only talking about his
chronological age but stating what he feels about his own
capacity.

For an adult more than a child, the investment of time in
an activity may be as important a decision as the investment
of money or effort.

Time may take on a new meaning as there is more leisure
for more people. The problems that are sometimes associated
with "leisure" grow out of the perceptions that adults have
about time, and the somewhat limited experience they may

have known in having large amounts of time under their own direction.

Hypotheses about the meaning of time, its relation to such notions as continuous learning, or to a concept like self-adequacy, are beginning to be investigated.

The Personality Structure of the Learner

Earlier we noticed that some kinds of learning seem to happen because the person, because of the kind of physical make-up and the personality structure he has, tends to behave in a way which we have described as leading toward "maturation." What else can we know about a learner growing out of study of his personality?

Philosophers, psychologists, anthropologists, and therapists have postulated theories about personality of a multitude of shapes and kinds. A large number of these have appeared in the years since World War II. This is not the time and place to undertake a major formulation in regard to personality structure. Rather we shall summarize a few principal concepts. These have been selected because they seem helpful in establishing a screen upon which to view the more detailed evidence about learning in the subsequent chapters. None of these statements, of course, is original with the writer: he has borrowed extensively, particularly from the field of counseling.[26]

The learner reacts to all experience as he perceives it. The learner is at the center of experience; in a very real sense he occupies a "private world." No one but the individual himself can truly feel an injury suffered in a factory, or approval from his shop steward, or appreciate the emotion resulting from a pay raise or a demotion. However, experience is only potential; he can deny it to consciousness, or distort it, or modify it. One man can react to an identical experience in a way markedly different from another. For an American watching a "Western" movie on television, observing the familiar scenes, and the highly stylized characters and action, the symbols and events have one kind of meaning. But when the viewer lives in some Asian or eastern European country the same happenings may support his belief that lawlessness, murder, and disorder are a commonplace in North America.

The learner reacts to experience as an organized whole. Later we shall encounter theories of learning that suggest that there are minute and discrete units of learning behavior involving a restricted part of the individual—for example, a nerve-muscle combination. However, most of the evidence from research now indicates that the total organism is involved in almost any activity. We now know a great deal more about psychosomatic medicine. Medical research is full of cases such as that of a schoolteacher who dreaded the visit of the inspector and who would wake up with a paralyzed leg on the occasion of his expected visits, but would be free of such a malady on the following day. A corollary of this notion is that what leads to the *organization,* rather than the *fragmentation,* of the person tends to support constructive behavior.

Learning (and any other behavior) is essentially an attempt by the person to satisfy his needs as he perceives them. Learning happens readily where the individual perceives that his needs can be satisfied by certain courses of action. This is not to argue that there can never be learning unless the person is interested or is aware of the value of what is to be learned. The adult student may not know in advance how fascinating or difficult a particular study may be. But it does mean that effective learning depends upon the learner's being fully engaged. When this occurs the accompanying emotion tends to support the achievement of the action. The intensity of the emotion will depend upon how important the person feels the expected achievement to be in terms of his own development.

The behavior of the learner can be fully understood only from his own point of view. Many a teacher or reformer has been perplexed or scornful because an adult is resistant to learning something new. This action, or refusal to act, can be understood only in the individual's own terms. If a workman were to develop radically different interests in art or religion or politics, this might cut him off from the intimacy of his circle of workmates. Peasants in underdeveloped countries have been taught new agricultural practices that increased their yield and income. But sometimes they have reverted to old practices and accepted a lower living standard when they discovered that certain old and valued social customs were destroyed or jeopardized by the new practice.

Any teacher or foreman must always try to understand how the individual views the learning situation. What does it mean to him?

Gradually within a human being there is the development of the self, and this development is crucial for all learning. All through life, but particularly in the days of infancy and early childhood, a portion of the total world of the individual becomes recognized as "me, myself, and I." First comes simple awareness of experience; then likes and dislikes. "I experience cold, or wet, and I dislike it." Of course the infant is not able to verbalize, but this seems to be his response. Later the reactions of others are added—"I hit my brother, and my mother called me a wicked boy." The self is built up not just with what is experienced directly but with the meanings concerning that experience that one may accept from others. Here is the stage for the drama on which Freudian interpretation is based, the interaction of the *id*, the *ego*, and the *alter ego*. The self may be based upon the perception of actual experience or feeling, or upon distortions. For example, what has been termed a "rejecting" mother may have built up a picture of herself as being loving toward her child. With this concept she is able to accept and live with the sensations of affection which she feels toward her child. However, the organic experience of dislike, distaste, or hatred toward her child is something which she must deny to her conscious self. Yet her need may be to express these feelings of distaste or worse by some aggressive act. She must search for some act which will bring release from intolerable tension, but her action must somehow conform to her view of the good mother. If a good mother in her view can be aggressive to her child only if the child has been *bad* and merits punishment, much of his behavior is seen as bad and punishable. This behavior is found beyond the parent-child relationship. One famous banker used to claim that he never foreclosed unless the man was given to dishonesty and dissolute habits. But it was also said of him that he found a surprising number of men who were thus afflicted!

All new experiences for the learner are symbolized and organized into some relationship to the self, or are ignored because there is no perceived relationship, or are denied organization, or given a distorted meaning because the experience seems inconsistent with the structure of the self. We are all aware of how selective is our attention. A friend recently joined a committee which is planning educational projects for the North American Indian. In the first week after beginning this work he was conscious that the radio and newspapers seemed to be full of references to the Indian, but he had never noticed these references before. One listens, sees, perceives selectively. Many sensory experiences are ignored until they are required to give meaning or content to some need of the individual. The seaman perceives meanings not seen by the landlubber; the Australian bushman can follow tracks imperceptible to anyone else.

Much is ignored and some experiences are even rejected and distorted. Notice that what is rejected is what is *inconsistent*, not just what is unflattering. The person whose self-concept is of failure and inadequacy cannot accept praise as being true or honest. He may need to be helped to a different picture of self before he is able to accept or assess either praise or blame.

Out of this condition flow many of the opportunities for both the teacher and the therapist.

Perhaps the most important task in learning is the development of a self that can deal with reality. The learner is able to move toward maturity, as discussed earlier, only when the self is able to perceive experience for what it is—not as threatening, or not in distorted symbols. This is not so obvious as it may seem. Many a person seems unable to deal with the subject of communism, or homosexual behavior, without employing distorted symbols. Or there may be outright rejection. The condition for effective learning is a self that is so constituted, and so *self-understood,* that even changes or a reorganization of that self can be faced without fear or flight.

A Reminder

It is self-evident that learning is something that happens to *a* person, it is an *individual* thing. It is equally true that one cannot have much understanding of learning unless he sees how the "self" is engaged in the changes we call learning. But it would be wrong to conclude that there is no more to learning than internal changes. How then could we explain the role of the teacher? Or the fact that much learning comes about through what transpires in a group? Or such phenomena as that in some societies extraordinary adaptations are made much more rapidly than in other societies? For example, we note the astonishing speed by which industrialization occurred in Japan, with all the learning that was entailed in that immense social revolution.

The self is never isolated; it takes part in various social situations, and is found in various social roles. "I am a part of all that I have met," sang the poet. Gardner Murphy puts it another way. "Paradoxically," he says, "it is often through the creation of the right group atmosphere that individuality can best be released."

The concept of the isolated individual as sitting behind a book or listening in his study to a radio or watching TV strips off the social clothing which gives context and meaning to the learning process. The individual learns as a member of a group, shares with others the goal of learning, interprets the material as something with respect to which he agrees or disagrees with others, constantly gauges for himself the implications of the knowledge or skill for his own action or place in the group. The types of investigation done long ago by Thorndike with reference to individual learning ability are important, and there must be much more study of what the adult can learn and how his learning depends upon constitutional factors, age, sex, experience and motivation. It is however, time for a broader view which considers the whole person and his social context as the subject matter for research in adult learning. Everything in clinical and social psychology should ultimately be made useful.[27]

In our inquiry we shall consider the factors mentioned by Murphy and also what can be learned by other students of man, both social scientists and artists—at least so far as space will allow.

Summary

Now that we have had a brief sketch of the personality of the learner we shall begin to observe, in some detail, physical and sensory factors affecting learning as well as intellectual factors, and the role of feelings and motives. In doing so we shall need to keep in mind such questions as these:

- changes during different stages in life and over the life span
- what is involved in "maturity"
- the use and reorganization of experience
- the perception and meaning of time
- how the self can face reality and can face change.

REFERENCES

1. See the review of research in adult education published annually since 1955 in the summer issue of *Adult Education* by the Adult Education Association of the United States. One section of this review is labeled "Clientele of Adult Education."
2. Malcolm Knowles, "An Overview and History of the Field," *Adult Education* (Chicago: AEA), Vol. 7, No. 4.
3. John Holden, "A Survey of Participation in Adult Education Classes," *Adult Leadership* (Chicago: AEA), Vol. 6, No. 10.
4. Harold F. Clark and Harold S. Sloan, *Classrooms in the Factories* (New York: New York University Press, 1958).
5. Robert Love, "The Use of Motivation Research to Determine Interest in Adult College-Level Training," *Educational Record,* July 1953.
6. Bernard J. James, "Can Needs Define Educational Goals?" *Adult Education* (Chicago, AEA), Vol. 7, No. 1.

7. Herbert Sorenson, *Adult Abilities* (Minneapolis: University of Minnesota Press, 1933).

8. John P. Dyer, *Ivory Towers in the Market Place* (Indianapolis: Bobbs-Merrill Company, Inc., 1956).

9. W. C. Hallenbeck, "New Needs in Adult Education," *Teachers College Record,* May 1947.

10. Ordway Tead, *College Teaching and College Learning* (New Haven: Yale University Press, 1949).

11. A. I. Lansing, ed., *Problems of Ageing* (Baltimore: Williams & Wilkins Company, 1952).

12. Sidney L. Pressey and Raymond G. Kuhlen, *Psychological Development Through the Life Span* (New York: Harper & Brothers, 1957).

13. A. Angyal, *Foundations for a Science of Personality* (New York: Commonwealth Fund, 1941).

14. Donald Snygg and Arthur W. Combs, *Individual Behavior: a New Frame of Reference for Psychology* (New York: Harper & Brothers, 1949).

15. Robert J. Blakely, "What Is a Free Society?" *Adult Education in a Free Society* (Toronto: Guardian Bird Publications, 1958).

16. David Riesman, Nathan Glazer, and Reuel Denney, *The Lonely Crowd* (New Haven: Yale University Press, 1950).

17. Karen Horney, *Self-Analysis* (New York: W. W. Norton & Company, Inc., 1942).

18. Carl R. Rogers, *Counseling and Psychotherapy* (Boston: Houghton Mifflin Company, 1942).

19. Harry Overstreet, *The Mature Mind* (New York: W. W. Norton & Company, Inc., 1949).

20. William S. Gray and Bernice Rogers, *Maturity in Reading* (Chicago: University of Chicago Press, 1956). Copyright 1956 by the University of Chicago.

21. John Schwertman, *I Want Many Lodestars* (Chicago: Center for the Study of Liberal Education for Adults, 1958).

22. James B. Whipple, *Especially for Adults* (Chicago: Center for the Study of Liberal Education for Adults, 1957).

23. C. O. Houle, "An Exploratory Study of the Self-Educating Person," reported in *Adult Education* (Chicago: AEA), Vol. 8, No. 4.

24. Robert J. Havighurst, *Social Roles of the Middle-Aged Person*

(Chicago: Center for the Study of Liberal Education for Adults, 1953).

25. Howard McClusky, "Central Hypotheses About Adult Learning" (Lafayette, Ind.: Commission of the Professors of Adult Education, 1958).

26. Carl R. Rogers, *Client-Centered Therapy* (Boston: Houghton Mifflin Company, 1951).

27. Gardner Murphy, *Psychological Needs of Adults* (Chicago: Center for the Study of Liberal Education for Adults, 1955).

Suggested Reading

AUCH, F. L., "The Differential Effects of Age upon Human Learning," *Journal of Genetic Psychology*, 1934.

BEAL, GEORGE M., and BOHLEN, JOE M., *The Diffusion Process* (Ames: Iowa State College, 1957), Special Report No. 18.

BERELSON, B., *The Library's Public* (New York: Columbia University Press, 1949).

CARTWRIGHT, MORSE A., *Ten Years of Adult Education* (New York: The Macmillan Company, 1935).

ESSERT, PAUL, *Creative Leadership in Adult Education* (New York: Prentice-Hall, Inc., 1951).

FARNUM, HOLLIS B., *A Study Comparing the Academic Aptitude of University Extension and Campus Students* (Ph.D. dissertation, University of Rhode Island, 1956).

GREENWOOD, WALTER, *A Study of Persistence of Public Evening High School Students* (Ph.D. dissertation, University of Pennsylvania, 1932).

HAVIGHURST, ROBERT J., and ORR, BETTY, *Adult Education and Adult Needs* (Chicago: Center for the Study of Liberal Education for Adults, 1956).

KALLEN, HORACE, *The Liberation of the Adult* (Chicago: Center for the Study of Liberal Education for Adults, 1954).

KAPLAN, ABBOTT, *A Study of the Liberal Arts Discussion Program for Adults in the Metropolitan Los Angeles Area* (White Plains, N.Y.: Fund for Adult Education, 1958).

KNOWLES, MALCOLM, "Adult Education in the United States," *Adult Education* (Chicago: AEA), Vol. 5, No. 2.

McGHEE, PAUL A., *A School for Optimists* (Chicago: Center for the Study of Liberal Education for Adults, 1953).

MORTON, J. R., *University Extension in the United States* (Birmingham: University of Alabama Press, 1953).

SIEGLE, PETER E., "The Adult Learner," *Adult Leadership* (Chicago: AEA), Vol. 3, No. 9.

SILLS, D. L., *The Volunteers: Means and Ends in a Voluntary Organization* (Glencoe, Ill.: The Free Press, 1957).

Chapter 3

PHYSICAL AND SENSORY CAPACITY

In this chapter we shall consider the relation of physical and sensory capacity to learning and note the changes in capacity that go on throughout life.

Nowhere have these changes in human life been more forcefully described than in a memorable passage from Shakespeare's *As You Like It:*

> . . . one man in his time plays many parts,
> His acts being seven ages. At first, the infant,
> Mewling and puking in the nurse's arms:
> Then the whining schoolboy, with his satchel,
> And shining morning face, creeping like snail
> Unwilling to school: and then, the lover,
> Sighing like furnace, with a woeful ballad
> Made to his mistress' eyebrow: Then a soldier;
> Full of strange oaths, and bearded like the bard,
> Jealous in honour, sudden and quick in quarrel,
> Seeking the bubble reputation
> Even in the cannon's mouth: and then, the justice;
> In fair round belly, with good capon lin'd,
> With eyes severe, and beard of formal cut,
> Full of wise saws, and modern instances,
> And so he plays his part: The sixth age shifts
> Into the lean and slipper'd pantaloon;
> With spectacles on nose, and pouch on side;
> His youthful hose, well sav'd, a world too wide,
> For his shrunk shank; and his big manly voice,
> Turning again toward childish treble, pipes
> And whistles in his sound: Last scene of all,
> That ends this strange eventful history,
> Is second childishness, and mere oblivion;
> Sans teeth, sans eyes, sans taste, sans everything.

This sounds a trifle bleak and threatening, but it is a reasonably accurate description.

To many people the fact that there is change and the fact that there is death is enough evidence that the powers in the later period are not equal to those during youth. In a society such as ours in which the attributes of youthfulness are highly esteemed, anything that is different from the quality of the young is inferred to be inferior. It *may* be of less value, but it is also possible that it may be of a *different* value.

Not all societies in the past, and not all cultures today, place the same premium on youthfulness as we do. For example, the largest number of our teachers are comparatively young, and we tend to think that this is an appropriate arrangement, perhaps even an inevitable one. But in some societies only those of the richest experience and ripest judgment are ever allowed to have any part in the teaching of the young.

We have no intention here to discuss the comparative advantages or disadvantages of the different stages in life. It is important, however, that as we study changes we try to do so with as little bias as possible. We should see these as changes that may have desirable *or* undesirable effects, depending in considerable measure upon the person himself; not as inexorable loss and decay. Browning was as accurate a student of the changes in human life as any psychologist and his findings are expressed in the lines:

> Grow old along with me
> The best is yet to be.

Accordingly, we are going to try to look calmly at the effect of the changes that occur during human life. This is no attempt to glorify what are sometimes referred to as "the golden years" of middle and old age. Nor is it a dirge or requiem, simply a search for understanding. We shall try to see what happens to the learner and in what way, if any, the changes that occur within him affect the amount and quality of his learning.

Scarcity of Data About the Later Years

There is no longer much mystery about the way that a baby grows, changes, and develops, before birth and through childhood and adolescence. Millions of children have been carefully observed directly and by camera, studied, measured, tested. They have been under the scrutiny of thousands of patient, trained observers, in every country in the world.

The main fact about this stage in life is that almost from the moment of birth there is a rapid upsurge in every capacity and this continues throughout childhood, though at differing rates. At puberty, for example, there is an acceleration of bodily growth and around the ages of eighteen and twenty there is a general leveling off in most capacities.

When we come to study the development beyond the twentieth year, what a contrast! Here, there is no mountain of books, films, studies, reports. In the past decade there has been more attention paid to the last years of life, and gerontological studies now are of considerable number, though but a tiny fraction compared to those associated with the child. But, as noted earlier, the middle years still constitute a desert.

> Middle age is unknown territory to the social scientist. Although he is thoroughly familiar with the length and breadth and depth of childhood and adolescence, and he has made intensive explorations into the domain of old age, his knowledge of middle age is limited to a small amount of highly specialized knowledge gained from marriage counselors, psychiatrists, and social workers, about small and non-representative groups of middle-aged people.[1]

What we do have is not very well organized nor is it readily available. It consists of charts about average height and weight, and insurance tables. These are useful guides if we want to predict what may happen to a few thousand people in a much larger population, but not very helpful in counseling a single individual. There is much additional data in some medical journals and reports of medical research, but little of this is generally accessible. However, it is now possible to secure much more information than ever before; and one of the increasingly difficult problems for the teacher of adults is to keep up with, and arrange in some pattern, what is coming to him from many different sources.

The Body

The activities that we call learning take place in a total organism. It is a common view that the mental and emotional attributes of a human being are highly complicated and unstable but that at least one can count on some stability in regard to the body. However, as Walter B. Cannon once pointed out, any constancy in the body itself is a kind of miracle:

Our bodies are made of extraordinarily unstable material. Pulses of energy, so minute that very delicate methods are required to measure them, course along our nerves. On reaching muscles they find there a substance so delicately sensitive to slight disturbances, that, like an explosive touched by a fuse, it may discharge in a powerful movement. . . .

The instability of bodily structure is shown also by its quick change when conditions are altered. For example, we are all aware of the sudden stoppage of action in parts of the brain, accompanied by fainting and loss of consciousness, that occurs when there is a momentary check in the blood flow through the vessels. We know that if the blood supply to the brain wholly ceases for so short a time as seven or eight minutes certain cells which are necessary for intelligent action are so seriously damaged that they do not recover.

When we consider the extreme instability of our bodily structure, its readiness for disturbance by the slightest application of external forces and the rapid onset of its decomposition as soon as favoring circumstances are withdrawn, its persistence through many decades seems almost miraculous. The wonder increases when we realize that the system is open, engaging in free exchange with the outer world, and that the structure itself is not permanent but is being continuously broken down by the wear and tear of action, and as continuously built up again by processes of repair.

Here, then, is a striking phenomenon. Organisms composed of

material which is characterized by the utmost inconstancy and unsteadiness, have somehow learned the methods of maintaining constancy and keeping steady.[2]

As one might assume, the health and efficiency of the body affect profoundly the quality of learning. What about physique? The studies of L. M. Terman[3] have demonstrated quite conclusively that the gifted and superior children tend to be somewhat larger and heavier than those who are dull. However, correlations between physique and intellect are so low, and there are so many exceptions, that no inference is permissible in regard to a single individual child. Is this equally true of adults? Studies are inconclusive, but all of them point in the same direction. There is some evidence to show that people in positions of authority tend to be somewhat larger and heavier than the average. In one study it was found that bishops were two inches taller and almost twenty pounds heavier than rural ministers in the same denomination, and that university presidents and school superintendents tended to be greater in physique than men on their staffs. Still, too much ought not to be made between the correlation of positions of prestige and the physical superiority of the incumbent; the exceptions are so numerous. Yet, on the other hand, there is very little support for a commonly accepted stereotype, that a man of intellect invariably has a weak flabby body. Brains and brawn are as often, more often, found together than separately.

It has also been found that in elections, or in appointments where the characteristics and qualities of the various candidates are not fully known to those making a decision, factors such as height, appearance, carriage, vigor, are given much more significance than if all factors are established.[4]

We shall see later that such environmental factors as family, social position, economic and social status have an equal or greater influence on learning than does physique.

Early Studies of Growth

We have already noted that artists and writers often choose as their field of interest the kinds of changes that occur in human beings, particularly in such critical stages as puberty, at the time of choosing a mate or establishing a home, and when growing old. One might almost claim that the novel in literature was created as a special form for dealing with the changes and continuity of living, rather than just with moments of high dramatic tension which are likely to be the theme of poetry and drama. Conscientious artists like Leonardo da Vinci left many records of growth changes; diarists such as Pepys and Boswell also left faithful written accounts of growth and change. Still, most of this information was piecemeal and had little order or system. Atoms of experience were preserved, but these had insufficient meaning in isolation and there was little permanent gain in understanding.

One of the most notable accretions of knowledge about growth came through the work of a gifted and inquisitive amateur scientist, Sir Francis Galton, whose curiosity and interests ranged over many fields. Galton was not a man to speculate while lolling in an armchair; he developed a knack for testing out his hypotheses in many ingenious ways. He had no captive audience in a school or institution, and so he devised a human "laboratory" at a great national fair, a health exhibition held at South Kensington, England, in 1884. Galton set up his observations and experiments in a tent booth at the fair. He had collected various gadgets and measuring devices which would measure aspects of physical performance. Where no gauges existed he invented them. He must have been very persuasive, for, despite competition from all the other booths, more than 7,000 individuals offered themselves or were enticed to submit to measurement of seventeen different characteristics such as height, sitting height, weight, vital capacity, visual acuity, auditory capacity, strength of pull, strength of hand grip, span of arms, and swiftness of blow.

Galton wrote extensively and published the results of his measurements. Stimulated by his results and his speculation, other men began to observe similar phenomena. The most impressive use of such information was achieved by insurance companies who soon had quite reliable tables to guide them in the prediction of length of life and thus a more accurate estimate of the premiums to be paid for insurance protection.

Kinds of Changes

On the average, the female reaches physiological maturity around the twelfth and thirteenth year, the male about a year or two later. Of course, individual differences are enormous, and there are cases of some individuals at twenty-one who are not physiologically "of age."

From maturity on, it is *normal* for the human organism to undergo the following kinds of changes, most of which occur *gradually*:

- Cell tissues become dryer, they do not grow so rapidly and the repair of cell tissues proceeds more slowly.
- Bodily cells become somewhat less elastic.
- The rate of basal metabolism is lowered.
- There is some decrease in strength.
- There is a decrease in the speed, intensity, and endurance of neuromuscular reactions.
- Vision and hearing become impaired.

STRENGTH

There are many measures of strength—the weight a subject can pull, press, lift, or jerk, the grip of the hand measured in pounds, the thrust of the legs. Galton's data, supplemented by more recent observation, shows that the maximum performance in these motor abilities comes relatively late, close to the thirtieth year, and the decline thereafter is gradual. But we must remember that these are averages. In a recent study two men over 65 registered scores for strength that exceeded any of those in their twenties.

A few studies exist concerning the capacity of people to do "hard" physical work. Considerable research has gone on at the "Fatigue Laboratory" at Harvard. The curves of decline vary somewhat, but the loss until age 70 is gradual. At 70 or 75, however, capacity for such work may be half of what it was at 35 or 40.

What is equally clear is that several nonphysical factors influence output markedly, particularly the amount of skill and experience a man has for a given task, and his motivation. For many tasks that are rated as "light" physical work, his output may not show any decline.

In a recent study in England where the task was sorting blocks, the men over 65 took much longer *on their first attempt* than those under 25. But as the work continued the oldest group increased their output. At the conclusion of the study their production was only slightly lower than the youngest group and the men of 46-64 had the best score of all. One man well over 70 was the third quickest in the entire group. It is obvious in this test that dexterity is a more important consideration than strength or endurance. And most studies indicate that losses in dexterity are negligible up to 70 and over, and that these losses can be retarded by training and practice.

SPEED AND REACTION TIME

As people grow older they slow down. This bald statement is somewhat ambiguous and it may seem trite and obvious. From our own observations we know that it is true. Yet the failure to recognize its importance has led to many misunderstandings and misinterpretations about people as they grow older.

Slowing up seems to take many forms. One is in regard to the speed of the flow of blood in the veins and arteries, others have to do with the passage of "messages" through the nervous system, the reaction of both voluntary and involuntary movements, and the time necessary for damage in the body to be repaired. We apprehend and perceive more slowly, we act more slowly, we think more slowly.

Ours is an age and a culture which is very "time conscious." When it is said of us that we are always "in a hurry" we take this as a compliment, whether it was meant so, or not.

The medieval man, or many a man in Asia today, would not be so prone to equate speed with quality of performance; they would be much less likely to measure "efficiency" in units of time.

Psychologists also contributed to this practice. In their studies of children they found that for many tasks, the child who performed correctly, also performed quickly. In their publications and through the results of timed mental tests that some of them devised, the notion was circulated that there is a close, direct relationship between speed of response and correctness of response.

This is true, within limits, when applied to children. It is *not* true about adults, particularly the older adult.

Accordingly, in every activity in which people participate, attention needs to be directed to the factor of speed and its importance.

For example, studies of automobile driving have shown that a driver of age 60 travels many yards farther before taking action after receiving a warning signal than a driver of 20. The increased time necessary for stimulus to reach his brain center and for him to respond by applying the brakes can be an appreciable distance in a car traveling at a high speed. Galton published some observations about reaction time by calculating the swiftness of a blow, and expressing it in a series of comparisons, using age 25 as 100—as in the following table:

age 15= 84	age 35=99
age 20= 98	age 40=98
age 25=100	age 45=96
age 30=100	

We shall discuss more fully the factor of speed in estimating mental ability in Chapter 4, but it is equally important in learning new skills involving dexterity, or sight and hearing.

CHANGES IN VISION

Traders in horses will invariably examine the animals' teeth with the utmost care to determine age and health. Probably the best index of the soundness of the human animal is the health and capacity of the eye. There are more substantial changes associated with aging of the eye than in almost any other characteristic. Walter R. Miles[5] has stated that visual function is a clear measure of physiological age, and others have used visual acuity as a basic index for bodily aging. Growth in function is very rapid in early childhood; there is a slow but continuous gain between the thirteenth and eighteenth year. This is followed by a gradual decline until the fortieth year. After 40 there is a sharp decline till age 55 and continuous decline at a decreased rate beyond 55.

This decline of function is not only general but there also seems to be a steady decline in efficiency in specific visual functions. There is increasing density of the eye tissues, loss of water, accumulation of amounts of inert material in the eye tissue, as well as loss of fat and elasticity. With advancing years the pupils become smaller and react feebly, the cornea tends to lose in luster and transparency, the eyelids become thin and less elastic. In terms of function, older eyes suffer a greater proportionate loss of visual acuity when the illumination is dim. There is also a narrowing of the field of vision, and a slow-down of the adaptation to dark. There is an increasing incidence of cataracts and of defective color vision, the latter reaching as high as forty per cent of men over 70.

However, as noted in the table, the greatest amount of decline occurs in the years 40 to 55. Studies have shown that over the age of 35 there is a marked preference for more illumination for reading than in earlier years. Beyond the age of 20 every person shows some decline in visual acuity; beyond age 40 the decrease is considerable. That visual regression is a characteristic of normal healthy people is illustrated by one study of industrial workers:

Age group	Per cent with normal vision
below 20	77
20-24	68
25-29	61
30-34	60
35-39	55
40-44	50
45-49	35
50-54	25
55-59	18
60 and over	6

Some people become very much concerned about this decline, particularly if the facts are not understood. However, as in most circumstances in life, when people know what may be expected, their adjustment may be accomplished with dignity and without damaging misapprehension.

We shall summarize, at the end of this chapter, some of the practical common sense procedures which to a considerable extent can minimize the effect of losses in sight and hearing, as far as learning is concerned.

CHANGES IN HEARING

In no capacity except sight are there greater changes at different stages in life than in hearing acuity.

In most people the peak of performance seems to be reached before the fifteenth birthday, and there is gradual but consistent decline until about 65.

Auditory disability sufficient to create difficulties in understanding an interview or a telephone conversation increases from about five per cent in children under 15, to about 65 per cent in adults of 65 or over. Older people tend to slow up in their reaction to sounds. That is, not only do we decline in our ability to hear sounds but we are slower to hear— to translate the meaning of the sound, and to act in response to it.

In the years after 20 the nerve cells in the ear gradually seem to atrophy and there is a gradual loss of acuity for all tones, particularly high tones.

It seems clear from the evidence that women lose acuity for lower pitch and men lose acuity for high pitch. An interesting consequence of this fact is that older women can, in general, communicate more readily with women and older men with men. Some attention has been given to this factor as a case of disharmony among older married couples, but no conclusive results have been found. People over 65 have somewhat less sensitivity to the richness of complex tones in high fidelity recordings.

In terms of the effect upon one's behavior, the psychological implications may be more significant than physical. Hearing loss can have a marked influence upon an individual's confidence or insecurity. It may increase his feeling that he cannot learn new things. He may be more reluctant to venture into a new situation because of the apprehension that he might not be able to cope with it, particularly if the activity occurs in a setting of crowding and confusion.

Hearing loss may have other effects. A man who doesn't hear well may feel left out, isolated, cut off from his associates. He may even come to believe that people are whispering about him. Some who have suffered losses in hearing have developed symptoms of a kind of paranoia. Others display the reactions of people who are isolated, they withdraw into themselves, or retreat. The querulousness which, in literature, has often been associated with old age, so far as this charge is true, may be caused in part by a decline in hearing.

ACHIEVEMENT IN WORK

We have already summarized the results of some studies of the success of older workers compared with younger. If strength is an important factor, or speed is at a premium, the older worker is at a disadvantage. But if these are relatively unimportant, he can expect to perform well. If there is emphasis upon such significant though hard-to-measure attributes as judgment, steadiness, reliability, the older worker usually outstrips younger workers.

There are few if any jobs, the learning of which will not be possible if his attention is gained and if he is given sufficient time. During World War II many older men and women were trained or retrained for a wide range of jobs.

ACHIEVEMENT IN SPORTS

In a later chapter we shall consider in a general way the development of special abilities of all kinds. Here we shall note briefly physical performance in sports.

At present, most of the world's records in swimming are held by a boy of 16, and teen-age world's champions have been known in women's tennis and figure skating. Activities which require energy in bursts place a premium upon youthfulness.

Sprinting champions, both in running and swimming, are usually youthful; achievement in middle distances and long distances is common by those who are older. Most boxers are finished by 30 or 35, but professional wrestlers may continue to perform night after night well into their forties or even fifties. The most consistently able performances by baseball players in the big leagues are given by athletes in their thirties but in all probability a baseball player attained his best batting average for a single year before he reached 30.

Golfers rarely reach their peak in tournament skill until after 30; one four-time winner of the American national championship, Walter J. Travis, did not take up the game until he was 37. Billiard championships are usually won by those in their late twenties, but many fine billiard players have continued to excel at ages 40, 50, or even 60. Winners in curling are found in all ages; "skips" are usually men in their later thirties or older.

In such activities as checkers or chess there are far more cases of success by the elderly than by youthful prodigies. One hears of only a few examples of older people mastering musical instruments, but this seems best explained by the small number of those who try. Here, as elsewhere, the belief that one cannot succeed results in refusal to try.

Sports championships are won by people who range in ages from 15 up to 40 or 45, but most championships are won at the ages of 25 to 35. However, if experience and dexterity are the main requirements, the employment of all physical resources rather than the quick release of nervous or physical energy, excellence may be maintained throughout most of life. Games and other physical activities can also be learned relatively late, but we shall see later how success in learning a new game or physical skill may depend on the degree of interest in that skill.

Some Common-Sense Practices for Minimizing Losses Associated with Age

In Chapter 11 we shall deal with many implications for the teacher or leader. Here we wish to list only a few "rules of thumb" which, if followed, can help to eliminate most of the effects of physical and sensory losses in respect to sight and hearing. We do not mean to suggest that learning happens as a result of a few simple changes in the environment; it is much more a matter of motivation than that. But such shifts can offset what some have regarded as serious deficits.

PRACTICES FOR OVERCOMING SIGHT LIMITATIONS

a. *Illumination.* One generalization may seem obvious enough, the need for adequate illumination. It is still common to meet the attitude that although good illumination must be provided for children, any old corner, no matter how dim, is good enough for adults. This is to put things backwards. Older people need better illumination than younger. Where premises are used for both children and adults, the best rule is to provide sufficient illumination to suit any adult member and the children will be well served. Not only should the illumination be sufficient (if in doubt consult any lighting engineer) but it should be constant, without flicker. Do not have your audience face direct light.

b. *Glare.* Have you ever noticed in how many conferences or meetings some members of the group are compelled to face glare, either direct or reflected? Usually a simple change in seating will reduce or eliminate this. Glare will cut down the total efficiency of your group; it is usually unnecessary and is an insult to your audience.

c. *Blackboards.* Have you ever made a census of blackboards used for adults? You may be astounded to note how many of them are shiny (glaring) or, even more common, are "tattletale" gray in color. Dirty chalk or dingy boards give you a result like automobile plates in one state during a particular year when the colors were described as "blur on blur." Chalk boards, or large paper pads which allow maximum contrasts should *always* be used; white on black, yellow on black, white on green make useful combinations.

d. *Other Factors. Arrange* seating so that people are close to speaker or demonstration. *Use* sharp color contrasts. *Enlarge*—if you use mimeographed material, choose pica type (at least) and double-space. *Simplify*—use simple words or phrases on chalk boards. Where possible avoid use of abbreviations. If possible remove everything from the board or chart except the relevant items.

PRACTICES FOR OVERCOMING HEARING LOSSES

Much can also be done in classes or conferences, to offset hearing losses:

a. *Organization and Atmosphere.* People with hearing loss will respond better and feel less isolated or threatened in small groups than in mass groups. In a face-to-face, informal group some hearing loss may not seriously matter. The conditions which are usually prescribed for effective small group discussion have even greater relevance for older people.

b. *The Teacher or Leader.*

- The teacher or leader should *stand still* in a position to be observed by all, so that the listener can adjust to the source of sound and also watch face and gesture which may provide him with visual cues to meaning.
- He should *speak slowly, clearly, distinctly, loudly.*
- He should *talk directly* to the group, using conversational manners and avoiding a monotone.
- He should *use simple, clear,* and *meaningful* words or phrases.
- He should *use* blackboard, wall paper, flannelgraph or other means to provide *supplementary visual cues* whenever new, unusual, unfamiliar words or numbers, titles, or ideas are introduced.

c. *Additional Checks for the Teacher or Leader.*

- Note and try to eliminate outside noises that may distract or interfere with the hearing of the group.
- Watch the faces of the group members to see if they are hearing.
- Ask someone in the back of the room to call attention when any members cannot hear.

- Questions directed to the teacher or leader by members of the group should be repeated for the benefit of the others.

It may take a minute or two for people to get used to the acoustics in a room or hall. Producers of training films do not put their important message in the first three minutes of the film; they allow time for people to "warm up" as it were and become accustomed to the acoustics. This is equally important in a class or meeting in which older people are present.

Summary

Throughout this chapter we have noted that in most physical characteristics there is some decline in the years after 20. In some capacities such as visual acuity this is considerable; in others it is very gradual.

The losses are most marked if they are measured in terms of time units, but these may be of little or no importance if measured in terms of quality. Indeed, some of the slowness of the older adult is itself caused by his concern with being accurate and thorough. Studies of the older worker indicate that he can learn and can perform well in most vocations. He can also begin relatively late in life to take part in leisure-time activities of many kinds.

For very few activities that adults may wish to learn, is the factor of decline of physique of such magnitude that they need to be discouraged from any attempt. In many cases the effects of decline can be overcome, to a considerable extent, if they are understood by the teacher and if some elementary adjustments and adaptations are made.

REFERENCES

1. Robert J. Havighurst, *Social Roles of the Middle-Aged Person* (Chicago: Center for the Study of Liberal Education for Adults, 1953).
2. Walter B. Cannon, *The Wisdom of the Body* (New York: W. W. Norton & Company, Inc., 1932).

3. L. M. Terman and M. H. Odin, *The Gifted Child Grows Up* (Stanford, Calif.: Stanford University Press, 1947).
4. Alvin W. Gouldner, ed., *Studies in Leadership* (New York: Harper & Brothers, 1950).
5. W. R. Miles, "Psychological Aspects of Ageing," *Problems of Ageing*, A. I. Lansing, ed. (Baltimore: Williams & Wilkins Company, 1952).

Suggested Reading

DONAHUE, WILMA, *Education for Later Maturity* (New York: William Morrow & Company, Inc., 1955).

HAND, SAMUEL E., *A Review of Physiological and Psychological Changes in Aging and Their Implications for Teachers of Adults* (Tallahassee: Florida State Department of Education, 1956).

LANSING, A. I., ed., *Problems of Ageing* (Baltimore: Williams & Wilkins Company, 1952).

McGEOCH, JOHN A., and IRION, A., *The Psychology of Human Learning* (New York: Longmans Green & Co., Inc., 1952).

MILES, WALTER R., and MILES, CATHERINE, C., "Mental Changes with Normal Aging," *Geriatric Medicine* (Philadelphia: W. B. Saunders Company, 1949).

PRESSEY, SIDNEY L., and KUHLEN, RAYMOND G., *Psychological Development Through the Life Span* (New York: Harper & Brothers, 1957).

RUGER, HENRY A., and STOESSINGER, BRENDA, "On the Growth Curves of Certain Characteristics in Males," *Annals of Eugenics*, Vol. II, Parts I and II, 1926.

Chapter 4

INTELLECTUAL CAPACITIES

We have established that as far as bodily and sensory functions are concerned, though there is decline all through the years of adulthood, it is not of a nature that need eliminate people from very many activities. Adults at any age have an excellent physical basis for learning.

But this fact has often been granted. And most people will also grant that *a few exceptional* men and women may continue their intellectual pursuits till very late: Goethe, Robert Bridges finishing his greatest poem at age 85, Tennyson's last volume coming out when he was 80, Verdi composing sacred music when 85, Wundt completing his memoirs at 87.

But what of ordinary people? Is there a decline in intellectual capacity throughout life as there is in physical capacity? Many people think so. We have noted that this belief is firmly rooted in myth, fable, and proverb.

But what do those say who have given serious study to the question? Some of them also believe that there is decline in intellectual powers, and therefore in the ability to learn, throughout adulthood. (One can make a distinction between intellectual capacity and the ability to learn, but these are often treated as synonymous, and we are using the terms in this fashion.) But many others do not. This subject has been one of controversy all through the present century. Much of the evidence from the earliest researches *seemed* to support the view that there is substantial loss.

Increasingly through recent years, and by increasing numbers of psychologists and other students of the learning process, the second notion has been gaining ground. This is the view that age, in and of itself, does not significantly affect the ability of adults to learn. One needs to keep an open mind in regard to this matter, since able, conscientious scholars are divided in their interpretation of the data, but this latter position seems to be well supported by research and experience.

Considerable evidence now exists. However, certain difficulties still remain.

Limitations in the Study of Intellectual Ability of Adults

Intellectual ability is "measured" by achievement on selected tasks which are included in "intelligence tests."

Most of the difficulties arise from the nature of the tests, the subject matter of the tasks, the basis on which the test has been validated, the factor of time, and the adequacy of the motivation of the adults in performing these tasks. The tests measure performance at some selected moment. Performance of one individual is compared with a large sample of individuals and is usually expressed as an "intelligence quotient" or IQ. It was once assumed that a person's IQ would be constant, at least throughout childhood and youth. But this could be established only if the same individual were tested again and again, as he grew older, on identical or similar tests. Such a testing program of the same individual at different stages in his life is usually called "longitudinal."

There are very few "longitudinal" studies, although such a study is a most reliable way of noting actual changes in intellectual performance or capacity. Instead, most of the studies we have are what are called "cross-sectional" studies.

In the "cross-sectional" study, there is no measure of the change or growth in learning ability or intellectual capacity of a particular individual throughout his lifetime. What we have are the scores of one group of people, achieved at one point in their lifetime, compared with the scores of an entirely different group of people at a single point in their lifetime. For example, the scores of men and women of 25 are compared with the scores of different men and women of 50. This comparison will be meaningful only if the compared groups are closely alike in *all* significant details. But in many important respects these groups may not be alike. For example, we can expect that the younger group will have had considerably more schooling since the average school-leaving age has arisen considerably since the 50-year-olds left school.

Fortunately, however, some psychologists like L. M. Terman[1] have begun to observe or test the same individuals a second or third time during their life span. We shall note the significance of such "follow-up" studies and the increased knowledge about changes or persistence of the ability to learn that they bring.

On "intelligence tests" the performance of the individual is compared with the sample of people upon whom the test was tried out and validated.

Sometimes the scores and the "norms" of tests have been based upon the performance of a special group of adults, a "captive audience" as it were, men and women who are available to the experimenter in such places as prisons or hospitals. The experience of such people, to say the least is atypical. However, in recent years more evidence has been accumulating from observations and tests of people who are *living ordinary lives* rather than as a patient or inmate. One such study, carried out in England, dealt with every thirtieth man or woman in that country who was receiving some kind of pension. In commenting upon this study of "normal" people, Professor Lorge of Columbia University made the observation that if the data secured can be applied to older people in general, "many of the so-called deficits of old age, which are now commonly accepted, are exaggerated."

In addition to the reservation that one may have about "intelligence" tests because of the sample of adults on which the results of these tests are based, there are some significant limitations in the tests themselves. This is in no way to suggest that such tests are valueless. Undoubtedly they have been of considerable importance in education, clinical work, and personnel management. However, they need to be used for adults with the most rigorous care because of a number of characteristics.

- Many of them are based on tasks associated with school rather than with real life situations.

- Many of them rely on a motivation that is characteristic of youth but not necessarily of adults.
- Many of them are based on the experience or performance of children and adolescents rather than upon the study of those who are adults.
- Many of them measure performance in units of time, which, as we shall see, is an inevitable handicap for an older person.

With these reservations we shall now review some of the evidence that has come from various studies that employed "intelligence tests."

The Conrad and Jones Study

One study that received considerable attention in the years after World War I was that of Harold E. Jones and Herbert S. Conrad, reported under the significant title "The Growth and Decline of Intelligence."[2] We are mentioning it here not because we accept the assumptions on which it was based or the conclusions reached, but because the results have been quoted so frequently, what we believe is a misinterpretation of the data has been so widely believed, and because the study raises clearly some fundamental issues. The tests were administered with considerable ingenuity. In selected New England communities a free motion picture was offered. During the intermission members of the audience were invited to take some tests. Individuals who did not attend the movie were visited in their homes and also invited to take part.

In this way the *Army Alpha* tests of mental ability were administered to 1,191 selected subjects who ranged in age from 10 to 60. When the scores were plotted against chronological age the results seemed to show rapid intellectual growth to about 16 years, some growth to about 18 to 20 years, and a gradual but steady decline thereafter. At about 50 years, performance matched that of 16-year-olds. Performance on all the subtests was not uniform, and scores on "information" and "vocabulary" *did not reveal any decline*. However, deficits on such subtests as "numerical completions" were considerable.

On the basis of these findings the authors stated that tests of vocabulary and information were the *least* valid indications of intelligence and that speed was a factor of major consequence in the measure of intelligence. As we shall see, these two conclusions, or assumptions, are perhaps the two most important aspects of the whole problem. The authors acted on one other important assumption: namely, that all adults could be considered equivalent in all respects. This was despite the fact that at the time of testing, the 20-year-olds had had considerably more formal schooling than had the 60-year-olds. The close relationship between success achieved by a person on an intelligence test and the amount of his schooling will be noted later.

We shall see below that the interpretation given by the authors no longer seems an adequate explanation and that with the same data one will probably arrive at a completely opposite conclusion.

Thorndike Studies

The studies of learning carried out by E. L. Thorndike and his associates were so substantial in result, were conducted over so many years, and were so ingenious and varied in design that they have been the subject not only of serious inquiry but also of fable and anecdote. How Thorndike progressed from the studies of fowl and animals to the human animal; how he arrived at Columbia with a taxi load of chickens ("the best-educated hens in the world, every one a graduate of Harvard"); how the chickens roosted on the Columbia University running track until a laboratory was built for them; how chickens, mice, snakes, football players and co-eds were all instructed in fascinating combinations in a series of experiments—these are now a rich part of the record and the folklore of psychology.

Thorndike's conclusions were based on the performance of people from 14 to 50 years old in tasks of many kinds, such as learning to write with the nonpracticed hand, to translate a message into code, to acquire an artificial language, to judge weight, to memorize poetry, to perform disagreeable tasks, and many others.

One used to hear these experiments described as the "foundation stone" for adult education. With great care, and in considerable detail, Thorndike showed that the age of a person is *not* a very significant factor in regard to learning; that *all* men and women can learn.

> In general, nobody under 45 should restrain himself from trying to *learn* something because of a belief or fear that he is too old to be able to learn it. Nor should he use that fear as an excuse for not learning anything which he ought to learn. If he fails in learning it, inability due directly to age will rarely, if ever, be the reason. . . . Teachers of adults of age 25 to 45 should expect them to learn at nearly the same rate and in nearly the same manner as they would have learned the same thing at 15 to 20.[3]

Thorndike made three general observations about adult learning:

1. The most advantageous period for learning is between 20 and 25 years of age.
2. There is a decline in capacity for learning from this period to about 42 years, of approximately one per cent per year.
3. The influence of intellect upon the curve of ability to learn in relation to age is slight. The ablest man and the ordinary man show very nearly the same curve.

Another psychologist, W. R. Miles, summarizes these studies, and his own, when he says that "age has no veto power over learning, for any period in the natural life span."[4]

As we have seen, Thorndike's research provided a factual basis for a more optimistic view about adult learning. However, it was limited by the very concepts and assumptions on which it was based.

- Thorndike's results were based on *rate* or *speed* of performance. Efficiency was calculated according to the amount produced per unit of time.

- Subjects of different ages were selected on the assumption that they were equal in all respects save chronological age.
- The tasks selected were laboratory or schoolroom tasks, not those of "real life."
- Thorndike's studies seemed to assume that learning is primarily a matter of practice regardless of the quality or character of the teaching.

In more recent years further experimentation has been carried on by many psychologists. Thorndike's own work has been continued by an associate, Irving Lorge who has employed substantial modifications, both in assumption and in approach.

Using the same basic data as Thorndike but employing many adaptations, Lorge has secured results that indicate even more positively than those of Thorndike the possibilities of excellent learning by adults.

A Shift in Opinion

Differences still exist about how well adults can learn. However, evidence continues to come in that tends to support the views of Lorge and others who have contended that capacity of adults to learn is much more significant matter than any deficits which may be a function of aging.

One of those who differed with Lorge is David Wechsler[5] who developed the Wechsler-Bellevue intelligence scale.

This excellent test of adult mental ability is now used very generally. It contains several subtests. Some of these are timed and some untimed. The collection of test results in aggregate provides important information about human capacity and growth. In the earliest publication of results about twenty years ago, Wechsler interpreted the data as evidence that intelligence was at its maximum on or near the twentieth year but from this point it declined steadily. But upon a recheck of results of his test in 1950 the Psychological Corporation (which distributes the test) issued revised information indicating that the total score *increases steadily from the teens to about age 35 years*, and that the subsequent decline is very much less than Wechsler had predicted. It is possible, indeed quite likely, that later revisions will put the "limit" many years further on.

Most test results in recent years have followed the same trend; namely, they tend to show that intelligence or learning aptitude does not or need not, decline in the years of adulthood. But this is a generalization. Test results for any individual are affected considerably by a number of variable factors which we shall now consider. These include previous schooling, speed, vocabulary, and attitude of adults to learning.

EFFECT OF SCHOOLING UPON ACHIEVEMENT IN INTELLIGENCE TESTS

As we have seen, it was once assumed that an "intelligence test" measured something that was constant and unchanging. It was supposed to be an index of "native" capacity regardless of experience or training, and it was assumed that a person would have the same IQ throughout life. The IQ or Intelligence Quotient, was computed by taking the score that was made on an intelligence test and comparing it with the scores made by others of the same age. If this assumption were correct, the amount of schooling that a person had would make no difference to the IQ. However, no such claim would now be made. It is quite clear that there is a direct and intimate connection between education, experience, *and practice* in the development and maintenance of intellectual capacity. Second, most of the tasks employed in intelligence tests are based on school experience. The performance of any individual on such tests is demonstrably affected by the amount of schooling he has had.

A number of studies bear out this general contention. Dr. Lorge had the records of boys and girls tested in the eighth grade, and was able to test them again at age 34. Those of equal mental ability as measured in the eighth grade, but who had continued longer in school, performed very much better at 34 than those who were equally "bright" but had enjoyed less schooling. He also found a high correlation between scores on the Army General Classification Test and "the highest grade completed."[6] John W. Tilton has published results showing that adolescents today perform significantly better on intelligence tests than those of the same age in the 1930's, the difference being that on an average boys and girls go to school longer now than twenty-five years ago.

Read D. Tuddenham showed that the poorest group of soldiers in World War II did as well on the same tests as the average soldier in World War I. The middle score in 1943 would have ranked 88 per cent in 1918. Troops in World War II had an average of ten years of schooling, those in World War I had an average of about eight years. Tuddenham concludes: "The present population is superior in mental test performances to the population of a generation ago . . . a large proportion of this superiority is a consequence of more and better education for more people." Alas for him who claims that adults have a low mental age, basing his findings on test results in World War I. If he will check the data he will be confounded to discover that the "mental age of the average adult" jumped at least two years between the wars!

In appraising the results of any studies of the capacity of adults, one needs to have precise information about the amount of schooling of the individuals. It is significant to note that when this factor is taken into account, most of the data pointing to decline in the mental ability of adults ceases to have any point.

SPEED

We have already seen that as people grow older their reaction time, speed of perception, and speed of task performance all decline. In regard to performance a number of studies have shown that the decline is not solely for physiological reasons. It has been found, for example, that older people may be more concerned about accuracy than younger subjects and thus inclined to take more time for the task.

But whether for physiological or psychological reasons—*speed does decline.*

Most of the earlier tests of mental ability were based on

the view that there is a very high correlation between speed and power. Thus if you tally the number of correct responses per minute or hour you will have an index of capacity. We have seen that there is general agreement that this is a valid assumption in regard to normal children. Many of those who, as in the Jones and Conrad study cited earlier, have measured the "intelligence" of adults likewise, seem to assume that for adults as well speed and power are also closely related.

Of course, if one assumes such a relationship one is forced automatically to accept the consequent view that the mental *power* or *capacity* of adults declines, since it is clearly established that slowing down occurs.

But suppose one lays aside such an assumption for a moment. Suppose one sets out to measure power or capacity separately from speed by giving subjects sufficient time needed to complete the tasks.

This is substantially what Lorge did in a series of experiments. He selected four tests—one *untimed* test of performance, and three *timed* tests of speed *and* power. The subjects were laborers of various ages. On the *timed* Otis Tests subjects of 20-25 years scored, on an average, 44.4; subjects of 27½-37½ years scored 39.3; subjects of 40 years and over scored 33.4. The scores for the same groups on the *timed* Army Alpha were 149.6, 142.3, 128.7. But on the *untimed* CAVD test *there was little or no change.*[7]

One can see from these results that a test conducted with a time limit supports the conclusion that there is a steady decline with age. But when a test is employed where time is *not* a factor there is *no* significant decline associated with age. This kind of study has been repeated on several recent occasions with similar results. Lorge concludes that there is a decline in the rate of learning as age progresses, *but that intellectual power in and of itself does not change from 20 to 60.* Lorge attributes the decline in rate of learning to losses in visual acuity, auditory acuity, and reaction time. He also refers to such factors as increased fear of failure and a different attitude that older adults have toward learning.

We have already noted the different ways in which younger

or older people may view "correctness." The matter is of some importance, worth an additional reference or two, even though this anticipates to some extent what will be discussed in Chapter 5.

A. T. Welford summarizes results from a large number of studies of job performance conducted in England:

> It appears that the older subjects' performance tends to be slower and more deliberate than those of the younger, but subsequently be more accurate. . . . If we are interested in the total amount achieved regardless of any other consideration, then the younger subjects must be regarded as better, though not markedly so. However, the older subjects achieved their results with much less effort wasted on small errors, so that their performance can at least be said to have been more *efficient.* Finally if we are concerned with accuracy, as we should be if every error represented waste of valuable industrial material, we must regard the older subjects as, on the average, clearly superior. . . . Although speed may decrease among older people, this deficiency is often more than offset by gains in quality and accuracy. . . . Also, it seems, there is a substantial number of individuals who maintain performances comparable with those of people in their twenties or thirties.[8]

But this is performance, in the main, on industrial activities. What about those of a more "academic" kind? Robert Peers has reviewed a number of studies of tests of "reasoning," where older people seemed to perform less well than younger:

> The statements from which the groups were required to make logical deductions were involved and questionable in themselves, so that the older subjects, with their greater range of experience and stronger convictions, were inclined to question and comment on the statements rather than make the logical deductions required by the instructions.
>
> A quotation from one of the older subjects (aged 57) seems to make this clear: "I find this work more difficult because I am inclined to question several of the statements, instead of accepting them and drawing the conclusions, if any, which may justly be derived from them." It is difficult to see how, in the circumstances, the results can be regarded as demonstrating any less ability on the part of the older subjects to make logical deduc-

tions; it may merely indicate their unwillingness or even in-ability to do so from hypotheses which are not justified by their experience or which conflict with emotional and moral "sets."[9]

The factors which are usually expressed as the "rigidity" of older people will be discussed later. It is quite clear that measuring intellectual performance in time limits without tak-ing such factors into consideration creates an added difficulty for the older person.

Wechsler, and several others, though accepting the evi-dence that there is no loss in correct responses or quality if the time factor is eliminated for the older person, still main-tain that speed should be retained as a component in adult testing in order to give a measure of efficiency—that is, the number of correct responses per total unit. Wechsler has de-fined intelligence as "the aggregate or global capacity of the individual to act purposefully, to think rationally, and to deal effectively with his environment."[10]

But whether this notion of "efficiency" is particularly use-ful or not, by far the most important point is that intellectual capacity *can be maintained.*

Some psychologists believe from the evidence so far that although with increasing years "slowing down" happens, the loss is considerably less significant in activities with which the individual is already familiar. There is also some evidence to suggest that loss of speed may be less for people of higher mental ability.

VOCABULARY

Many people seem to lack confidence about their speech and vocabulary. In part at least this may result from the widely advertised claims that some new book, or encyclopedia, or training scheme will increase vocabulary, give "word power" and bring about vocational and social success. One result of such clamor is confusion and insecurity. We may have a vague fear that we are lacking the rich, selective, compre-hensive kind of vocabulary that everyone should have. In addition to these fears we are all conscious of how often we forget. We forget names of people, we can't think of the right word when we want it, we no longer remember the French or Spanish we learned at school. What we don't use regularly we tend to forget. For all these reasons, our feelings about our own capacity regarding vocabulary are often quite negative.

Consequently it comes as a surprise, almost as a shock, when we hear that *in capacity to use vocabulary*, adults do not show the decline that is characteristic of many kinds of capacity. If anything they tend to improve throughout life, right up to the later years.

We have already noted that in the Jones and Conrad study adults of any age continued to do well in vocabulary although other scores were down. This was explained by the assertion that vocabulary is *not* a reliable test of intelligence.

Studies by Lorge and others all show some improvement with age in scores on vocabulary. In one such test given recently to over 2,000 industrial workers in Scotland, the 30 plus, 40 plus, 50 plus, and 60 plus all had better scores than the 20 plus group. In another study of university professors, one of the 80-year-olds made the highest score, and the older men had better scores than the younger on synonym-antonym tests and equaled the younger men on a test of word meanings. Now, if Jones and Conrad are right in asserting that a vocabulary test is not a useful index of intellectual capacity, the results above would be interesting, but not very important to our discussion. But if capacity in using vocabulary *is an important aspect* of mental ability, the persistence of this capacity throughout life is of the utmost importance.

On this particular point, there really isn't much difference of opinion. One might assume that the mastery and use of one's mother tongue would be as valuable an index of intelligence and ability to learn as it has proved to be a guide in the understanding of personality. And so most psychologists believe it. As a matter of fact, many of them regard the vocabulary test as the *most significant single test of intelligence*. If possible, psychologists will use a battery of subtests, rather than a single one, when they attempt to assess the mental ability of anyone. But if one is compelled to choose one single test as a measure of intellectual capacity, the most satisfying is that of vocabulary. And it is on this supremely important kind of test that adults perform successfully throughout their life span.

Of course, as we might expect, performance is related to *practice*. In one study, for example, it was found that professional persons progressively increased vocabulary through ages 60 to 70 years, and that persons for whom language was not a major factor in daily living showed an opposite trend.[11]

ATTITUDE OF ADULTS TO LEARNING

Most of the comparisons that have been made of the performance of young people and adults on mental tests have not only assumed equal school preparation but also equal or similar motivation. But the attitude of an adult to a test may differ markedly from that of an adolescent. It may be stronger or weaker. He may take the test seriously, with indifference, or even with hostility.

It can be predicted, however, that such tests do not always engage the fullest effort of an adult. Will a banker, or housewife or garage mechanic respond with much effort or enthusiasm when he is asked to learn Esperanto or the fact that K x G = Z? Contrast this with the attention that one sees being given to a complicated mathematical problem at a horse race, or stock market, or the capacity of a political agent or recent convert of a church to master extraordinary amounts of complex information.

Being able to see results has a positive effect upon performance. In tasks where men and women have been informed that they will be given the results of their work they tend to achieve more, more quickly. As we have noted earlier, being aware of the purpose of a task is likely to increase efficiency. Where work seems to be without aim, output is less and fatigue seems to be greater. If the subject knows or suspects there is no possibility of accomplishing the task, there is a decline in the amount of effort.

The direction and intensity of the adult motivation will markedly affect his success. Any results of adult performance on mental tests cannot be appraised without reference to the seriousness with which the adult undertook the tasks. We shall deal with this in greater detail in the next chapter.

Evidence from Follow-Up Studies

We have noted that there are few *longitudinal* studies of mental ability where the performance of individuals on the same or similar tests are noted regularly over the entire life span. However, there have been a number of valuable "follow-up" studies in which individuals were retested at least once after a period of intervening years.

As mentioned earlier, Dr. Terman has been able to test the same men and women at different ages. All the subjects showed gains in test scores. Using one of Terman's tests, Boyley and Odin obtained scores from a group of men, and their wives, all about 41 years of age, who had taken the same test twelve years before. Scores on the second test were consistently higher.

Another investigator, Dr. W. A. Owens, retested 127 males using the same form of the Army Alpha which they had taken as an entrance examination for college. Individuals were carefully selected so that they could be considered representative of the entire group of candidates. The result, after thirty years, was that the individuals all showed a significant increase in total score. It is relevant to our earlier discussion that even with this select sample, the more schooling that had been taken, the greater gain in test score.

Most of the follow-up studies of Terman and others have had subjects of high intelligence. Would there be different results with average, or below average, adults? No conclusive answer can yet be given to this question. However, what evidence exists is again positive.

Two follow-up studies have dealt with cases of low intelligence.

In the first study the same battery of tests was given to adults who had taken them eighteen years before. All showed gains, the average increase in IQ amounting to 15 points. Similar results were achieved in the other study. No conclusions can be reached on such small samples, but the results are worth some consideration until more evidence is in.

Interest and Learning

One of the curiosities of human growth is that power in the use of verbal symbols persists throughout life, but there seems to be considerable decline in the use of mathematical symbols. When, for example, the scores of adults taking college courses are compared with those of younger undergraduates, the adults invariably tend to do better work in literature, philosophy, and history and less successful work in mathematics and physics. The problem itself is a complicated one. The less favorable scores could be substantially affected by lack of practice, lack of interest, or even the resigned acceptance of older people that they cannot do mathematics.

One of the reasons that adults continue to learn well, according to W. R. Miles, is that they concentrate their learning in the areas of experience in which their interests also lie. Thus their motivation is substantial and, as everyone knows, wanting to learn is the greatest aid to learning. During childhood, varied learning is common; in maturity, active learning is usually practiced in areas defined in terms of interest.

We shall examine these factors of interest and motivation in much greater detail in Chapter 6.

Summary

Some differences of opinion still exist in regard to the maintenance or decline of intellectual capacity, or learning aptitude, throughout life. But there has been a dramatic reversal in the trend of interpretation. Increasingly evidence is coming in to support the view that adults of all ages can learn effectively (that age has no veto power over learning).

In respect to tests of *vocabulary* adults, if anything, show improvement, not decline.

In giving the *same* tests taken earlier to adults a decade or so later (in follow-up and longitudinal studies) the individuals have usually registered a better performance when older.

This seems to be true for individuals of slender as well as of excellent intellectual ability.

The amount of schooling that a person has had modifies considerably his performance in such tests. Indeed, a critical factor in many tests of ability seems to be the amount of practice of the particular task. When people "keep in training" in intellectual as well as physical tasks, their capacity is maintained.

Motivation of the adult undertaking the test is a major factor in performance. Also of importance is the development of well-defined goals for any program of studies, of clear statements about the difficulties or possibilities of succeeding in these objectives, of planning the enterprise in clear stages that can be attained, and involving the learner in some process of appraising his accomplishments.

REFERENCES

1. L. M. Terman and M. H. Odin, *The Gifted Child Grows Up* (Stanford: Stanford University Press, 1947).
2. H. E. Jones and H. S. Conrad, "The Growth and Decline of Intelligence," *General Psychological Monographs* XIII, 1933.
3. E. L. Thorndike, *Adult Learning* (New York: The Macmillan Company, 1928). By permission of Teachers College, Columbia University, New York, copyright owners.
4. W. R. Miles, "Psychological Aspects of Ageing," *Problems of Ageing* (Baltimore: Williams & Wilkins Company, 1952).
5. David Wechsler, *The Measurement of Adult Intelligence* (Baltimore: Williams & Wilkins Company, rev. ed., 1955).
6. Irving Lorge, articles in *Review of Educational Research:* XI December 1941; XIV December 1944; XVII December 1947; XX June 1950.
7. Irving Lorge, *op. cit.*
8. A. T. Welford, *Skill and Age: An Experimental Approach* (London: Oxford University Press for the Nuffield Foundation, 1951).
9. Robert Peers, *Adult Education—A Comparative Study* (New York: Humanities Press Inc., 1958).
10. David Wechsler, *op. cit.*

11. C. Fox, "Vocabulary Ability in Later Maturity," *Journal of Educational Psychology*, Vol. 38, 1947.

Suggested Reading

DONAHUE, WILMA, *Education for Later Maturity* (New York: William Morrow & Company, Inc., 1955).

HAND, S. E., *A Review of Physiological and Psychological Changes in Aging and Their Implications for Teaching of Adults* (Tallahassee: Florida State Department of Education, 1956).

HAVIGHURST, ROBERT J., *Human Development and Education* (New York: Longmans Green & Co., Inc., 1953).

LORGE, IRVING, "Adult Intelligence," *Encyclopedia of Educational Research* (New York: The Macmillan Company, 1952).

——, "Never Too Old to Learn," *Baltimore Bulletin of Education*, June, 1956.

MINER, JOHN B., *Adult Intelligence* (New York: Springer Publishing Co., Inc., 1957).

NATIONAL EDUCATION ASSOCIATION, "Twenty-five Years of Educational Research," *Review of Educational Research*, Vol. XXVI, No. 3, 1956.

OWENS, WILLIAM A., "Age and Mental Abilities," *Genetic Psychology Monographs* XLVIII, 1953.

Chapter 5

FEELINGS AND EMOTIONS

We have already made considerable progress in our search for understanding about adult learning. It is well established that the physical basis for learning is adequate, and we have just been noting that the intellectual capacity for learning is satisfactory. Adults can, and do, learn well all through life.

Now we shall begin to consider what are the conditions of good learning. How does learning happen in some cases and not in others, if the physical-mental equipment is similar? Earlier we observed that the "self" had to be *engaged* if there was to be effective learning. In the next two chapters we shall consider the part that feelings, interests, motives, and attitudes play in this engagement.

Feelings and Learning

There never was a time when it was not understood that emotions played an important part in learning. This is expressed in a hundred aphorisms in various languages, "Spare the rod and spoil the child" just being the crudest, and the one with the widest currency. For centuries some people spoke and acted as if learning was not possible unless accompanied by pain and beatings. This is developed explicitly by novelists like Dickens and Marryat. Many a parent and teacher believed that a boy could not learn unless he was belabored with various kinds of weapons.

The interests, needs, and motivations of any student, child, or adult, are primarily a matter of the emotions, not of the intellect. Any student brings to a classroom his feelings regarding authority, self-esteem, fear, jealousies, status, prestige, and so on. Writing in 1924, Drever clearly identified the importance of nonrational factors:

The fact must be emphasized once more that an individual's tendencies are educationally and socially more important than his capacities, however important the latter may be, and despite the contrary belief on the part of the man in the street. In school, and in life no less, it is the driving power that counts in the long run.[1]

But, as we have seen, learning is often looked on, and spoken of, as if it were entirely an intellectual exercise. A well-known psychologist, L. K. Frank, recently said in an address: "The dilemma of education arises from a belief in man as a rational being in whom emotion can be controlled by reason and intelligence. Educational programs shrink from any frank acceptance of the underlying personality make-up and emotional reactions of students as entering into the educational situation because to do so would bring widespread collapse of the whole educational philosophy and undermining of approved pedagogy." This is not the place to argue about the consequences of not recognizing the place of emotions in learning. At any event, they are being given increasing recognition. Though psychologists differ in many respects, on a point like this there is general accord, even though the consensus may not yet be represented in educational practice.

We shall not, therefore, do much more than assert that feelings and emotions are to be found in any learning situation. The matter is discussed in considerable detail in the suggested readings. The reader can also gain further understanding for himself by observing or remembering his own learning behavior under such circumstances as the last-minute preparation before an exam, at the time of news of military victory or defeat, hearing about the fortunes of his favorite team during the World Series, the occasion of a death in the family, or by recalling his behavior in the classroom after receiving more than usual praise or rebuke from a teacher.

What is important, is to understand some of the main emotional influences on learning, to note the part that interests, attitudes, and motivation play in learning, and the way in which changes in these respects are brought about.

It is also worth noting not only that emotions influence

learning, but that there are many similarities between the "field of emotion" and the "field of learning." Both learning and emotion are aspects of the same process of adjustment to environmental situations which the person must make continuously. Feelings are not just aids or inhibitors to learning; the goals of learning and of emotional development are parallel and sometimes identical and can probably be most conveniently stated as self-realization and self-mastery.

At the outset, it should be acknowledged that our knowledge about this is still rather embryonic. We notice the power and effects of the emotions even though we don't know too much about the causes, or precisely how they operate.

Feelings of Adults

It is a common view that the child is a "bundle of emotions," but some people seem to assume that the adult is lacking feelings, or somehow "got over them." Of course, the reverse is true, as Gardner Murphy points out. "The adult has not *fewer* but *more* emotional associations with factual material than do children although we usually assume that he has less, because the devices of control are more elaborate and better covered in the adult."[2]

The adult carries one load or stigma from which the child is free. He is marked, for good or for ill (and it is mostly for ill), with the prevailing view that he and all other adults are not efficient learners. We have seen in the preceding two chapters that the facts contradict this assessment, but here we have an example of a case where the assumption has just as much influence as if it were true.

The adult may bear one additional burden, that of failure or unpleasantness associated with learning during childhood. Adults in the future may not have so many negative feelings about their schooling. But many men and women, in the present day, though they might subscribe to the notion that "school days are the happiest days of life," still carry some feelings about the school they attended that range from mild dissatisfaction to hatred and loathing. If learning is associated with past defeats and failures, the adult will stay away, or be "too busy." After all, he has had a lifetime of experience in fabricating protective devices to protect his "self" from threat or defeat. Sometimes the first essential step is to make him feel that the new learning situation is indeed *new*, that it is planned for him, that it has no association whatsoever with failures in the past.

The common view about the weaknesses and failings associated with older people is very strong and is widely held. Irving Lorge and Jacob Tuckman once prepared a questionnaire employing such stereotypes as "Old people . . . are absent-minded." The questionnaire was presented to both children and adults. The results showed that as early as 10 years of age children have a negative picture of old age, and that graduate students hold such a stereotype so tenaciously that even a course on the psychology of aging does little to remove the negative picture. Not surprisingly, older adults also have a similar view themselves.[3]

Few of us are fully able to understand or accept our own feelings. Often we don't understand other people or why we feel about them as we do:

> I do not love thee, Doctor Fell,
> The reason why I cannot tell.

Nor do we understand ourselves.

Most of us are capable of, and do have, what are sometimes called the "finer feelings." We like to think of ourselves as being kindly, reasonable, and loving. At times we may be shocked to find that we are also capable of being hateful, wicked, cruel, unreasonable. The inward struggle, the need to cover up our shortcomings from others, and particularly from ourselves, leads to a defensive behavior which deeply affects our freedom to engage in the adventure of learning.

For learning involves change. Who wants to change? No one really does. We all wish that the popular song "Just keep on doin' what you are doin'" could be our theme song. Newton's first law of motion is, "Every body persists in a state of rest (or of uniform motion in a straight line) unless compelled by external force to change that state." One need not accept this as a law to explain all human relationships, but human beings too, seek to remain in a state of equilibrium. No one wants to change but everyone must change. We must adjust to other people. We must take into account time and place and things. Change means disturbance, and a human being is ready to bear disturbance only under some conditions, and not at all under others.

This is not the place to attempt a catalogue of all the emotions. Moreover, they seldom present themselves in any simple form. They are nearly always mixed and complicated. The young man who has been summoned for an interview with his boss may feel—If-he-balls-me-out-I'll-throw-his-job-in-his-face-I-hope-I-get-a-raise-I-wish-this-was-over. . . . Or the same young man on his way to see a young lady may feel—Will-she-go-with-me-to-the-dance-I-don't-care-if-she-doesn't-I'll-take-that-blonde-I-love-her. . . .

Constellations of Feelings

There are three, at least, emotional foci or constellations of feelings that are of constant influence on learning:

- love and associated feelings such as respect, admiration, generosity, sympathy, friendliness, encouragement
- rage and similar attributes such as sense of frustration, being thwarted and rejected
- fear and such concomitants as suspicion.

The first group in the many forms in which these factors are found, leads to calm, serenity, hope, joyousness, confidence, happiness. To the second and third the response is anxiety, withdrawal, despair, greed, hate.

As we have seen and shall see later, the first tends toward learning of quality and endurance, and the second and third tend toward resistance of learning and forgetfulness as a means of ending the pain.

Welford[4] has reported a number of studies in which it was shown that anxious individuals learned less rapidly than others. However, we say *tends* because the process is not a simple one. There are as many paradoxes in the field of learning as in any other area of human experience.

In a recent book by Ashley Montagu the author takes a strong position about the place of affection in learning:

> . . . to teach is to love. And in the final analysis, as Goethe said, we learn only from those whom we love. . . . My greatest teachers have been great lovers. The very interests I have in this world I can trace directly, in almost all cases, to the moments when my teachers with love and reverence spoke to us of some great figure or event. . . .[5]

Or, as Carlyle wrote: "Love is ever the beginning of knowledge as fire is of light."

Throughout life, of course, there are many changes in the kinds of situation or stimulus in which fear and anger are invoked.

Fear of the dark is characteristic of the child. But as his size and strength increase, and as intellectual maturity is reached, many fears simply "drop out" because the growing child becomes able to understand and to handle situations that had formerly resulted in fear. In later years declining physical or intellectual capacities may induce fear. There may be increasing anxiety about decline in sexual competence, or a new form of fear of the dark or of slippery streets on the part of a man or woman whose sense of balance is deteriorating. There is not yet much evidence about this, but it seems that anxieties are greatest in *anticipation* of the decline; that the adult *facing the fact* of decline is able to manage it with less actual stress than he displayed when he first began to be concerned.

Many studies have shown that older people seem less self-confident than at an earlier age. Undoubtedly this is a result not only of decline in some capacity but because of their acceptance of the stereotype of loss to which we have already directed so much attention. In a recent study it was seen that a group of older professors made twice as many remarks belittling themselves when taking an "intelligence" test as did a group of younger professors.

There are also changes in the conditions that result in anger. Studies of college students have indicated that for them causes of anger usually come about from the thwarting of plans or wishes. Sometimes this happens as a result of the action of other people, sometimes through such institutional factors as college regulations, railroad schedules, and the like. Personal inadequacies and chance factors also make some contribution. As people grow older, there seem to be no fewer causes of anger, but most adults have learned something about the control of anger. However, anger resulting from a threat to one's values in areas like politics and religion seems to become of greater significance in later years. To put it another way, such attacks are seen as jeopardizing the "self."

Many studies and observations have reported that older people are rigid and inflexible. The word "set" is invariably applied to an older person. For anyone planning a program or curriculum with older people this is a factor which cannot be neglected. Views about politics, religion, morality, duty may be held fixedly; they are not subject to question or review without displays of emotion. But there is enough evidence to question if this "crystallization" or "integration" happens invariably and inevitably, or results because of waning contacts with ideas or with stimulating social groups. The provision of educational opportunity for the old seems to inhibit somewhat the onset of such rigid behavior.

We shall, of course, return from time to time to the ways of reducing the inhibitions to learning which result from fear and anger.

Learning Associated with Pain and Fear

But is there no learning at all if pain or fear is associated with the learning experience?

Of course there is. For generations children and adults have learned some subjects, or lessons in life under the most threatening conditions. "The burnt child dreads the fire" and learns not to touch the stove. A child in fear of physical beatings may learn his arithmetic or irregular Latin verbs. But he may also—not always—learn to dislike or hate the teacher, to dislike or hate the school, dislike or hate the subject, dislike or hate studies in general. He may learn to defend and protect himself in the present and to avoid similar experiences at all costs as soon as he is able to escape. The adult whose honest questions are ignored or disregarded may learn that some foreman, or some professor, leans on and is circumscribed by his particular field of knowledge or his skill, or that such teachers are not really themselves interested in learning. Such disinterest is infectious.

Rogers has made a useful distinction between threatening conditions in life which result in learning directed to self-preservation, and learning under threat in the classroom:

> It may be objected that learning goes on in spite of or even because of, threat. Witness the platoon which is likely to be fired upon as it goes into enemy territory, and because of this threat learns rapidly and effectively about the terrain. It is true that when reality provides the threat, the learning of behaviors which will maintain the self goes on apace. If the desired training has no other goal than to maintain the self as it is, then threat to self may not impede the progress of learning. But in education this is almost never true. What is desired is growth, and this involves change in the self. Whenever such a broader goal is envisaged, then threat to the self appears to be a barrier to significant learning.[6]

Four Aspects of Self

We have, of course, been talking all along about the "self," for that is what feels. It is important to recognize that there are four selves or, more correctly, there are four different aspects of self:

- What the person actually does and says
- How the person views and feels his own behavior
- How what the person does is perceived by others
- The ideal self (the superego) which each of us carries all through life.

The differences, even the conflicts between these aspects of self have long been the main field of attention for the novelist and dramatist. The learner must cope not only with what emotions are present or released at the time of an action, but how others expect him to feel and how he idealizes himself as feeling. The housewife looking at a contemporary painting (or considering joining such a course as "Understanding Modern Painting") is the subject of a complex of feelings associated with the painting itself, what her friends or her husband will say about such painting, what she has read in her magazine, what view she has of herself, or what is her understanding of such terms as culture.

Two other matters also modify feelings. One is usually called "level of aspiration," the other is the "social class" of the individual.

Level of Aspiration

Much that has been said about the "level of aspiration" is now being comprehended under such notions as "self-image." We shall not deal with these related concepts fully, but they are very important for learning. What does the learner feel that he might achieve? How far does he think he can go? On the whole is he "optimistic" or "pessimistic" in his view about his own potentialities? Does his view about his possibilities correspond with reality?

We can see many examples of the way that "level of aspiration" modifies feelings and behavior.

It used to be thought, for example, that all people in tropical areas are indolent because of the heat and the ease of living. This is far from true. Some are, and some are not, as in other parts of the world. Indolence is not unusual in the tropics, but where it is found it may be a matter of inadequate diet and is frequently associated with the "self-image."

Our own culture is one in which there is quite general acceptance of such slogans as "The sky is the limit," "The incredible we will do now, the impossible will take a little longer," "Any man may become a millionaire," "Anyone may become president." But, though holding such notions in part, the adult may also have deep-seated feelings of personal inadequacy, all the more poignant because they conflict with what he feels he ought to be able to accomplish. After all, if you lived in another country and belonged to a restricted class, expecting always to live in that class and in that manner, you would not be assailed by guilt feelings for not doing better. In our relatively open society, such feelings are more common. Class and social position have much to do with anyone's level of aspiration.

Effects of Social Class

A number of studies have shown that the factor of social class may have as much to do with success in school as "intelligence." Boys and girls from certain homes tend to do better schoolwork and stay in school longer than boys and girls, with the same aptitude, who come from other homes. Farmers of a certain kind make full use of agricultural extension services, others do not. By class we mean simply what Morris Ginsberg described in the *Encyclopedia of the Social Sciences*:

> . . . groups of individuals who, through common descent, similarity of occupation, wealth, and education, have come to have a similar mode of life, a similar stock of ideas, feelings, attitudes, and forms of behavior, and who, on any or all of these grounds, meet one another together on equal terms, and regard themselves altogether with varying degrees of explicitness, as belonging to one group.

It used to be commonly believed that there was no such thing as class in the equalitarian society of North America, that such things had been left behind in Europe. Robert and Helen Lynd, in their two books on *Middletown*, have many references to this. They observed:

> To most of its people in whatever group, "class differences" and "class consciousness" are vague, unfamiliar, and, if recognized, unpleasant and sinister terms. . . . Any talk about "class differences," a "class struggle," and similar unpleasant things is

attributed to "reckless outside troublemakers." Officially Middle-town scoffs at the "class struggle."[7]

This attitude went so far that anyone who was concerned about class differences was considered somewhat unreliable; he might have had some contact with subversive ideas. However, with the publication of many social studies such as those of Lloyd Warner and his associates this situation is probably changing. Nevertheless, a public opinion poll question employed not very many years ago which asked, "To what social class do you belong—the middle class, the upper class, or the lower?" drew the following answer:

- willing to identify themselves with upper class   6%
-    "   "   "   "   "   middle class 88%
-    "   "   "   "   "   lower class   6%

Where people place themselves is not so accurate but is just as revealing as where they are placed by an outside observer. Warner's famous classification is:

Upper-upper	1.44%
Lower-upper	1.56%
Upper-middle	10.22%
Lower-middle	28.12%
Upper-lower	32.60%
Lower-lower	25.22%
(unknown)	.84%[8]

This discrepancy between how people class themselves and where Dr. Warner placed them is exceedingly interesting. Of the utmost significance is the feeling of people in the different classes both about each other, and about other groups. One can and does hear such remarks: "All the people on this street are a nice class of people," "They are honest enough, but nobodies," "I would rather not have my daughter go to a party on that street," "Boy, are the kids in that school a bunch of squares," "They are too rich for my blood," "Down in that section they live like animals."

One is influenced in making or resisting changes in behavior by the very strength of one's group or cohesiveness of one's neighborhood. For example, Duncan and Kreitlow found that where the bonds of religion and ethnic societies are strong, the men are less likely to adopt new attitudes and new techniques.[9]

Where and how one lives has a crucial effect on feelings about events and activities. When adolescents become men and women they may change their economic and social position since mobility is one of the main features in our society. But whatever social position they are in, markedly affects their feelings about participation in such activities as violin playing, golf, going to races, kinds of music that one listens to, art, reading or discussing philosophy, choice of magazines, courses in parent education, and so forth.

It is quite possible to conduct activities in most of these fields for people in most social positions. But the way in which they are approached and encouraged to take part must take into account their present feelings about such matters and the light in which that participation will be viewed by others around them.

Their social position will therefore also influence the satisfaction that they may receive from an activity, although other factors also modify satisfaction.

Sources of Satisfaction

We pointed out earlier that the individual will tend to persist in a task, no matter how difficult, if he is getting enough satisfaction from it. To continue may cause him physical pain, like practicing rowing when his hands are covered with blisters, or struggling to master a multitude of new words and constructions, despite previous failures, when he is preparing for a fellowship to study in another land. He may, by continuing, even endanger his life, or bear endless routine and boredom in connection with scientific experiments. But if he is not gaining satisfaction, on his own terms, he tends to reject, to forget, to excuse himself. This is all part of "normal" behavior. The abnormal person may develop the ability to blot out whole scenes and episodes from his experience if, instead of satisfying, it is threatening or painful to him.

Satisfaction, whether it is about physical or intellectual activity, is itself an emotional matter, not an intellectual one. We *feel* satisfied, *and* this gives us some release from tension or we *feel* the discomfort of dissatisfaction.

In a class, or learning group, there are three sources of relationships in which satisfaction may or may not show itself. First, there is the relationship between student and teacher; second, the relationship between student and other students; and, third, the relationship between the student and the subject matter of the course.

In his relationship to the teacher, to his fellow students, and to the subject being studied, the student, consciously or unconsciously, always hopes to demonstrate his worth and to feel enlarged. Accordingly, if he perceives that he is under attack by the teacher, or threatened by his fellow students, or certain to appear in an unfavorable light in his handling of the subject matter, his mind and his energies will be engaged in covering up and protecting himself, not upon opening himself up to change and growth. How much can he be himself? Will the teacher accept anything he may bring to the discussion? Will his fellows think him queer if he really says what he thinks? These are questions he wants answered even before he permits his curiosity in the subject matter to be displayed.

In his approach to subject matter, whether as individual student or as class member, the student is an explorer, a discoverer. If he finds that there is no adventure, if the teacher is weary of exploration, or always has some *truth* up his sleeve to play if the student is not following a prescribed pattern, if the student is denied any opportunity for discovery, much of the satisfaction of learning is dissipated. Most of us have seen an older brother spoil a great adventure for a younger by revealing its climaxes too soon, or by belittling, by saying that all this is "old stuff." This can also happen in the classroom or laboratory.

Fellow class members can be seen as colleagues, collaborators, allies in a joint undertaking. If so, the class is a place where one can try out ideas—even though to try means to risk failure. But if class members are perceived as competitors or critics, as hostile, one will not venture much, or one may become aggressive in attacking them or in defending one's present position.

It is also possible, of course, that relationship with the class members may become so supporting, the attitudes and experience of all class members may become so much alike, that little learning is possible. But such an eventuality will happen only if the teacher abdicates *his* responsibility and if the subject matter is not used with judgment and effectiveness.

There must be some dissatisfaction, unrest, desire for something else, if there is to be learning. It is in the balanced relationship of these three factors, that learning is made effective and enduring.

Strong feelings may also be associated with different subject matters. An engineer may get a sense of completeness, symmetry, well-being, delight in solving a difficult but orderly mathematical problem. When he is studying modern history or economics and at the end of a session there seem to be more unanswered questions than when he started, he may have feelings of actual alarm and pain, rather than well-being. In both cases the learning may be substantial and significant, but in the latter condition the result may be a conflict in feelings. And as we have seen, the presence of these feelings may sharply influence whether he will undertake a further learning experience in such a subject.

Recapitulation

It is now time to recapitulate something of what we have been saying about the relationships of feelings to learning and begin to get a somewhat clearer picture of how learning actually happens. There will be effective learning, the self will tend to be engaged, if the following conditions are realized:

stimulus-and-security
dependence-and-independence
reorganization of previous experience
relevance of relationships
satisfaction, in terms of the learner.

Both security and stimulus are essential. Much that has been written or said about learning has concentrated on the stimulus. It has been argued that if you make the stimulus strong enough, or challenging enough, or threatening enough, that will produce good learning. Does it? Not always. The child that is to be punished in the event of mistake, the salesman who will be fired if he does not reach his quota, may be thrust down into failure due to fear and nervousness. The result of a strong stimulus without *something else* may be rebellion, withdrawal, rejection, or apathy. The something else needed is a condition of security. By this we mean that the learner needs to feel at home with himself, sufficiently confident that he can meet the challenge successfully, or he may make no effort at all. He must have enough well-being *and* enough challenge or he will not dare the pain or discomfort that, in little or in large, always accompanies any learning.

The learner has two opposite needs—dependence and independence. He wants to lean on the parent or teacher, or foreman or coach, to be guided by him. He would like to have the hard tasks done by someone else. At the same time he wants to assert himself, he is fed up with being a "yes man," he wants to dominate, to have people know that he is "quite a person." Sometimes one of these opposing tendencies is stronger, sometimes the other, but both are always present. The learner who understands that he has such counterpoised drives, is already in a better position to bring them into some kind of equilibrium. Conversely, neither the situation in which dependence is always penalized, nor the one in which independence is always punished, gives much opportunity for effective learning.

Learning depends on previous experience. Of course, you will say. But this is a qualitative matter as well as quantitative. It is much more than how much experience—it is what *kind* of experience and what *meaning* it has, how it affects the self. One of the earliest concepts of learning was that called the *tabula rasa*, in which it was alleged that a human being could be likened to a fresh and empty sheet upon which are written all the lessons in living. A second concept was that the human being is like a sponge, soaking up facts and skills, and releasing them (forgetting) under pressure, or through aging. We know that the process of learning is not passive reception of experience, or passive absorption of facts. The human being is active, it reaches out, it seeks, it selects experience and relates and integrates new experience into its being. What that being is, how it has handled previous experience, what are its feelings from previous learning encounters—these are matters of utmost significance.

Any student of any age brings his experience to the classroom or seminar. But the experiences of the adult may be extensive and varied. This may be the richest source of his learning objectives as well as a resource for testing out hypotheses growing out of the subject matter. To the extent that this is achieved, the adult is likely to take a responsible part in the learning transaction.

Learning depends upon the relevance of relationships. We have all heard that the "3 R's" have a central place in learning, and we know what they stand for. R might equally stand for *relevance*. We have seen that the human learner is not a sponge, soaking up all experience, but a subtle selecter of experience. One of the principles of selection is relevancy. Children expect to have to learn things, whether or not they see any meaning in the learning; adults are much less ready to accept learning without clear relevance. It has been pointed out frequently that teachers of mathematics, diligent as they may be in teaching the steps or processes in mathematical problems, will not have much success unless they explain what is being attempted, what is the nature of the problem, and what is the purpose of the exercise. In addition, the way the proof of a problem is arranged makes a marked difference between success in understanding the problem. Otherwise there may be some memorizing (quickly to be forgotten) of certain mechanical steps.

Adults expect to find relevance both in the objectives and in the methods employed. For them, evaluation often means reassurance that what they are doing is relevant.

Continued learning depends upon the achievement of satisfaction. The satisfaction must be felt in terms of the learner's own expectations and needs. Satisfaction should obtain in his relation to the teacher or leader (recent studies of "leadership" show that all successful leaders have at least one trait in common—that the followers attain satisfaction in the relationship).[10] It should also come about in relation to the other participants and to the subject matter itself.

REFERENCES

1. J. Drever, *An Introduction to the Psychology of Education* (London: Edward Arnold, Publishers, Ltd., 1924).
2. Gardner Murphy, "Social Motivation," *Handbook of Social Psychology* (Cambridge, Mass.: Addison-Wesley Publishing Company, Inc.), Vol. II.
3. Jacob Tuckman and Irving Lorge, "The Influence of a Course on the Psychology of Adults on Attitudes Toward Old People and Older Workers," *Journal of Educational Psychology*, Vol. 43, 1952.
4. A. T. Welford, *Skill and Age: An Experimental Approach* (London: Oxford University Press, 1951).
5. Ashley Montagu, *Education and Human Relations* (New York: Grove Press, 1958).
6. Carl R. Rogers, *Client-Centered Therapy* (Boston: Houghton Mifflin Company, 1951).
7. Robert S. Lynd and Helen M. Lynd, *Middletown* (New York: Harcourt, Brace and Company, 1929).
8. W. Lloyd Warner and Paul S. Lund, *Social Life of a Modern Community* (New Haven: Yale University Press, 1943).
9. James Duncan and Burton Kreitlow, "Selected Cultural Characteristics and the Acceptance of Educational Programs and Practices," *Rural Sociology*, December 1954.

10. Murray G. Ross and Charles E. Hendry, *New Understandings of Leadership* (New York: Association Press, 1957).

Suggested Reading

HAVIGHURST, ROBERT J., and ORR, BETTY, *Adult Education and Adult Needs* (Chicago: Center for the Study of Liberal Education for Adults, 1956).

MURPHY, LOIS B., and LADD, HENRY, *Emotional Factors in Learning* (New York: Columbia University Press, 1944).

PRESCOTT, DANIEL, *Emotion and the Educative Process* (Washington, D.C.: American Council on Education, 1938).

STOCK, DOROTHY, and THELEN, HERBERT A., *Emotional Dynamics and Group Culture* (New York: New York University Press, for National Training Laboratory, 1955).

WAYLAND, SLOAN, AND BRUNNER, E.DES., *The Educational Status of the American People* (New York: Teachers College Bureau of Publications, 1958).

Chapter 6

MOTIVATION, INTERESTS, AND ATTITUDES

In the preceding chapters we have given some answer to the questions *Can adults learn?* and *How well can adults learn?* Though we shall continue to be concerned with these questions we shall also consider some equally relevant queries such as *Do adults want to learn? How can the attention of adults be secured for learning?* and *How can adults be helped to become continuing learners?*

First, we need to win awareness. In a world in which all conceivable means of expression are being employed to capture attention, how can those interested in learning succeed in the competition? The press, posters, radio, movies, television spray a kaleidoscope of sounds and images upon the individual. How can his eye and ear and emotions be gained for the purposes of education?

What people will, or can be persuaded to, attend to depends very much on their interests and attitudes. These, and motivation, have increasingly become the chief subjects of the student of learning.

Early research about learning usually had to do with simple units of behavior like the "conditioned reflex" where a hungry dog who had been given meat, simultaneously with the ringing of a bell, would "learn" to display all the hunger signs whenever the bell was rung. But much recent research has been about social and human relations in which the primary attention is on motives and attitudes. Many writers have asserted that motivation will determine whether learning will happen at all, as well as the rate and the amount of learning.

In this chapter we shall review some general considerations about motivation, note the physical and social basis for it, and illustrate by pointing out the effect of such key influences upon motivation as time and money. A large part of our discussion will be given to interests and attitudes: how they develop, how they grow and change, how they affect learning. For illustration we shall note some recent studies that not only help us to understand attitude changes but that also suggest useful directions for education.

Why did she do that? What is it that makes a miser? or a millionaire? or a missionary? What started the man on "skid row"? In the words of the title of a well-known novel, "What Makes Sammy Run?"

Perhaps the most curious and fascinating part about human beings is the drives and needs and desires and interests that make them what they are. In previous ages this was the field for speculation by the theologian, philosopher, and novelist. Now it has become a primary interest of the psychologist, other social scientists, and lately of the practitioner of the new occupation known as "motivation research." Though a great deal more is now known about the motivations governing human action than heretofore much mystery still remains. But this need not daunt us. Alfred North Whitehead often said that he had a horror "about the teaching of inert or static ideas . . . that this is the correct thing to know! Once learning solidifies, all is over with it; when that happens, thought is dead." Fortunately, or unfortunately, there is still much more to be learned about motivation than is yet known.

Definitions Related to Motivation

Definitions can obstruct and confuse as well as clarify, but it may be useful to have a brief look at some terms that are in common use, alas, sometimes with very different meanings.

Motivation is usually employed as the general term to designate the active kinds of relationships that an organism has with its environment.

Motives are "a state or set of the individual which disposes him for certain behavior and for seeking certain goals."

Sometimes *motives* are distinguished from *drives* where

drives are used to denote such physiological needs as hunger or thirst, and motives to include interests, attitudes, and purposes.

Both wants and needs are included under motives. Strictly speaking wants are less forceful, they refer to desires, and may lead to action or may be accepted by the individual without his doing anything about them. Needs refer to demands and presumably always lead to some activity to satisfy or remove the tension.

Motivation seems to have two different though related effects directing and selecting, as well as re-enforcing. Motives may lead to either approaching or avoiding behavior, and sometimes both. One writer was recently recalling his behavior during college days. He claims that he developed surpassing skill, when Saturday night was approaching, in lining up and extracting loans from new prospects and, at the same time, avoiding all those from whom he had borrowed in previous weeks.

A person who has developed a strong interest in opera, or classic drama, may pursue these with great eagerness and avoid with equal passion the kind of music and drama which may have previously satisfied him.

Another distinction is between intrinsic and extrinsic motives. The first would be for the sake of the activity itself, such as the joy in playing tennis. The second might be pursued for some value associated with the activity, such as becoming club tennis champion.

It used to be commonly stated, though often denied in practice, that most extrinsic motivations were second-rate, if not downright harmful. Educational texts have been full of diatribes against special incentives even while educational practice placed an ever greater premium upon such incentives. The question is not quite so simple as some supposed. It is not always true that intrinsic motivation is superior in learning effect to extrinsic motivation. Thorndike noted long ago in his book *The Psychology of Wants, Interests and Attitudes*:

> In certain respects, intrinsic interests do possess greater merits. In so far as the task of education . . . is to develop or strengthen

certain interests as more or less permanent features of a person's make-up, the more intrinsic the interest can be, the less dependent upon outside aids and circumstances, the better.[1]

But, he goes on to show, these advantages have often been very much exaggerated, at least as far as learning is concerned:

If an educated adult for any reason is induced by any force, no matter how external, to want to learn a certain thing, no matter how remote learning it is from his other deeper, and more "real" needs, he can learn it provided of course that it is within his powers.

Riesman, in his book *The Lonely Crowd*, has discussed some of the ethical and practical issues involved in extrinsic motivation, in his discussion of "inner-directed" and "outer-directed" individuals.

BASIS FOR MOTIVATION—PHYSICAL AND SOCIAL

Motives can be labeled internal or external depending whether they develop within the organism or without. Hunger for food is an example of an originally interior drive but "hunger" for a good talk has an external origin. Sherif refers to the first as "unlearned biogenic motives" and to the second as the "learned, sociogenic motives."[2]

Primary Motives. There is the need of the body for food, drink, rest; for protection from threats in the physical environment (falling) and for elimination of waste products. For each of these there are characteristic intra-organic sources of stimulation, types of restlessness and tension, and characteristic acts which relieve tension and restore equilibrium. Of considerable importance, too, is the way that we experience some sensations associated with these drives as pleasurable and other as unpleasant. The strength of these drives varies in extraordinary degree throughout life. As a generalization it can be said that they seem to have greatest effect upon motivation and behavior in the early years of childhood and again in the very late years of life when physical losses may impose some limits upon behavior.

Secondary Motives. Beginning at birth there is also a complex of social motivations that are derived from biological urges, but that are equally based on the way a human being "gets along" with his family, in his school, in his job associations and on the way he manages the pressures of social living. These social motives are highly personal but at the same time are affected deeply by the culture in which the person lives. Some "cultural" needs are very powerful. This was seen clearly during the years of the depression when millions of people were out of work. As the Lynds reported in *Middletown*,[3] food sales declined nearly 50 per cent and sales of men and boys' clothing went down about 67 per cent. But gasoline sales declined only 3.6 per cent. The *secondary* need of gasoline, representing as it did social position as well as ability to see their friends, was actually a motive of extraordinary power in comparison with the primary needs of food and clothing. Both primary and secondary motives can be persistent or changing. Gardner Murphy once wrote that motivation

. . . never "starts" or "stops." There are rapid or slow rises in tension level, and rapid or slow transmissions of the tension. . . . But the essential fact about motivation seems to be the continuous instability or restlessness, and the consequent interstimulation which characterizes all living systems.[4]

Still, changing though these motives are, they do have the effect of organizing experience. One psychologist, A. H. Maslow, attempted to show how drives altered and matured into purposes by listing them in a kind of hierarchical order, starting with those appearing first in life and later those having significance in adulthood:

Gratification of bodily needs
Safety insurance against pain and danger of life
Love, affection, warmth, acceptance, a "place in the group"
Self-esteem, self-respect, self-confidence, feeling of strength and
    adequacy
Self-actualization, self-fulfillment, self-expression, use of one's
    capacities "to be the most one is capable of being."[5]

KEY INFLUENCES AFFECTING MOTIVATION—TIME AND MONEY

Motivation, then, is influenced by the physiological characteristic of a person. But it is equally influenced by such non-bodily factors as time or money. A man or a woman who is consciously seeking a mate or a new job, or who is responsible for the care of children, has a very strong goal. Demands upon them in terms of time may result in actually re-enforcing the motivation. Time is limited; if it is used for study, or for work, or for child care, this fact in itself acts to focus and intensify the motive. Other desired activities are forced aside, and, as this is done, the motivation associated with them may gradually be weakened and even replaced. When the person again has ample time for choosing a different activity this may be a time of bewilderment and frustration because the aims and appropriate motives that may be necessary to fill the void may have become diffused or even have disappeared. A woman whose family no longer needs her attention at every waking moment, a man or a woman about to retire, is sometimes facing a critical adjustment, basically a crisis in motivation. The person who has acquired or developed many and varied interests, desires, and goals more readily meets these periods of increased freedom.

But time is restricted in another way. The adolescent has all the time in the world ahead of him, nothing seems impossible to do. But the woman at forty-five, the man at fifty, now realizes that it may already be too late for the expression of some deeply felt needs, and that all future objectives will depend upon how much time is left for their expression. The intensity of motives may deepen or lessen; a man may be determined to finish some task before it is too late, or he may become resigned to the likelihood that it will never be finished.

The influence of time upon what a man will desire to learn, or attempt to learn, is obvious. Equally obvious are the secondary effects upon personality and upon self-confidence, when various forms of frustration accompany the inability to pursue cherished goals.

One aspect of time that has had insufficient study is *span of attention.* The child stays only a short time with one activity, then shifts his attention. As he moves through adolescence the span lengthens until in adulthood there may be several hours of deep, absorbed attention. Much laughter is devoted to the absent-mindedness of some adults, such as professors, but this is recognition of what may simply be a misapplication of a highly developed and highly desirable capacity. The span of attention seems to be related far more closely to interests than it is to the facts of physiology.

Money, or the relative freedom of an individual to choose what he will do, by being able "to afford it," with all the emotional as well as economic consequences that it may bring, is also an influence of considerable intensity. To anyone it is of vital importance to have the money to prepare oneself for a chosen vocation, or to make a change in vocation, or to proceed or not, with plans for establishing a family, or to undertake chosen leisure-time pursuits. The possession or desire for money and the complex attitudes built around its possession and use are a major modifier of motivation.

Motives are also deeply affected by one's age, culture, and social group. In general, middle-class people are more likely to act in greater awareness of time than urban, working-class people. They have more of a link with the past and are more willing to postpone gratification of desires for the future. For the working-class person future rewards or sanctions are too uncertain to have much motivational value. There is a distinct difference between a man of 50 and a man of 25 in his regard toward planning for the future, and toward such notions as saving and thrift. In general, the young man is prepared to use credit; the older man *may* do so but, perhaps, with some sense of impropriety or even guilt. Usually the older man will more readily accept the notion that saving is a good thing.

Learning to use credit is conditioned directly by one's experience and therefore by one's motivation. The young person in North America takes this easily in his stride. But a West Indian farmer, to whom his land is the symbol and guarantee of both freedom and status, and for whom the fear of the money-lender is very real, will try never to do anything which in any way threatens his title to his land. Great schemes for agricultural improvement may be held up because of widely held values, fears, and motives that may work against the proposed changes.

Some writers claim that educational motivations are quantitatively different from a buying decision or a choice of reading material, different not only in complexity but also in the length of time committed in the action. Entering a course or following some other educational venture requires a decision to accept behavior that is formalized perhaps highly regulated, and covering more than one episode. The individual will make such a choice only as he has imagined for himself the satisfaction to be gained from such a course of study. There is considerable doubt that attempts to influence motives toward education by those whose experience is selling a product will be notably successful, unless there is much adaptation of usual advertising practices. It is often urged that those who sell soap ought to be asked to sell education, but results, thus far, do not justify this optimism.

Some research has been made of why workers and farmers undertake study. For example, those in Canada's Farm Forums overwhelmingly said that they were motivated by "neighborliness and community spirit" but they also referred to educational advantages, better understanding of farm problems, achieving a unity among farmers and preparing for social action on behalf of rural people. Ten per cent of the farmers and their wives reported they joined because they enjoy discussion.[6] It is hardly *surprising* that "social" motives are often, or usually, present in most adult educational choices. Some people scoff at such motives as if they were unworthy, but they are to be anticipated and they provide as well an excellent basis for much learning.

Interests

In discussing motivation thus far we have, for the most part though not entirely, been dealing with needs. Now we shall turn our attention to interests and attitudes. We shall not try to distinguish fully between needs and these other responses; they are not identical, but neither can they easily be separated. An interest is often the direct expression of a need, but sometimes it is a substitute. There are, for example, many interests that are some form of substitute for sex hunger. But most interests and attitudes would be included in what Sherif described as sociogenic motives, not internal ones.

We shall not try to make much of a point of the difference between interests and attitudes. If you will search the dictionaries you will discover some variation but there is far from complete agreement. Perhaps the most useful distinction is historical. That is, the earliest research was in what were called *interests*. The results were important, even though the methods used and the conclusions reached were relatively uncomplicated. In more recent years, with refinement both of theory and method, the studies of *attitudes* have become much more subtle. A deeper understanding of what constitutes learning may be coming about through intensive studies of how attitudes are formed and modified.

Our own discussion of these responses will follow the historical precedent; we shall begin with interests and shift over into a consideration of attitudes.

INTERESTS AND LEARNING

Those concerned about learning have often speculated about the relationship between interest and learning. It has long been recognized that there may not be much learning of consequence unless a marked interest is present. The factor of interest was likened by early psychologists to a sentry at the gate, admitting certain stimuli and blocking out others. This is a rather mechanical metaphor; learning is much more dynamic than this interpretation suggests. Interests act not so much as sentinels as an impetus to seek out new experience, or as a favoring climate for change and growth.

Many writers on education, John Dewey for instance, have equated interest with discipline. Dewey often said that the price of self-discipline is the arousal of interest. Others have spoken of interest as an essential condition of responsibility.

There is no fundamental disagreement here although there is not too much knowledge about the nature of interest, and the exact ways in which it affects learning. More information is being sought about the changes in interests throughout life.

A number of psychologists have studied the role of interests, the name of Edward K. Strong[7] being the most prominent. Usually the study has been of those interests relevant to education, vocation, or leisure time.

Changes in Interests. Most observers agree that although interests change radically during life, these changes do not occur in any capricious or inexplicable way. Changes of interests are an accurate reflection of such things as changes in abilities and energy, outlets for the sex drive, modifications of the personality, and shifts in vocational and cultural expectations as youngsters become mature, middle-aged, and elderly. His vocation is much more likely to affect a man's interests than will his chronological age. But changes do occur during life. Older people are just as likely to have strong likes and dislikes as younger. Activities which require well-developed physical or sensory skill, daring, or stamina show the greatest change of all. For most men scaling a cliff or walking along a precipice might be considered a "normal" interest in the twenties, but exceptional thirty years later. Team sports, strenuous tests of endurance, driving a car, performing conjuring tricks may also decline, but bird watching or visiting museums may persist or increase. The older man is likely to be much more resistant than the younger to acquiring interests that interfere with established habits or customs.

One study suggests that a man's hobbies, which often require greater physical activity than those of women, are more likely to have to be given up in the later years. Thus a man who is limited to such hobbies may lose these interests at about the same time as he retires from work, constituting a serious double loss.

Interest in physical activity declines, but it should not be considered that older people ought never, or will never, take part in activities making some physical demands. Walking and visiting friends may be very pleasurable activities. An eighty-year-old widow recently received a power saw and lathe and has learned quickly how to make her own furniture. This is uncommon, but is far from an isolated case.

However, interests and recreations that have to do with talk, writing, reading, and that are carried on at a modest pace, are most likely to survive and even increase in intensity with the passing years. This means that most of the interests associated with most forms of learning endure or even intensify throughout life. However, some studies seem to indicate that there may be a lessening interest in linguistic skill and in efforts requiring writing. The older person, much more often than the younger, prefers interests that are carried on individually rather than in company. However, this finding ought also to be accepted with some caution. It may simply be related to the fact that at present many older people in our society lack congenial social groups. There seems to be a slight decrease in the total *number* of interests as one gets older chiefly because of the decline in those involving physical activity. But most observers agree that interest span, that is, variety and quantity of interests, is closely related to "intelligence."

For interests associated with reading of books and magazines there are considerable individual differences. But we have already seen that interest in reading tends to persist, perhaps to grow. So, in general, does attention to radio and television, though this is more likely to be done individually than in company. Attendance and interest in movies declines sharply after age 25. In the over-60 group 75 per cent of people never attend a movie.

The changes in interest do not take place at a uniform rate. E. K. Strong believes that at least half the changes are likely to occur between twenty-five and thirty-five, about 20 per cent in the next decade and about 30 per cent between forty-five and fifty-five. On the whole, as we noted earlier, the older adult seems to be more resistant than the younger if what is to be learned seems useless or meaningless. Moreover, the older person seems to apply stricter tests of relevancy than does the younger.

Interests and Emotions. The older person seems to suffer more anxiety as the result of poor success while following up an interest. The older person also seems to do less well than the younger where learning is carried out under conditions of mild bodily discomfort.

The generalization that breadth of satisfying interests goes along with happiness seems to be justified for all ages. One writer who has studied the lives of older people maintains that of the three factors that seem essential in a satisfying old age (namely economic security, freedom from physical hardship, and varied interests) the factor of interests is most important. Another who interviewed a large number of teachers concluded that those who were able to carry on wide, varied activities were much better "adjusted" than those whose interests were restricted to work. One does not have to accept the view that "adjustment" is invariably desirable to feel a sense of sorrow and pity for one whose interests have never ranged beyond his job.

Perhaps the most striking single fact about interests is that they are well established at an early age. Most observers believe that if an interest is to have much intensity it must have been established, with satisfaction, before the age of 25. To put it another way, if a man or a woman is to take a rewarding interest in the fine arts when he or she is 50, the beginning for this activity should have developed in the teens or twenties. If he has had no exposure to this interest, or has gained no satisfaction from its expression, he is much more likely to resist, to feel it is not for him, that "he has no time."

It should be pointed out, however, that people tend to read the books that are accessible to them more often than the books in which they say they are interested. This phenomenon seems to be paralleled by their choice of learning or leisure-time pursuits. In part at least, this is determined by what is easily available, not just by what they say they want.

Interests are very much a matter of culture and social position. The game of squash is played by those who belong to social clubs in which there are courts; polo is played by those of wealth and social position, as well as by a handful of cowboys. Some sports like bowling are played by everyone, but predominantly by wage earners. Playing cards are available to all, but the number of people playing poker, or bridge, or whist, is determined in considerable measure by the social position of the players. Interests in opera, symphony concerts, ballet, drama, libraries, used also to be very much a matter of social class, but there has been an expanding participation in these activities by all social groups.

Attitudes and Attitude Changes

Probably in no other field of human activity has there been more recent speculation and research than upon attitude formation and change. Attitudes are learned. They have been defined as "patterns of response which predispose the individual to rather specific behavior." Allport once said that the common element in all attitudes is "readiness for response."[8] Ideals, prejudices, and beliefs are often found together. They seem always to have well-defined objects or values, of either a favorable or an unfavorable nature.

It has long been realized that there is often a wide divergence between what might be called moral knowledge and behavior. Boys and girls quickly learn most of the facts of "right and wrong" in regard to living with their family and living in society. From that point on what they *know* may be distinguished from what they may *practice*. The extent of divergence between knowing and doing seems to bear no relation to age. However, it has been reported that young people seem to be more sensitive about ethical factors having to do with individual rights and with personal relationships, but to be less aware or concerned with either knowing or acting upon that which is associated with civic or social demands.

As a boy or girl goes through adolescence he modifies his views about what is right or wrong. He learned these by rote; he now modifies them by experience, and usually his moral values tend to become more realistic and more "liberal." These changes may continue throughout life but at a slower rate after the teens.

The behavior of children is markedly influenced by their own groups; particularly is this true of the various kinds of gangs to which boys may belong. Both attitudes and behavior of older people are also influenced by their social groups and the way in which they make a living. On the whole, older people appear to make more value judgments in terms of right and wrong. The younger are able to tolerate more reasons or excuses for certain acts.

Many of the most serious kinds of antisocial behavior occur in youth. Beyond the twenties the amount of crime declines steadily and rapidly. Some of the assertions that are sometimes made about the degeneracy of older people cannot be justified to any extent by statistics about crime.

Attitudes toward politics, science, or religion may and can influence what is learned since perception is modified by an attitude. We have seen earlier that pro- and anti-Communists learn more from a text depending on how closely the text conforms to their presently held position.[9]

Many or most young people are not well prepared to take part in civic and national responsibilities when they leave school. Adult ignorance and passivity may also exist, but the study of political issues and participation in local, regional, and national affairs grows steadily through the years, till age 50 or beyond. Voting and political interest often continue even when energy for political action may have waned. Interest in religion seems to follow two curves—one that rises sharply in childhood to slope off when other intense interests come along to compete in the late teens and early twenties, followed by another pronounced upward shift in the later years. The attitude to religion is often accompanied by an interest in reading about or studies about religion, philosophy, and human relations on the part of the older adult.

AGE AND CONSERVATISM

As we have discussed before, in one respect the older adult seems to differ from the younger. He is more conservative. It is worth noting the reasons that are usually cited for this tendency:

- He was reared at an earlier time when, in general, attitudes were not so "liberal" as at present, and he has persisted in these attitudes.
- He learns more slowly.
- He has a more restricted social life, attends fewer movies and public meetings and may choose books, friends, and learning experiences to conform with well-established biases.
- He has a particular social role. The older adult has a position and is more apt to defend that position, and to maintain the attitude associated with it, than the youth who has no particular status.
- He has suffered some losses in sensory and physical capacity, with lessened self-confidence and therefore may feel that it is more necessary to cling to habitual patterns of behavior and display more tenacity in the face of threatened change. He finds the old ways more comfortable and less threatening.

CHANGES IN ATTITUDE

In general, changes in attitude can be brought about by lessening the tension and the conflicts with which the person is affected. For example, providing jobs and housing for older people will probably have considerable effect upon their attitudes. Much can also be done by increasing the number of opportunities where older people will continue to read, hear lectures, see films, take part in study-discussion groups. A major goal is to help them keep up with and take hold of life rather than sit back and submit to inevitable decline. Older people who have maintained an active interest in affairs rarely become the conservative or reactionary influences that sometimes act as a block to progress.

Some Examples of Changes in Attitude and Behavior

A good deal has been found out about attitudes through studying the ways in which people have approached certain situations, as illustrated in several experiments. Two of these have been selected for illustrative purposes: one where women learned new food habits and one where the subjects learned to do something that had previously been distasteful.

CHANGE IN HABITS

Stimulated by some extraordinary research projects conducted by Kurt Lewin[10] and his associates during World War II, there have been a number of studies of the way women learn about and change their habits of serving food. The experiments have been conducted somewhat as follows. The immediate object of the project was to teach the *facts* about nutrition, and the desirability of serving certain kinds of foods while cutting down on the use of other kinds. The content was presented according to two plans. In the first, the women in a large group were taught by excellent instructors who used charts, films, and demonstrations. Under the other plan the women covered the same content but under the guidance and direction of discussion leaders. In each case an effort was made to provide the best possible instruction for the same amount of time. At the conclusion of the course, the women were tested to determine *what facts they had learned.* The results have been about the same. All the women learned a good deal. As far as facts are concerned it seems to matter not at all whether they are taught in a large or a small group. But after an interval of weeks or months, the women were tested once more. This time they were not asked to recall *facts*, but to report on changes in *practice*. Did they now serve less starches and more vitamins, or did the course produce little or no change in their behavior? Now it was found that the women in the small groups who studied the same content and learned the same facts, *had changed their practice* demonstrably more times than those taught in large groups.

Several explanations have been offered for this variation in behavior. Most observers who have studied the results conclude that the significant factor lies in the attitude that is encouraged and developed through a *different quality of participation* in the small group. For some of the women in the large group the class was interesting enough, but it remained a *government* or *university* class. For most or all of the women in small groups, the group soon became *our group*, and the women developed a bond of relationship with other members. Accordingly, they began to assume some obligations to their fellow members, and to the leader. They seemed to feel that they must do something about what they had learned. Attitude change often seems to accompany the acceptance of responsibility or an obligation to oneself and to others.

One needs to be cautious not to extend too far the significance of these inquiries, but they have much to say about the ways in which attitudes of responsibility, as well as incentives for further learning, may be established.

ALTERING THE MEANING

We noted earlier that Thorndike and others conducted some experiments in which adults would "learn" to do things that at first were distasteful. Despite the supposedly universal aversion girls have for mice, women students were given white mice for pets to see what effect this might have on the girls (and the mice). It is amusing to note that this kind of experiment has often been thwarted because the students will refuse to give up their pets at the end of the trial period.

Other students have taken part in experiments designed to have them overcome their repugnance to snakes. This experiment has usually begun with a group of co-eds' being asked to handle snakes. All would refuse, even in the interests of science! Each day a similar attempt would be made but familiarity alone would bring slight, if any, improvement. Only a few girls would undertake to touch the snakes after many trials. At this point a number of *changes in the situation* would be introduced. Instead of "snake" the reptiles would be given names, chosen from movie stars and college football heroes. Second, the snakes would be tied with ribbons, and would be thoroughly saturated in perfume. As these successive changes were introduced, more and more, finally all the girls were able to handle the snakes without any outward show of distaste.

A pleasant story. But it has a very important lesson which goes far beyond the experiment itself. Notice what the changes introduced really were. At first glance they seem amusing and trivial, but this is not really so. What has been done is that the *meaning* of a situation that has deep significance has been radically altered. At the beginning of the experiment the meaning is snake-ugly-dirty-dangerous-slimy-odorous. With the changes introduced, the meaning changes substantially. Accordingly there is also a chance for behavior to change.

For many kinds of learning it may be necessary to alter the meaning of the situation. Another example of the same principle occurred in a community center in a large city. The staff person felt that an excellent activity for high school members was square dancing. But when first suggested, the proposal was greeted by the young people with hoots of derision. The staff member bided his time. At a dance at the center arranged several months later, he brought in a group of eight men and women who were to put on the "floor show" (the activity of greatest prestige, for the members concerned). The featured dancers presented square dances. In introducing the dance, the program director emphasized vigor, and the demands upon skill and energy. The "floor show" then demonstrated dances which exhibited these traits. Next, eight boys and girls, selected because of prowess in dancing, were invited to take part with the visitors. By this time the staff member had accomplished his main purpose. Square dancing which had conjured up a meaning of country-hick-oldfashioned-slow now had meanings derived from floor-show-speed-agility-endurance. From that point on interest in the activity itself was enough to ensure support for it.

Summary

The information about motives, interest, and attitudes is all very interesting. But some people have asked, What in practice does it have to do with learning? Some books on learning make no reference to it; others pay it but slight attention.

However, to anyone who has read this far, or who has reflected even for a moment about what learning means, it must now be unmistakable that the aspect of motivation is both significant and central. The crucial questions are those which deal with the way that the individual *becomes deeply* involved. This affects not only the present learning episode but all subsequent learning experience.

The student of learning must acquire an understanding of the sources of motivation in bodily and social needs. The needs and goals of the individual, how they are shaped, how they are expressed, for example, in the use of time and money, are factors of particular significance. But not only must motivation be understood: it is never static, it is possible to change motivation. Learning usually starts with such a change.

Both interests and attitudes are examples of learned motives. During a lifetime interests change significantly. In the main the shift is away from activities demanding strenuous physical effort, and toward those involving talk, reading, and similar pursuits. Interests and attitudes are closely linked with occupation, class, and culture; they may be influenced more by occupation than by chronological age. Many of the changes in interest as people grow older favor the conditions under which education is usually conducted. However, if experience in a particular activity did not occur, with satisfaction, in the first two or three decades of life, the development of that interest in an older person would be far from automatic. But interest can be created and can be changed, if the initiation of interest is undertaken with care.

Attitudes can also be changed. They are complex forms of response and they may serve many functions in the emotional life of a person. They are most likely to be altered when the person is not undergoing threat or tension; to solidify under overt or presumed attack. The tendency toward rigidity and conservatism that is often found in older people may have nothing inevitable about it. Where basic needs of older people are met, such as the provision of shelter and economic security, interesting employment, and the feeling that one is wanted, reactionary behavior is not common and more "liberal" attitudes can be expected. In changing attitudes, the *self* must be involved. This may happen through assuming responsibilities to oneself and to others. Change can also be achieved through modifying the *meaning* of the social situation.

A Pause

We shall now pause momentarily to look back over the ground we have covered.

At first glance, the track may appear twisting and obscure. There is little that is plain or rudimentary about learning or about the path we have taken in our exploration of it. The word does appear to mean different things to different people, in different situations. Neither formulas nor detailed guides have yet been presented.

However, a number of points are established. They have been presented again and again, in different forms. Perhaps the repetition has been boring, but one must risk that possibility sometimes with ideas that really are basic, particularly when, as in the present case, though they may have achieved *verbal* recognition, they are so frequently denied in people's feelings and habits.

- Continuing education has become an important enterprise for millions of adults, and the effectiveness of such education is a matter of the utmost social and national importance.
- The physical and sensory equipment of people of all ages is ample for most kinds of learning if it is used efficiently. (Of course there are substantial individual differences in capacity.)
- There is nothing about aging itself which prevents or seriously hampers learning.
- Many, perhaps most people, do not accept the facts above and act as if they are not so. In so acting, they handicap themselves for learning.
- A constellation of feelings associated with love (respect, admiration, generosity, sympathy, friendliness, encour-

agement) have much more "efficiency" for learning than have feelings associated with anger or with fear.

- Of all the factors pertaining to success in learning, the most critical are those of motivation—how a person deeply engages himself in the learning transaction. Subject matter, environmental factors, methods, and techniques are also important, but they must be seen in the light of the key word *engagement*.

So much is clear. What have we failed to do?

Many things. To begin with, little has been said about what some people describe as the "mechanisms" of learning. Neither have we, in any systematic way, indicated what writers, experimenters, and theorists in the field of learning have to say about it.

In Chapters 2 to 6 we have been talking about *the learner*. We shall now shift our focus a little, move outside the learner, and concern ourselves with what others have said about learning. The purpose here will be twofold. The first is to help us as practitioners with our own task of formulating for ourselves a satisfactory theory of learning. But those chapters will not be all theory. Considerable "classroom practice" will be presented and discussed for illumination and exemplification of learning principles. And we shall end by recapitulating what seems to be essential and central in the learning transaction.

REFERENCES

1. Edward L. Thorndike, *The Psychology of Wants, Interests and Attitudes* (New York: D. Appleton-Century Co., Inc., 1935.) By permission of Appleton-Century-Crofts, Incorporated.
2. M. Sherif, *An Outline of Social Psychology* (New York: Harper & Brothers, rev. ed., 1956).
3. Robert S. Lynd and Helen M. Lynd, *Middletown* (New York: Harcourt, Brace and Company, 1929).
4. Gardner Murphy, *Personality: A Biosocial Approach to Origins and Structure* (New York: Harper & Brothers, 1947).
5. A. H. Maslow, "A Theory of Human Motivation," *Psychological Review*, Vol. 50, 1943.

6. R. Sim, J. Nicol, A. Shea, and P. Simmins, *Canada's Farm Radio Forum* (Paris: UNESCO, 1954).

7. E. K. Strong, Jr., *Change of Interests with Age* and *Vocational Interests of Men and Women* (Stanford: Stanford University Press, 1931 and 1943, respectively).

8. Gordon Allport, *Handbook of Social Psychology* (Worcester, Mass.: Clark University Press, 1935).

9. H. Brewster Smith, "A Study of Attitudes Toward Russia," *Public Opinion and Propaganda* (New York: Dryden Press, 1954).

10. Kurt Lewin, "The Relative Effectiveness of a Lecture Method and a Method of Group Discussion for Changing Food Habits," *Readings in Social Psychology* (New York: Henry Holt and Company, Incorporated, 1947).

Suggested Reading

ADULT EDUCATION ASSOCIATION, "Workshop—Helping Adults Change Attitudes," *Adult Leadership* (Chicago: AEA), Vol. 5, No. 6.

BIRNBAUM, MAX, "Mind and Emotion in Adult Education," *Adult Education* (Chicago: AEA), Vol. 7, No. 3.

CALDWELL, J. P., "Action—Research on Apathy," *Adult Education* (Chicago: AEA), Vol. 5, No. 3.

DONAHUE, WILMA, and TIBBETTS, CLARK, eds., *The New Frontier of Aging* (Ann Arbor: University of Michigan, 1957).

FRIEDMANN, E. A., and HAVIGHURST, R. J., *The Meaning of Work and Retirement* (Chicago: University of Chicago Press, 1954).

KEMPFER, HOMER, *Identifying Educational Needs of Adults* (Washington, D.C.: Office of Education, 1951).

MILLER, NEAL E., and DOLLARD, JOHN, *Social Learning and Imitation* (London: Kegan Paul, 1945).

MURPHY, GARDNER, and KUHLEN, RAYMOND, *Psychological Needs of Adults* (Chicago: Center for the Study of Liberal Education for Adults, 1955).

STYLER, W. E., "The Motives of Adult Students," *Adult Education* (London: National Institute of Adult Education, September, 1950).

VERNON, COOLIE, and NEWBERRY, JOHN S., "The Nature of Adult Participation," *Adult Education* (Chicago: AEA), Vol. 8, No. 4.

Chapter 7

THEORIES OF LEARNING

We are now ready for what the composer or dramatist would call a change of pace—also of substance.

In our quest for understanding about adult learning we have made a beginning by getting some general impressions of the adult learner and then by considering different aspects of learning in somewhat greater depth.

We have discovered that learning, though it always involves changes, may mean changes of different kinds. We have also discovered that all our questions are not yet answered, that all that there is to learning is not yet known or applied, that "the greatest songs are yet unsung."

In many activities now going on, fresh evidence about learning continues to become available. We shall look at selected fields of work in Chapter 8 in order to get some impression of this evidence, and how one can apply it and keep up with it.

But to do that, as well as to organize what we have already been talking about, we need the kind of guidance that is usually supplied by sound theory. By selecting examples from a number of theories of learning we hope to attain two objectives:

- to derive considerably more information and perhaps insight, about the learning process
- to become more fully aware of the importance of theory and perhaps make a beginning in organizing what we know about learning.

The Place of Theory

We have already had some discussion of the value of theory to the research scholar and to the practitioner.

The research worker needs a set of assumptions as a starting point to guide what he does, to be tested by experiment or to serve as a check on observations and insights. Without any theory his activities may be as aimless, as wasteful as the early wanderings of the explorers in North America, or one's attempts to find his way around in a city he is visiting for the first time, if he has no street map.

A well-conceived system can encourage both study and action, as noted by Edna Heidbreder in her book *Seven Psychologies*:

> Systems of psychology are to be regarded not as statements of psychological knowledge but as tools by which psychological knowledge is produced; not as accounts of scientific fact, but as a means of acquiring scientific fact. . . . For scientific knowledge does not merely accumulate; it is far more likely to grow about hypotheses that put definite questions and which act as centers of organization in the quest of knowledge. . . . Frequently the victories of science are won through the use of conjectures that become the basis of active and ingenious research especially directed toward the particular body of evidence which will prove or disprove the point of issue.[1]

Most of us are ready to concede that a research worker ought to be guided by theory. The librarian or nightschool teacher needs it too. He also is dependent upon sound theory, if he is concerned in the slightest degree with the improvement of his own work. Let us start with an obvious example, a coach of diving. He has a student who is learning to do the one-and-a-half forward somersault. The coach gives careful instruction; perhaps he demonstrated correct form. The student tries it once, twice, three times, ten times, thirty times, without any noticeable improvement. He doesn't have the "feel" of it. Then, perhaps on the thirty-seventh attempt, his body rolls and opens out at the precise split second and he makes a tolerable entry into the water. Much more important, from that time on he is always able to perform this action. He can improve the grace of the act; he never again needs to learn the combination of muscular-sensory actions necessary for its execution. Now how does the coach go about teaching another boy to do the same thing? By the same long series of trials? But a coach who knows even the rudiments of *gestalt* theory will understand that for some kinds of learning, being told about performance or even thinking about performance is not enough; the senses and muscles must actually try out, trace out, "learn" the pattern of performance. Understanding this, even in an elementary fashion, will assist the coach to devise means by which the young athlete can go through the movement until his senses and muscles learn the pattern, while protected somewhat from the consequences of failure. This is why a "safety belt" is used for teaching many athletic skills. Protected in this way, the body is put through the correct motions and acts.

Some knowledge of theory always aids practice. It also may stimulate new forms of practice, just as the alchemists' theory that baser metals could be transmuted into gold stimulated the development of chemistry. The theory that the earth was round stimulated exploration, trade, and the opening of the new world. Practitioners are sometimes wary of theory, because, since it is an attempt to explain what is not yet fully understood, it frequently contains (is almost certain to contain) some error. Beware of the theorist, so we say, because later on he will be proved wrong in some of his speculations. But wrong theory is not necessarily or always destructive in its results. Nor does the lack of theory guarantee against undesirable consequences. Naturally one needs to approach any theory, particularly any new theory, with caution. To what extent does it seem to fit the facts? But in terms of its main effect, whether or not a theory is correct in every particular has little to do with the possible value of that theory in practice. It is possible that much of what Sigmund Freud once hypothesized as the basis for human behavior will be found to err. But the effect of Freud's work has been that most of us, or all of us, think or act in a different way than we had before; it has had enormous consequences for practice.

Just as we need not be upset because time may prove that there were errors in a certain theory, we do not need to reject one hypothesis that may appear to be confusing. There is not *a* theory of learning, there are several theories of learning.

We have noticed earlier that the word *learning* is used to cover a wide variety of experiences, such as memorizing a poem, acquiring a vocabulary, finding out how to use a typewriter, becoming more able at reasoning and deciding, acquiring the skill of swimming, acquiring preferences or prejudices, changing one's behavior or attitude toward other people. These activities are not all alike; indeed, we may be making an error of some magnitude in including all of them under a single term "learning." One psychologist, Tolman, has suggested that there may be as many as seven different kinds of learning. So our dilemma in gaining a theory of learning that will withstand critical inquiry may in part be one that we ourselves have created. Until we can reach more agreement about what constitutes learning we ought to expect that there will be more than one theory, to explain all that is meant by the term.

Actually, as we shall see, most of the theories, though they show discrepancies and conflict, tend also to be supplementary and complementary rather than antagonistic. Often it is really a case of *both and* or *yes but* rather than this-cannot-be-so-because-the-opposite-is-true. And most of the theorists draw closer together when they are formulating implications for the teacher or practitioner. Indeed, one of the gains that the practitioner studying the theories of learning may make is that he will find many of the *same* principles and good practices emphasized from different points of view. As time goes on these theories seem to be tending toward re-enforcement rather than mutual destruction, or the kind of stalemate or paralysis which is sometimes the result of conflict.

Our plan, then, is to look briefly at some characteristic theories of learning, note both their similarities and their differences, see how they help us to build generalizations from what we have ourselves experienced, and how they answer our questions or pose some fresh ones. With patience we may be able to struggle to some kind of formulation for ourselves that will not only give us better footing for our present work but help us to keep up with the explorations going on all around us.

We have noted earlier that learning theory, before the present century, was usually linked to philosophy or theology. What one thought about the nature, origin, character, and destiny of man determined what one postulated about how he learned. However, in the last seventy-five years or so, theory has been based far more directly on observed behavior and experimentation.

We sometimes think of learning theory as "belonging to" the psychologist. Indeed, for one psychologist, C. L. Hull, learning and behavior are hardly to be distinguished and one of his books on learning is entitled *Principles of Behavior*.[2] But others than psychologists have also made their contribution— philosophers, sociologists, anthropologists, psychiatrists, to name a few. To some of these we shall make reference in the next chapter; here we shall consider briefly the influence of some philosophies and later give our main attention to the psychologists.

Philosophers and Learning

In his introduction to the book *Modern Philosophies and Education* John S. Brubacher wrote:

> The study of educational philosophy has flourished in the twentieth century as never before in the whole history of education. Earlier centuries, no doubt, produced a fair share of famous essays on education, but relatively few of these essays were philosophical in exposition and intent. . . . The twentieth century, by contrast, has produced almost a plethora of publications on philosophy of education.[3]

We shall attempt no systematic treatment of any major philosophic points of view but instead shall simply single out some examples of philosophical positions that have specially affected learning theory and practice for adults.

One such group is the Catholic philosophers, men like Etienne Gilson and Jacques Maritain, and a long line of Catholic educationalists. Maritain summarized the central Thomist position on education:

Knowledge is a value in itself and an end in itself; and truth consists in the conformity of the mind with reality—with what is or exists independently of the mind. The intellect tends to grasp and conquer being. Its aim and its joy are essentially disinterested. . . . There is no other foundation for the educational task than the eternal saying: It is the truth that sets men free. . . . Education is fully human education only when it equips (the learner) for truth and makes him capable of judging according to the worth of evidence, of enjoying truth and beauty for their own sake, and of advancing toward wisdom and some understanding of those things which bring him to intimations of mortality.[4]

Some Catholic teachers, such as Dr. M. M. Coady of the Antigonish Movement in Canada, have emphasized that adult education "must begin with the economic." Unless learning is imbedded in man's everyday preoccupations, it may neither take hold nor move forward. But this does not mean that materialism occupies the entire field, or sets the limits, for adult learning. For Coady, learning is to make men "masters of their own destiny":

We have no desire to create a nation of shopkeepers, whose only thoughts run to groceries and to dividends. We want our people to look into the sun, and into the depths of the sea. We want them to explore the hearts of flowers and the hearts of their fellow-men. We want them to live, to love, to play and pray with all their being. We want them to be men, whole men, eager to explore all the avenues of life and to attain perfection in all their faculties. Life for them shall not be in terms of merchandising but in terms of all that is good and beautiful, be it economic, political, social, cultural or spiritual. They are the heirs of all the ages and of all the riches yet concealed. All the findings of science and philosophy are theirs. All the creations of art and literature are for them. They will usher in the new day by attending to the blessings of the old. They will use what they have to secure what they have not.[5]

A second group, sometimes referred to as "Aristotelians," are best represented by Mortimer Adler. Adler's speaking and writing are distinguished by two characteristics: the directness, forcefulness, certitude of his credo and assumptions;

and his emphasis upon the learning of adults. No one need be unaware of his position for long:

> The *ultimate* ends of education are the same for all men at all times and everywhere. . . . They are absolute and universal principles . . . absolute in the sense that they are not relative to contingent circumstances of time and place, universal in the sense that they are concerned with essentials.[6]

One may be attracted by such claims, or repelled, but they are not easy to ignore. About method he makes the same absolute claims as about aim:

> Similarly, it can be said that educational means *in general* are the same for all men at all times and everywhere. If the *ultimate* ends of education are its first principles, the means *in general* are its secondary principles and the scope of the philosophy of education goes no further—*to know these first and secondary principles in an absolute and universal manner.*[7]

Adler is equally insistent that learning is for the mature, and for developing maturity:

> In America today we are blinded by a romantic adoration of the child. We thus come to suppose that the most important problems of education concern the rearing of children, and we exaggerate the importance of the educational institutions which deal with children. But clearly the beginning of anything is not as important as the end, and the beginning can only be well thought about in terms of the end. The end of education is one of overcoming the deficiencies of immaturity.[8]

His insistence upon rigorous logic in the formulation of ideas about learning has been a spur, alike for those who believe as he does and those who are opposed, to state their positions equally clearly. The best-known example of an adult activity influenced by Adler is the "Great Books" program with its characteristic form of study based on the examination of "fundamental" problems and principles, employing a Socratic questioning style. (It should be added, of course, that although this program has been much influenced by Adler, many with a different philosophy participate in it.)

But if the "Aristotelians" have prodded and provoked friends and foes alike to further efforts, a similar claim can also be made for Dewey, Kilpatrick, and other experimentalists (or instrumentalists or pragmatists, for all these terms have been applied). Brubacher in the introduction already quoted asked, "What is the reason for this greatly augmented interest in educational philosophy?" and answered his own question, "Perhaps the simplest answer is the rise of 'progressive education' as a *cause célèbre.*"

In sixty years or more of prodigious scholarship, demonstration, and teaching, John Dewey achieved enormous influence over the theory and practice of education. Author of some of the most important books written on education (for example, *Democracy and Education, How We Think, Human Nature and Conduct, The School and Society*), author in his very last years of such a wide range of papers as "Democratic Faith and Education," "Authority and Resistance to Social Change," "Liberty and Social Control," "The Relation of Science and Philosophy as the Basis of Education," Dewey has both so many followers *and* critics that a balanced assessment of his achievement is hardly possible at present. But of his influence there is no doubt, in rethinking educational goals, in reshaping curricula, in underscoring the social context of thinking and learning, in bringing about shifts in method, in emphasizing science not only as a subject but as method and ethic:

> The sciences had to battle against entrenched forces to obtain recognition in the curriculum. In a formal sense, the battle has been won, but not yet in a substantial sense. For scientific subject matter is still more or less segregated as a special body of facts and truths. The full victory will not be won until every subject and lesson is taught in connection with its bearing upon creation and growth of the kind of power of observation, inquiry, reflection, and testing that are the heart of scientific intelligence. Experimental philosophy is at one with the genuine spirit of scientific attitude in the endeavor to obtain for a scientific method this central place in education.[9]

Like Adler and Catholic theologians in this one respect at least, Dewey often emphasized the importance of adult learning:

Education must be reconceived, not as merely a preparation for maturity (whence our absurd idea that it should stop after adolescence) but as a continuous growth of the mind and a continuous illumination of life. In a sense the school can give us only the instrumentalities of mental growth, the rest depends upon an absorption and interpretation of experience. Real education comes after we leave school and there is no reason why it should stop before death.[10]

William Kilpatrick has also had an impact on theory and practice in learning. Kilpatrick's emphasis was always upon living, upon a curriculum based on living, upon a school that provided rich experiences of living. "In a democracy," said Kilpatrick, "it is self-directing personalities that we try to build, the kind that can carry forward life ever more successfully in a developing world. Such a world calls for the experimental outlook and an experimentally directed education." The child "learns only and exactly his *own* responses."

> I learn what I learn as I accept it. I learn it in the degree that I live it, in the degree that I count it important to me, and in the degree that I understand it and can fit it in with what I already know. And what I learn I build at once into character— that, in fact, is what to learn means.[11]

This is a philosophy and practice deeply concerned with living, morals, ethics, and character. His talk and writing were usually about the child but there are many applications of his thinking to adults. One example of many is that in his description of how the school "must be a place where living goes on, the best and finest type of living we can help people create," he set down many of the conditions essential for an adult residential school.

Kilpatrick wrote often about individuality or selfhood and how it developed as the result of interaction with other selves, in a social process. How one becomes aware of self, how one knows about it, the values of the self—these are all social in origin. The self, from one point of view, is an expanding organization of experience and thought.

Education conceived in this way does not end at any prescribed period. It is as meaningless to say that a person has finished his education as that he has finished his experience of art. "I don't need a book, I already have one," is a very old joke; it is not a view of education that is satisfying in any respect.

Eduard Lindeman, through his teaching and writing, had an effect both upon the practice of social work and of adult education. Lindeman was deeply concerned with the relationship of study and action, and with the function of education in a democratic society.

> Learning which is combined with action provides a peculiar and solid enrichment. If, for example, you are interested in art, you will gain much more if you paint as well as look at pictures and read about the history of art. If you happen to be interested in politics, don't be satisfied with being a spectator: participate in political action. If you enjoy nature, refuse to be content with the vicarious experiences of naturalists; become a naturalist yourself. In all of these ways learning becomes an integral part of living until finally the old distinction between life and education disappears. In short, life itself becomes a perpetual experience of learning.[12]

A society that neglects education, for all people of all ages, runs a great risk, for action may thus be governed by expediency or worse. Education for adults is not just a pleasant conceit; it is an imperative if democracy is to survive, Lindeman believed.

> The key word of democracy is participation. It is at this point that education enters the equation. Social action is in essence the use of force or coercion. The use of force and coercion is justified only when the force is democratic and this means that it must be derived from intelligence and reason. Adult education thus turns out to be the most reliable instrument for social actionists. If they learn how to educate the adherents of their movement, they can continue to utilize the compelling power of a group and still remain within the scope of democratic behavior. When they substitute something other than intelligence and reason, social action emanates as sheer power and soon degenerates into habits which tend toward an anti-democratic direction. Every social-action group should at the same time be an adult-education group, and I go even so far as to believe

that all successful adult education groups sooner or later become social-action groups.[13]

Theodore Brameld, in more recent times, has been attempting what he terms a reconstruction of educational philosophy. Though deriving it in part from "progressive" theories, he has not failed to call attention to what he considers limitations or defects. "Progressivism," he believes,

> . . . is strong in scientific method—weak in concern for the concrete and comprehensive outcome of this method. Strong in teaching us how to think—weak in teaching us the goals toward which to think. Strong in characterizing as well as encouraging active intelligence—weak in estimating and counteracting the forces and restrictions that block its effective operation. . . .[14]

Brameld believes that "it is perfectly plausible that adult education, if properly organized, could attract literally hundreds of millions of students throughout the world. This is the ideal at which reconstructionists aim; indeed they are convinced that the cultural order they propose cannot be attained without adult education." In setting down educational goals Brameld states that "powerful national and international purposes must be the governors of education." Social processes provide the context for learning, and he identifies five main sources of content:

- through direct evidence of one's own experience as well as indirect experience of others
- through free process of communication, nonverbal as well as verbal, in the classroom and the community
- through reaching open majority agreement making allowance for minority disagreement
- through action
- through group dynamics.[15]

Perhaps the most eloquent of modern educationalists is Sir Richard Livingstone. He has not produced a systematic body of theory, but his ideas about adult learning have been widely quoted and practiced. One notion on which he wrote frequently is that only in adulthood is it possible for some kinds of learning to happen. Children and youths have not the requisite experience on which learning must build. In this he follows Aristotle's "A boy cannot be a philosopher," and Newman, writing in *An Essay in Aid of a Grammar of Assent*, who said:

> Let us consider, too, how differently young and old are affected by the words of some classic author, such as Homer or Horace. Passages which to a boy are but rhetorical commonplaces, neither better nor worse than a hundred others which any clever writer might supply, which he gets by heart and thinks very fine, and imitates, as he thinks, successfully in his own flowing versification, at length come home to him, when long years have passed, and he has had experience of life, and pierce him, as he had never before known them, with their sad earnestness and vivid exactness.[16]

Learning that is necessary for the good citizen is also something for maturity, Livingstone believes:

> What lovers of paradox we British are! Youth studies but cannot act; the adult must act, and has no opportunity of study; and we accept the divorce complacently. But action and thought, living and learning, naturally belong together and should go hand in hand. Instruction in civics at school, if you will. But when the children are adults and have votes, let such instruction be available so that their votes can be used with intelligence.[17]

A central idea for Livingstone is the necessity of the study of the "first rate." He quotes Whitehead: "Moral education is impossible without the habitual vision of greatness." This is true of *all* education, adds Livingstone:

> The way to acquire a good taste in anything, from pictures to architecture, from literature to character, from wine to cigars, is always the same—be familiar with the best specimens of each. Knowledge of the first-rate gives direction, purpose and drive; direction, because it shows what is good as well as what is bad; purpose, because it reveals an ideal to pursue; drive, because an ideal stirs to action. . . . The sight of goodness in life or in literature or history gives a standard and a challenge.[18]

A philosophy that has created considerable recent attention is just beginning to be applied to problems of learning. We refer, of course, to existentialism. The philosophy is concerned about the unfolding of the individual, as a whole, *in the situation in which he finds himself.* It is learning directed to the whole man, for the whole of life. And it is about existence, omitting nothing that bears on existence. The existentialist, like the psychiatrist, aims to free man from his isolation, from his anonymity, to free his mind from confusions that prevent him from accepting himself and releasing his own powers. Every man, it is urged, should try to learn what it is to be a man, including all the limitations as well as the potentialities. In the end, as one writer has put it, what counts is "education for character, for the habits that enable a man both to remain free and to remain with the truth when he finds it."[19]

These are meager samples of what men are writing and saying about educational philosophy. But they suggest what can be found in this field. It is exceedingly rewarding for a teacher of adults to probe deeply into the speculations of such men and to make detailed comparisons of the main claims of each.

In recent years more of the issues have been identified and studied, as *subjects* or problems and not so much as the *credos* of conflicting ideologies. An example of such thinking is the publication of the Adult Education Association entitled *Seeking Common Ground in Adult Education.*[20]

We shall not attempt it here, but similar informing concepts could be drawn from the writing of linguists, political scientists, sociologists, and anthropologists. Some examples will be found in the chapter on *practice.*

We shall now turn our attention to the endeavors in learning theory contributed by the psychologists:

- developments in psychological theory during this century
- some of the more important psychological theories of learning
- implications for the practitioner.

Developments During the Century

The first psychological theories concentrated attention on relatively simple units of learning, and were often based on observations of animals. Laboratory techniques, borrowed from physics and biology were employed, and the learner was treated as if he were an empty organism, responding to outside influences in ways that were more or less automatic, or even random. Usually a specific stimulus was assumed to be connected to a specific response and the observer would attempt to study the kind of stimulus, and the kind of response, S → R. The latter could be varied by rewards or punishment. Hungry rats or hungry dogs could be placed in one part of a maze and food in another. When the animals made a *correct* response they were rewarded with food or punished by not receiving it or even by loud noises, or electric shocks. The same procedure could be followed with human beings as subjects. Soldiers learning a signaling code would make certain motions until they had achieved the correct response whereupon the sergeant would bestow approval, or even extra privileges for good performance. Out of this kind of experimentation came what were sometimes called laws of learning.

It should be pointed out that the rudimentary nature of the mechanism studied, and of the explanation offered, was not just because psychology was at a much more primitive state than at present. In part, *connectionist* and *behaviorist* theory now seems oversimplified because the advocates of these theories were in rebellion, were reacting against sophisticated explanations of learning based on religious or philosophical interpretations and upon an assumption that an individual was possessed of certain properties and faculties. In attempting to overthrow theories that depended upon mystical explanations of human nature and conduct, an attempt was made to find explanations for man's behavior in the fact that he is a *human animal*.

But neither the so-called laws of learning nor the theories of connection and association could explain all phenomena. For example, lines presented in this fashion | | | | were perceived as four separate lines, but in this fashion □ as *one* square. Four circles presented in this form O 0 o o would be perceived as four circles, but arranged as two eyes, a head, and a body might represent a man. Or, on a standard test, a boy of ten might perceive a number of circles as just so many circles, whereas for a soldier these forms might symbolize woman. *Arrangement* of things could give an additional meaning to things.

Theories were now developed, or were given widespread circulation in which the arrangement or pattern of units was considered significant. Learning was no longer perceived as a simple relationship of experience-stimulus-response, but of ordering and structuring experience.

But it soon became apparent that it was even more complicated than mere patterning. If an instructor was talking about some mythical social system in which men and women shared the possession of all goods he could expect one kind of interest and attention. But if, in describing the same kind of social arrangements, he were to state that this was a *Communist* system, he could expect a radically different kind of response than before. Not only would the quality of attention alter but if he were to test his students the following day he might find that some remembered considerably more, some remembered considerably less, and some remembered things which he had not said! Learning, then, is something more than pattern: there are emotional factors that can markedly affect what is learned and what is recalled. As a result of studying the effect of emotions upon learning, the teacher became more interested in the needs of students, what experience the student brings to his study, and what is his social position. All these matters were seen to predispose the student to accept, reject, or distort material presented to him.

It was also observed that a man in one kind of group is awake, active, co-operative, participating; and in another he is silent, opinionated, or critical. Not only his behavior but how much he will learn is affected. A man who is a member of one workteam cannot seem to master the technique of assembling a radio component after two full days of trial. But when shifted to another team, he becomes proficient and speedy in the assembly work within a matter of hours. Learning for him may depend in large measure upon his associates.

Considerable study is now going on about the group as a place where learning happens.

Selected Theories of Learning

We shall now make a brief reference to a few of the psychologcial theories of learning that continue to receive attention and that have some implications for adult learning. Since there is space here to identify only a few of the leading psychologists, there will be inevitable distortion in the presentation. At a recent international conference in Paris, one teacher who is not at all a dogmatic person was able to use only the declarative form of the French language. After two or three statements she would pause, smile, and say "peut être?" ["perhaps?"]. In using these summaries the reader is warned to punctuate them with a few "peut êtres"! Better still, he should study the actual statements made by the writers referred to at the end of the chapter, as well as criticisms of these theories.

CONNECTIONS, TRIAL-AND-ERROR

For at least half a century there was one widely accepted explanation about learning called by the rather clumsy term *connectionism*. As early as 1898, E. L. Thorndike, in his book *Animal Intelligence*,[21] asserted that the basis of learning is an association between sense impressions and impulses to action. The association became known as a "bond" or "connection," thus the name. Sometimes it was also referred to as the stimulus-response or S-R psychology of learning, and much of it had to do with learning through trial-and-error.

Tolman, who was often critical of Thorndike, once said: "The psychology of learning has been and still is primarily a matter of agreeing or disagreeing with Thorndike, or trying in minor ways to improve upon him. All (psychologists) seem to have taken Thorndike, overtly or covertly, as our starting point." There were a number of reasons for the predominance of the views of Thorndike and his associates, in addition to the brilliance and versatility of the man himself. His position was established early, and his theory, more than any other was linked directly with classical *association* and thus with the learning theories of scholars going right back to Aristotle. Thorndike, however, carried association far beyond the rather crude formulation known prior to 1900 by such men as John Locke, Thomas Hobbes, and John Stuart Mill.

All people are familiar with the idea of learning by association—"once burned, twice shy." To many boys of all ages the month of October always suggests "World Series." Long ago John Locke had written in his *Essay on the Human Understanding:*

> The ideas of goblins and sprites have really no more to do with the darkness than light: yet let a foolish maid inculcate these often on the mind of a child and raise them there together, possibly he shall never be able to separate them again so long as he lives. Many children imparting the pain they endured at school to their books they were corrected for so joining these ideas together that a book becomes their aversion and they are never recovered to the study and use of them all their lives after.[22]

Thorndike's was a view of learning that seemed to be well grounded in physiology; its experimental methods and use of mathematics also won respect. It dealt with a unit of learning—a stimulus, an organism, and a response—that could be comprehended. It was established just at the time when teacher-training was being developed on a much wider scale than ever before and Thorndike's psychology became almost the *official* psychology in many a school system. He was often criticized but seemingly without much loss of position or prestige. It was as a result of no outside attacks, but a consequence of his own integrity that he strode to the platform of one great international convention to announce boldly, "I was wrong." Subsequently he made substantial corrections in many of his most important conclusions.

We noted in Chapter 3 that much that we know about the learning of adults started with Thorndike's investigation. His studies covered a wide range of learning situations and his ideas were stated in an extensive series of papers and books.

The focus for much of his work was on the rate of learning. Thorndike did not develop a single, consistent theory; yet, considering the breadth of his interests and his courage in changing his opinions in the light of new evidence, there is a remarkable coherence in his position.

In addition to what came his way through traditional association psychology, Thorndike was influenced strongly by research on animals by the early experimenter Wundt and others. He himself devised many of the most typical and most used problem situations for studying animals, such as the maze and the puzzle box. Concern with individual differences which he derived in part from Galton was another factor in his development. For the rest there was endless experimentation, insatiable curiosity, and the ability to prize discovery far more than consistency.

Connectionism, as Thorndike developed it, links human behavior to that of lower animals. Thorndike's "laws of learning" were developed from animal experiments. He put it that *learning is connecting* and the connections have a basis in the nervous system. Those things which we call intellect and intelligence can be thought of as quantitative rather than qualitative—a person's intellect is the sum total of the bonds that he had formed, and the greater the number of bonds the higher is his intelligence.

> A man's life would be described by a list of all the situations which he encountered and the responses which he made to them, including among the latter every detail of his sensations, precepts, memories, mental images, ideas, judgments, emotions, desires, choices, and other so called mental acts.[23]

One of the most influential, even though most criticized, activities of Thorndike was the stating of three "laws of learning." These are not laws in the sense that this term is used in physics but statements about the directions in which learning happens. These concepts were stated in language meant to be intelligible but not technical; they were aimed at helping teachers in the classroom and did not attempt the precision favored by the psychologist in his laboratory. We have already noted they were modified somewhat in the last years of Thorn-dike's life.

Effect. The bond between a stimulus and a response is strengthened or weakened because of the satisfaction or annoyance that accompanies the action.

Exercise or frequency. It is often said that practice makes perfect. But it *doesn't* matter how much we practice something that pains us deeply, we may never attain much skill in it. Repetition by itself does not produce effective learning. But repetition with meaning results in substantial learning.

Readiness. If the organism is ready for the connection the result is pleasurable (therefore enhances learning); if not, the result is not pleasurable and learning is inhibited.

Thorndike was opposed to meaningless drill. "Arithmetic consists not of isolated unrelated facts, but of parts of a total system, each part of which may help to knowledge of the other parts, if it is learned properly. . . . Time spent in understanding facts and thinking about them is almost always saved doubly. Drill and practice are necessary but only when employed with meaning." Another problem in which his influence was shown was in regard to "transfer of training." Does the learning of Latin improve one's ability to learn English? This was a common enough assumption. "No," said Thorndike, "improvement in any single mental function need not improve the ability in functions commonly called by the same name." At first this denial resulted in acrimony, but it helped teachers and psychologists to study the conditions under which there might be transference—when Latin was taught in such a way that learning English would be improved. In the profitable observation and study that was touched off in this way, much of the nonsense that once had been believed and solemnly asserted about the value for learning of certain forms of discipline were undermined or washed away. One still hears some teachers and others aver that to do something distasteful, because it *is* disgusting, will result in strong character and effective learning, but such talk is rare indeed. Of course we are not here concerned with its possible ethical effect, but its relevance, if any, to learning.

Most critics of Thorndike charged that his theory is too mechanical, oversimple, and atomistic. In his later years Thorndike himself talked more and more of broad patterns of response. A colleague, Woodworth, rejected the notion that the connections were one-to-one:

> Either S or R may be as big and complex as you like. Such a performance as lifting a heavy weight by the co-ordinated action of arms, legs and trunk is properly regarded as a single response. And such an aggregate of stimuli as is presented to the eye on looking out of the window works as a single combined stimulus when it arouses the response "What a beautiful day."[24]

Thorndike was well aware of the importance of purpose even though he seldom emphasized it:

> The influences which co-operate with the situation to determine their response are as complicated, variable, purposive and spiritual as the learners themselves are. The chief role in the drama of learning is not played by external situations, but *by the learner*. The reason why I have said so much about frequency of connections, satisfyingness of connections, identifiability of situations, availability of responses and the like, and little about the purposes or mental sets or total minds which direct and organize them is not that I belittle the latter. It is rather that the general importance of the latter is obvious.[25]

Thorndike laid great stress upon rewarding—stating that a reward acts directly upon the neighboring connections and thus strengthens them. Punishment is much less effective in his view. Punishment does not have a direct weakening effect although it may cause the learner to do some other act which, if rewarded, will attain the re-enforcing effect. This aspect of Thorndike's work has had considerable influence. The evidence he adduced from his experiments had some effect in banishing or limiting some of the more brutal or futile uses of punishment in schools and training situations.

Some of what Thorndike taught we might now reject; for some of what remains valid we might favor a different explanation. But Thorndike's influence on the teaching and training in the classroom, playing field, and factory has been endless; spelling, arithmetic, reading, modern languages, science, music, shopwork, and many of the practices he fostered are now regarded as standard.

CONDITIONING-BEHAVIORISM

Perhaps the simplest way to describe some aspects of learning is *conditioning*. This is also based on association. Conditioning theories were first developed in the laboratory, where animals were forced to salivate, or escape from electrical shocks. This seems far removed from human life and yet theories derived in this way have been not only influential but continue to be employed in learning activities for adults.

To those who based their theory on conditioning, it was not necessary to postulate a purpose for either learning or conscious thought. As in connectionism the drama of learning is played by the organism, the stimulus, and the response.

From experiments on dogs by Pavlov, the resulting notion of the *conditioned reflex* or *conditioned response* was chosen as the significant unit of learning. In training by conditioning one starts with a response already well established that is related to a stimulus or cue, and then proceeds to fix the same response with a different cue, or produce a different response to the same cue. Thus, in an anecdote told by the psychologist, Guthrie, the horse of a village parson had been properly trained to halt at the cue word "whoa." Alas, the village boys began to prod him with a pitchfork as they shouted the word "whoa," and before long the horse would bolt and run, instead of halt at this command, thus producing a calamitous result. Boys have also taught parrots to swear in a similar way. Conditioning has been used not only to fix desirable habits, but to break undesirable ones. Several of the cures for alcoholism are based on the use of various drugs that, in the presence of alcohol, make the patient uneasy and violently ill. After exposure to this cure for a while, the patient is supposed to reject the alcohol itself. Of course, attempts are made simultaneously to help him gain new satisfactions in life and not be forced to rely upon some addiction or substitute. Cures for smoking have also been devised in which every act (cue) associated with smoking, such as drinking coffee or having matches easily available, is listed and the patient systematically begins to prevent these cues from occurring or to replace them with others. Guthrie has told an amusing anecdote about himself:

> Drinking or smoking after years of practice are action systems which can be started by thousands of reminders. . . . I had once a caller to whom I was explaining that the apple I had just finished was an excellent way of avoiding a smoke. The caller pointed out that I was at that moment smoking. The habit of lighting a cigarette was so attached to the finish of eating that smoking had started automatically.[26]

BEHAVIORISM

Two of the most influential psychologists whose work was based on conditioning are Watson, who has been best known for the theory called "Behaviorism," and E. R. Guthrie.

For Guthrie, learning is primarily the alteration of behavior that results from experience. Responses are of at least two kinds—the *outward act,* such as reading, writing, speaking, sitting, rising, and the *inward bodily reaction* such as increased supply of oxygen in the blood, or glandular secretion. Emotions are also of two kinds—those that *excite* and lead to the altering of behavior and those that *depress* or hinder the alteration.

For Guthrie association happens because the pattern of stimuli at the time of a response tends on the recurrence to be followed by the same response. What could be simpler? The only elements are stimulus and movements. No mention of goals, of drives, of many repetitions. No mention of either reward or punishment. According to Guthrie we learn only what we do, not what we accomplish. That is, we learn specific responses. These can be errors, or bad habits, as well as good. Responses can be associated or they can be disassociated from the stimulus. Forgetting, Guthrie says, happens not because of the passage of time but because disassociation has taken place for one or more reasons:

- The correct response is blocked by an inhibitor such as fear or disgust, e.g. in the treatment of alcoholism.
- The response is blocked by fatigue—applied particularly in the training of horses (also in some modern applications of "brain washing").
- The stimulus is repeated with such slight intensity that it is soon associated with a different response—such as getting the horse used to the saddle by starting with a light blanket.[27]

Guthrie also believes that learning occurs at once (in a single association episode) but if it is to be strengthened the correct response must be attached to a whole series of stimuli. Accordingly a skill is not a simple habit but a collection of habits. Practice, Guthrie pointed out, can be wasteful in time and result unless it is the correct response to a number of cues. Practice should be in the specific situation where we expect the response. If a man or a group is to perform in a variety of places or situations, the practice should take place in all these situations.

Guthrie does not believe, with Thorndike, that punishment has an effect which is much less significant than reward. Punishment can be influential, depending upon the circumstance.

Sitting on tacks does not discourage learning. It encourages learning to do something else than sit. It is not the feeling caused by punishment but the specific action caused by punishment that determines what will be learned. To train a dog to jump through a hoop, the effectiveness of punishment depends on where it is applied, front or rear. It is what punishment makes the dog do that counts, or what it makes a man do, not what it makes him feel.[28]

Guthrie's ingenious statements help us to understand some phenomena of learning, but fail to account for others. Still, their lucid presentation and their practical application to many training problems have won attention by teachers and trainers who have tended to reject other psychologists because the latter have used language or symbols that are difficult to follow.

Clark Hull's contribution was quite different from that of Guthrie. We have all heard the saying, "He is a lawyer's lawyer" or "a poet's poet." This means that the man referred to is a master of his craft to a degree that can be appreciated only by fellow craftsmen. It takes a psychologist to appreciate the importance of Hull's work. His theories were as mechanistic as other behaviorists, his central concern was habit, and he dealt with conditioned responses, not with consciousness as such. His particular field of study was a narrow one—rote learning. But he set out to state the conditions under which the investigation of learning theory ought to be carried out:

- State carefully all definitions to be used.
- State hypotheses.
- Derive theorems from logical expression of hypotheses and state the theories in terms that can be tested.
- Proceed to test the theorems rigorously and in this process gradually refine the theory.[29]

He employed mathematics for stating and explaining most of his formulations. He did not live to carry his own work very far but he did set out the paths by which learning theorists may be obliged to proceed, and may also have prevented some of them from taking the wrong short cuts.

Curves of practice or performance. The "curve of practice" (often wrongly called the "learning" curve) is usually associated with the conditioning theory of learning because it was applied successfully by many psychologists who were interested in conditioning and bond theories. The use of such curves goes back many years, even before the turn of the century when two men, Bryan and Harder, were conducting a study of learning telegraph language and were confronted by the difficulty that is usually termed the "learning plateau."

In many learning situations the subject makes some initial gains, then there will be a period of no gain, followed by further progress, punctuated by periods of no gain. The record of the practice of the skill or knowledge can be charted and the occasions on which the subject's performance levels off or shows actual decline are called *plateaus*.

There are as many practice curves as there are subjects and kinds of learning. But, in the main, these curves follow two fairly general patterns. In one, the initial learning is rapid and the plateau does not appear in the early stages. But when it does appear it tends to be wide, and this phase can be exceedingly frustrating to the learner. In the other pattern, the early gains are slow, but after a certain stage is reached progress is rapid and the plateaus may be of slight dimension. Type A is found in learning of some relatively simple subject matter where the principles can be readily grasped, or some physical skill which is like the skills that the subject has already learned. Type B is found (a) where the principles are difficult to grasp (b) where the skills are of a different order from those already experienced (c) where, as in the learning of a language, there must be a certain amount of learning of words and ear training before any real progress is possible (d) or where extensive unlearning is necessary to remove old habits that interfere with the new, such as changing the hand grip in golf.

Why should anyone go to the trouble of charting one's progress in this way? The answer is plain. The curve is one of the most effective means, not of teaching, but of helping the teacher or the learner to sense when "something must be done." If the performance of a subject is steadily rising one might assume that the learning is proceeding in satisfactory fashion. If, however, a plateau has been reached it may be the signal for a change in the learning practice. The curve warns the teacher about this; it can also give the subject a much better understanding and awareness of his progress.

Of course, it may be essential to continue for a time at the plateau if, as some psychologists argue, the plateau represents the period in which the person is integrating the new experience. But the plateau need not be unduly protracted. How can the learning plateau be interrupted? There are many possibilities. It may be accomplished by increasing the motivation. It may be by improving some of the methods of working. Another means is seeking to see the problem *whole* in order to understand where the particular information or skill is related or by a better distribution of practice with shorter periods of activity repeated more often and with greater relaxation between. The curve is the guide to improvement.

With no attention to it, the learner may begin to feel he has reached his limits, that he has achieved "good enough." As one writer put it, "If John Bunyan had written a *Learner's Progress* he would have noted Mr. Faint-Heart and Mr. Fairly-Good stopped here."

The most common use of conditioning is in animal training, such as by a cowboy who is breaking in an untamed and fearful horse. To the wild horse a man, noise, the bind of the harness or of the saddle are all equally stimuli that will bring about a response of fear and flight. Accordingly, the horse is given time to become used to having the man touch and fondle him, so that the cue *man* does not bring the response of *fear*, or *run*. Next the horse is saddled, and additional time is allowed until this act no longer brings about a negative response. Finally, the man climbs astride the horse. Each step in the conditioning, where different responses are learned, is accompanied by support and reassurance to the animal, while the doses of fear-producing stimuli are slowly increased. The impatient or clumsy trainer, who gives too little support, or allows the tension cues to come too quickly, may jeopardize the training, for if the horse is again frightened the original strength of the fear cues may be re-enforced.

This can and does also happen to human beings. The child, even the adult, introduced to Beethoven, or Shakespeare, or baseball, under conditions which threaten him, pain him, or humiliate him, will carry a conditioned response against such activities until reconditioning takes place. A famous conductor once said, "They don't like Brahms, so we will play them Brahms." Exposure to the stimulus, under conditions in which approval can develop, resulted in a growing appreciation and later enthusiasm for Brahms. But exposure under conditions of threat, or pain, or humiliation can result in reactions against "good" music, or new tastes in food that can be eradicated only with the most careful reconditioning.

WHOLE LEARNING

Those who emphasized conditioning were often criticized because they were concerned about atoms or particles or pieces of learning. The group of men who were particularly concerned about the *whole* rather than its parts, and to *patterns* of learning rather than to a single incident, have been called *Gestalt* from the German word meaning shape or form. Much of their research consisted of studies of movement, or rhythm, and of the properties or configurations or patterns of action. One of the most influential of the early Gestalt psychologists, Wolfgang Kohler carried out much of his work while interned in the Canary Islands during World War I. Kohler's book *The Mentality of Apes* won immediate attention. The stories of animal behavior were themselves impressive, and there always seems to be widespread curiosity about the great apes. Moreover, this represented the first forthright attack on the then well-accepted position of Thorndike and others who were within the general framework of association psychology. It is easier now to see complementary relationship between these theories; at first, all that was noticed was the conflicts.

Research by the Gestalt psychologists is almost as well known as that of Pavlov or Thorndike. Frequently apes or gorillas were employed as subjects. A typical kind of experiment would go somewhat like this: A hungry ape is placed in a cage, and on the roof of the cage is a stem of bananas. In the cage are a long stick and a heavy box. For a while the ape paces around eyeing the bananas. Then he jumps and tries to reach them. He may jump again and again, failing each time. After a while he may take the stick and try to knock down the bananas, try and try and try, but he fails each time. Up to this point there has been no step-by-step learning that could be charted on a practice curve, no apparent gain and plateaus; there has been only failure. But suddenly, all at once, the ape grabs the stick, climbs to the box, leaps up swinging the stick, and knocks down the bananas. He has grasped *the pattern of action* required and from that time on he can repeat the pattern. He may improve his performance in climbing or hitting with the stick but he is always able to co-ordinate the parts of the whole. These experiments took many forms such as reaching through the cage bars with a stick, piling one box upon another, even on one occasion, joining two sticks together, which seems to have happened by chance but continued thereafter to be repeated. Note three attributes here:

- The solution seems to come abruptly as a flash of insight.
- It seems to be permanent and to carry over into other experiences.
- It seems to come about because the learner perceives the relationship of the different factors in the scene rather than responding to isolated stimuli.

The Gestalt descriptions and explanations differed most from those of Thorndike in insisting that the trials of the learner were by no means random. . . . One might describe their earlier behavior as trial-and-error but, as one writer put it, the apes "made clever errors." Changes in spatial relations would alter the nature of the problem: a stick placed out of sight and out of reach might not be employed at all, or only very late in the process; but a stick placed close to, or in line with, the food was resorted to relatively early. Once the relationship is seen the stick could be moved away or hidden, and the animal would search for and use it. Kohler maintained that this happened because the objects become endowed with new meanings, that a stick which before was just something to bite upon now took on the character of thing-to-get-fruit-with. Kohler says:

> What the animal has actually learned is to make an irrelevant object relevant to the situation.
>
> . . . only one conception of the performance is possible; that the animal has acquired an ability to introduce "tool" into certain situations. Nor is this ability limited to the particular thing with which it was acquired; on the contrary, it is an acquisition of a much more general nature.[30]

The emphasis at every stage is upon perceiving relationships, rather than responding to isolated objects or stimuli. Factors which hinder the understanding of this relationship are these:

- The animal may lack sufficient motivation. (Gestalt psychologists put special emphasis upon motivation.)
- The elements of the situation may be scattered too widely for the relationship to be perceived—for example, when the stick was out of sight.
- The organism may have insufficient experience to be able to master the skills needed.

A fourth factor occurs when old habits block the acquiring of new. The context is important. An ape which had been using one box to get food would not employ another when the familiar one was in a corner and another ape was lying upon it. The second box was apparently perceived not just as something-to-aid-in-getting-food but as having a different meaning. Context is even more important with human beings and, as we noted in Chapter 6, learning may happen only as, and when, the social context is given a new meaning.

Gestalt psychologists have not explained with complete satisfaction how insight happens. But they have contributed considerably to learning theory and practice. Theories such as conditioning and trial-and-error could explain, with some success, the learning of animals but they do not begin to comprehend much of human learning, particularly of mature and experienced people. For notions such as insight and the role of motivation the Gestalt ideas are much more relevant. Gestalt theory emphasizes that problems are to be solved sensibly, with concern about structure and organization. Learning does not happen mechanically, they insist, or simply by repetition or drill. The subject will behave as intelligently as he can under the circumstances. There may be fumbling and trial-and-error but only when the problem is too difficult, and only till a solution can be achieved. Gestalt theory also stimulated considerable speculation about whole learning which soon became a part of the theory and practice of many teachers and trainers. It is now a commonplace in the teaching of reading, or tennis, or a foreign language, or the use of a micrometer, to begin with meaningful wholes while watching for the points at which practice is needed on specific aspects, whereupon these acts are worked back into broader wholes. The attack is on the larger patterns first, even if they seem to be complex. For example, in teaching badminton, an attempt is made to give some impression of the whole game, its ebb and flow, its strategy, whereupon specific attention is directed to teaching the serve, or footwork, or the forehand smash. Sometimes the learning may seem slower at first if this method is followed; actually it is only the performance that is slower. Eventually, before very long in fact, there is accelerating achievement.

Another lesson, useful for athletic coaches and others teaching physical and motor skills, has been described earlier: namely, that some kinds of skills can best be learned, perhaps can only be learned, by tracing out the desired action in such a manner that the muscles and senses become familiar with the desired pattern. As we have noted, with a complicated bodily skill such as a somersault dive from a springboard, the body may be put through the action several times while the person is protected by a safety belt from harm, fear, or the development of repugnance. When one hears a coach talk about "the feel" of an activity, this is what he may be referring to.

Gestalt psychology also played some part in stimulating an approach to learning which is usually referred to as "field theory" and which we shall deal with later.

PURPOSE

Most of the men who are concerned about some form of association have tried to explain learning in ways that did not depend upon cognition or purpose. Thorndike did not repudiate such aspects of learning, but he felt that he could explain what happened more satisfactorily in other ways. The Gestalt psychologists showed the place that purpose and goals have in the selection of responses that an animal would make in a particular situation.

Edward C. Tolman took the conception of purpose a little further. He chose *Purposive Behavior in Animals and Men*[31] as the title for his most important early book. Tolman found many affinities between his own system and other schools of psychology, including psychoanalysis.

Tolman insists that behavior is directed in relation to goals. It is always moving toward something or away from something. What is significant about what an animal or a man is doing is *what he is doing it for*. The learner selects the means or tools for achieving his purpose and he chooses what he will learn in relation to some purpose; learning doesn't happen by chance. For him there is also a principle of least effort: the learner tends to select the means which will most easily and most quickly achieve his purpose. Because this is so, Tolman believes, people are teachable; they make good learners.

Instead of believing that the learner is being goaded by stimuli to choose certain responses and having them stamped in by repetition and rewards, Tolman believes that the subject is learning, not specific responses, but a *map or path*, is learning not just to move but the meaning of the movement. Tolman placed considerable emphasis upon the use of creative inference in learning and upon all aspects of cognition.

Tolman's second contribution to learning has been to bring into some common exchange theories from several fields of psychology. By calling attention to purpose he cleared away much that was sterile about behaviorism. By attempting to study and describe how it works he devised some means of observing some of the subtler kinds of human experience.

FIELD THEORY

A number of psychologists have been contributing to what is generally called "field theory." The most influential has been a German, Kurt Lewin, who spent his last years in the United States. We shall deal with the application of some of Lewin's principles in a later chapter. Much of what is now termed group dynamics or group development grows, indirectly or directly, from his speculations and early experiments.

Lewin has identified four kinds or aspects of learning:

- change in the cognitive structure (knowledge)
- change in motivation (learning to like or dislike)
- change in group belongingness or ideology (example: an immigrant coming to terms with and integrating in a new culture)

- achieving voluntary control of body musculature (example: speech skills).[32]

At the beginning of his work Lewin was not interested in learning as such. Part of his approach to the study of psychology was borrowed from physics. Quite early he set himself to the analysis of the *actual* situation, *what was happening*, rather than the result. For example, he would not be particularly concerned with measuring the difference in achievement between a housewife and an actress in memorizing poetry. The usual means of measuring performance would reveal that each was learning so many words, or sentences per hour of time, as though each task were identical. His more subtle analysis showed that what each is doing is really very different, so different it can hardly be compared. The housewife is mainly searching, she is groping, beset with fears and anxieties which inhibit learning. On the other hand, the actress has a well-developed technique for the study of words; with her the whole process is almost mechanical. What interested Lewin was always what was actually happening to a subject, with *his* experience, in a particular social setting. What forces are at work upon the individual? What stresses are there for him?

It is interesting to note the relationship between field theory as applied to learning and the now famous speculations of Dr. Hans Selye about *stress*. The implications of this have been alluded to by Professor McLuhan:

> Selye has come up with the first non-visual disease theory since the Greeks introduced the image of the skin as an envelope enclosing organs. His *stress* theory is entirely a *field* view of disease. The body is part of a total field.
>
> The Greek view of the body as a package of organs and humours got cut down, at the Renaissance, to the view of the body as a pumping station. Then with the rise of chemistry in the nineteenth century the body became a chemistry factory. Everybody was loaded with germs. But the rise of field theory in physics now has its medical counterpart in Dr. Hans Selye's stress view. He rejects the idea that each disease has a specific cause which must be found and isolated in order for cure to occur. In a word

he regards as unreal and outdated, the lineal view of disease as a specific target for which a specific shot is indicated.[33]

Lewin in describing his own work has said that he used a "constructive" method rather than one of classification. By "constructive" he means studying an individual case rather than an abstract one, but studying it with the aid of such concepts as psychological tension. Second, he chose a dynamic approach, one that attempted to get to the depths and not be satisfied with superficialities. Third, he chose a psychological rather than a physiological approach—he showed very little interest in minutiae of what happened in the nervous system, or the glands, or the blood pressure. Two other characteristics were the attempt to analyze the system as a whole, not in separate parts, and, like Hull, the attempt to make a mathematical representation of the field of inquiry. He tried to represent some of these dynamics by borrowing concepts from mathematics and physics. The accuracy of his formulae, and the suitability of using such analogies, has often been criticized; but this theory does not depend upon the analogies he uses or upon his mathematical presentation.

For Lewin the chief area of attention is the psychological field, *the life space*. The life space is where the person lives psychologically, as seen from his own viewpoint. The famous *New Yorker* cartoons of Cobean show a man in the real world seeing some reality, usually an attractive blonde, in his own special way. This is not a dream or a delusion; the man is not withdrawn from reality but is living in a real world and responding to it rationally while, at the same time, perceiving in his own characteristic fashion. A man interacts with the real world, and this produces some changes in his psychological world. The teacher, says Lewin, must never forget both realities, the real world, and the life space of the child. He must try to understand the psychological world of the child. If instead of dealing with the world of the child, he substitutes the world of the teacher, or of anybody else, "he is not being objective, but wrong."

The life space is influenced and altered by the physical,

social environment but is not identical with that environment. The most interesting psychological problems, therefore, have to do with the person in his life space. The person may be attracted by an object, and Lewin described this attraction as showing *valence,* of course borrowing the term from chemistry. This provided him with a means of describing and observing different kinds of conflict:

- Two positive valences, e.g. a student must choose between basketball and going to a dance.
- A simultaneous positive and a negative valence. A workman is offered double-time for over-time when he wants to go to a ball game.
- Two negative valences. A man is threatened with the loss of his job if he doesn't report the negligence of his work partner.[34]

Using the concept of valence, adding to it concepts of direction, distance, and time, Lewin was able to identify and describe many kinds of social problems in terms precise enough so that they have been studied experimentally. One classical investigation was conducted by associates of Lewin on the effect of three kinds of leadership upon learning and character changes.[35] This experiment has many implications, but we shall describe it briefly as it relates to learning. Groups of boys in a clubhouse are learning to use carpentry tools. They are subjected, in turn, to three different kinds of leadership. In one—*autocratic*—the leader decides what will be done and what will be learned, assigns all the tasks, instructs in considerable detail, and gives praise or blame according to his own standards. In a second—*laissez-faire*—the leader leaves all decisions about what is to be done, what is to be learned, how it is to be done, up to the boys. In the third—*democratic*—the leader and the boys discuss and reach decisions about the ways in which their tasks will be carried out. All the boys are organized in small groups and in turn are subjected to each of these kinds of leadership. Their behavior and how it is altered, what they do, how they react to each other and to the leader, was recorded by observers and by a moving picture camera focused through a one-way glass screen.

The research team were thus able to study the behavior of the boys and make inferences about changes in what they did, how they felt, how they acted toward each other, how much they accomplished, how much they learned. It was found, for example, that the productivity in the craft activity was greatest in the early stages by the boys under authoritarian leadership, and least under laissez-faire, but that at a later point the boys under democratic leadership outstripped the others in things done, as well as in learning how to deal effectively and wholesomely with themselves, their fellows, and their leader.

Some psychologists claim that Lewin's theories have little or no relevance to learning. This seems far from correct. Even if this were so it is still true that the experimental work which he originated, and the "small group theory" about which we shall deal later, have made a substantial impact upon adult education.

OTHER APPROACHES

a. Psychoanalysis. Sigmund Freud was not specially interested in learning as such and made no systematic attempt to understand or write about it. But since his dynamic conception of psychology has so influenced every nook and cranny of the field, it is impossible to write of any part of it without at least a passing reference to him.

A number of basic concepts of Freud have direct application to learning, for example:

- pleasure principle—the law of effect
- fear and anxiety as a drive or inhibition
- unconscious influences upon word association, recall, and forgetting of names and events
- fixation—either meaning an arrested development in which an adult may continue at an adolescent level of behavior or meaning fixed habits
- regression, where a person returns to earlier modes of behavior
- learning as an aspect of psychotherapy.

Freud's work gave a considerable support to all who place primary attention upon the emotions and motivation in learning. Despite his preoccupation with the irrational, his suggestions with respect to learning all play up the rational, cognitive aspects of learning and play down simple or irrational elements. The aim of psychoanalysis is to get rid of the blocks to rationality and, therefore, to rational learning. An important step on the way to rationality is self-understanding, which in itself, as we have seen, is a powerful aid to education. Most of all, psychoanalytic thinking has opened up the entire field of human behavior to scrutiny. Learning is not relegated to a portion of life, not even bounded by such a distinction as what is *neurotic* and what is *normal*. The range of subject matter for students of learning now includes symbolism, repression, and the factors which tend to change and distort perception.

Many other psychoanalysts—Horney and Fromm, for example—have also made several applications of therapeutic principles to learning.

In a larger way so have some men whose work is more closely identified with Jung than with Freud. One of these, Rank, has had a marked influence on both theory and practice in school, particularly of nursery and infant schools. Another, W. R. Bion, has made many contributions to group therapy and understanding the small group, with some practical applications to education. He postulated that in a group, the learning activity is always influenced to some extent by certain emotional stakes. The drive toward learning may be purposive; the emotional preoccupations are nonpurposive and not under conscious control. In understanding the behavior in a group the interplay between task and feelings must be noted. Behavior by members of the whole group which, on the surface, appears contradictory, may thus appear to have consistency. Bion's theoretical concepts have recently been tested out systematically by Thelen and Stock and reported in a book entitled *Emotional Dynamics and Group Culture*.[36]

Of even wider application are the therapeutic principles of Carl Rogers, often identified as "nondirective" counseling. Since these are mentioned in other chapters we shall only refer to them here. Associates of Rogers have made direct applications of nondirective principles to learning. He himself has also done so, particularly in his book, *Client-Centered Therapy*.[37]

b. Functionalism. An eclectic, middle-of-the-road view of learning has been the approach of more psychologists than ever became partisans of any particular theory. R. S. Woodworth[38] is only one of many who were of the temper to examine the work of many schools and systems and to choose what seems to be most relevant and satisfying.

These men never operated within a school of psychology although there were many points of agreement in their work. Significant interests have been in motivation, how adequate responses are established, how inadequate learning can be improved, "transfer of training," and the amount and distribution of practice. These were not men who compelled others to think in new ways as did Freud, and to a much lesser degree Lewin, nor did they range across many fields of learning as did Thorndike. They did, however, critically test and make applications of various learning theories and they did help the partisans of clashing opinions to maintain some form of communication. They have recognized the need for an integration of learning theory. Most of them have been men who have the temper and capacity for helping such an integration to take place. Often, too, their writing provides the clearest exposition of contending theories of learning; the layman can turn to them for more understanding sometimes, than to primary sources.

c. The emergence of mathematical models. Any reader of science fiction knows that many problems in the physical world are first stated and solved by using the language of mathematics, before there has been any laboratory work or pilot projects. Can such methods be applied to the social sciences?

In fact, one of the earliest applications of this attack was in the field of learning theory when Ebbinghaus in 1885 found that the curve of forgetting of facts that had been memorized was roughly in logarithmic form. Accordingly he fitted a logarithmic equation to it.

$$b = \frac{100\ k}{(\log t)\ k}$$

where b = per cent retained by the savings measure,
t = elapsed time, and c and k are arbitrary constants.

This may not mean very much to most of us but it was highly suggestive to later psychologists. We have also seen the attempts by both Hull and Lewin to use mathematics to represent central ideas and relationships. Numerous attempts have been made to present learning curves in precise mathematical form and to employ the result in predictions of future learning. So far the results may have been disappointing but at least have been highly suggestive. An example of the use of mathematical principles in another field occurred when life insurance companies began making actuarial curves or tables and employing them in determining the likelihood of insurance risks.

Mathematical models, developed from success in games such as chess and from the study of communication, may still yield important data about learning.

As W. K. Estes[39] points out, information that is incorporated in such a model is in a form that is suitable for prediction, the results of different kinds of experiments are more nearly comparable when referred to such a model, quantitative analysis of data is usually facilitated by having such a model, and the very rigor associated with constructing the model itself leads to precise testing of any assumptions.

It may be that this mode of theorizing holds much for the future. Naturally it will not and need not replace other kinds of investigation. Mathematical models are far from foolproof; they are useful so far within a limited range of phenomena. Moreover, as E. R. Hilgard[40] reminds us, the most arresting theories are still, and may still be, made without benefit of mathematics, as were Freud's.

For the Practitioner

Earlier we asserted that the foreman, basketball coach, or nightschool teacher requires good theory. How has this worked out? Is there any direct application of these theories to the practitioner? Much!

UNDERSTANDING AND APPRAISING CURRENT LITERATURE

The practitioner needs some background before he can appraise or use books in his library. He might pick up a recent book such as *The Learning Process*[41] and find that it deals almost exclusively with such matters as conditioning, repetition, memory, distribution of study time, doctrine of formal discipline, and transfer of training. Or he may open another book on learning in which none of these factors is mentioned. One recent psychological text asserts that nothing that happened before the end of World War II has much practical significance as far as learning is concerned. This is an extreme view; but the practitioner needs some guidance in appraising such claims.

THEORY TO GUIDE PRACTICE

We have indicated that some of the explanations given with respect to once accepted theories could scarcely now be countenanced, but neither do we need to discard or disregard totally such theories. We could hardly accept *conditioning*, for example, as a single explanation for all learning. Yet there are a number of direct outcomes from this theory:

- It has focused attention upon the learner's responses and helped to bring about an understanding that if the learner is himself aware of his responses and success, learning can be more efficient.
- Attention has also been directed to unlearning—and to the fact that learning needs repeated re-enforcements to consolidate and maintain performance. This notion led logically to the development of workbooks, and other kinds of auxiliary aids, and to the study of re-enforcing that using various media of communication can have.

- The conditions under which undesirable responses can be unlearned, or replaced, are better understood. Unlearning does not happen by chance but in ways that can be predicted.
- It has become increasingly evident that simply increasing the intensity of the stimulus (threat, fear, pain) without attention to motivation can have negative results; this in turn has led to more attention to motivation.

The study of conditioning, even though it may have resulted in some oversimplifications also led to greater concern about the student and his individual problems.

Other examples are the application of connectionism in the understanding of learning by rote, and in animal training. There have been many applications of Gestalt theory to physical education. Field theory, as we have seen, is the basis for several current experiments and developments. The success of men like Tolman and Woodworth in achieving some integration can be a guide to the practitioner in attempting the same task.

THE BEGINNINGS OF FORMULATION "ESPECIALLY FOR ADULTS"

We saw in Chapter 2 that theorizing based on the particular and special characteristics of adults is now beginning. Peter Siegle,[42] for example, has developed in some detail the notion of *horizontal* learning, rather than vertical, taking into account the richer associations and relationships that an adult can bring to anything learned. Howard McCluskey has been developing a concept of *self-adequacy*, which may have some parallels with that of maturity. McCluskey and Gale Jensen have been stating and enlarging their formulations in annual conferences with professors of adult education drawn from many universities. Jensen has stated that the content for an adequate theory of learning must come from four main kinds of phenomena:

- the structure and dynamics of face-to-face groups
- the social processes, structures and activities found in the formally organized social systems (church, school, military

organization, industry or government agency) in which adults spend much of their working hours
- personality organization, including the kind of integration that takes place between the cognitive, emotional, and motor aspects of human learning
- community institutions and ideologies.[43]

Leland Bradford[44] and others have been making application of small group theory to adult learning.

Those who are concerned about the creative process also are uncovering new notions about learning. Sometimes they are dismissed with scorn as charlatans or "brainstormers," but they are exploring a valuable and fascinating field.

In developing novel approaches to teaching, in testing out notions and hypotheses, and in describing and analyzing his attempts and results, no one has been more active than Nathaniel Cantor.[45] This author has been able not only to give a lucid account of his teaching but to illustrate it with many transcripts from class discussion.

AN INTERESTING FIELD OF STUDY

Learning theory, and how it has evolved, is a fascinating study, and the practitioner deserves an opportunity to know it better simply because of the interest afforded. How some men have been able to gain an increasingly better understanding of what constitutes learning is as exciting a chapter in man's progress as many that are frequently celebrated in novel and drama. To supplement the brief references that have been provided here the reader can follow up some of the recommended readings.

REFERENCES

1. Edna Heidbreder, *Seven Psychologies* (New York: The Century Co., 1933). By permission of Appleton-Century-Crofts, Incorporated.
2. C. L. Hull, *Principles of Behavior* (New York: Appleton-Century-Crofts, Incorporated, 1943).
3. John S. Brubacher, *Modern Philosophies and Education* (Chicago: National Society for the Study of Education, 1955).
4. Jacques Maritain, in *Modern Philosophies and Education* (Chicago: National Society for the Study of Education, 1955).

5. M. M. Coady, *Adult Education in Canada* (Toronto: Canadian Association for Adult Education, 1950).

6. Mortimer Adler, in *Modern Philosophies and Education* (Chicago: National Society for the Study of Education, 1955). Permission granted by The Great Books Foundation, Chicago, copyright owners.

7. *Ibid.*

8. *Ibid.*

9. John Dewey, *Problems of Men* (New York: Philosophical Library, Inc., 1946).

10. John Dewey, *Democracy and Education* (New York: The Macmillan Company, 1920). By permission of The Macmillan Company.

11. William H. Kilpatrick, in *Modern Philosophies and Education* (Chicago: National Society for the Study of Education, 1955).

12. Eduard Lindeman, *The Democratic Man,* Robert Gessner, ed. (Boston: Beacon Press, Inc., 1956). Used by permission.

13. *Journal of Educational Sociology,* September, 1945.

14. Theodore Brameld, *Philosophies of Education in Cultural Perspective* and *Toward a Reconstructed Philosophy of Education* (New York: Dryden Press, 1955 and 1956, respectively). By permission of Henry Holt and Company, Inc., copyright owners.

15. Theodore Brameld, *Philosophies of Education in Cultural Perspective* (New York: Dryden Press, 1955).

16. J. H. Newman, *An Essay in Aid of a Grammar of Assent* (London: Longmans Green, 1891).

17. Richard Livingstone, *On Education* (New York: The Macmillan Company, 1945).

18. *Ibid.* Cambridge University Press, copyright owners.

19. Ralph Harper, in *Modern Philosophies and Education* (Chicago: National Society for the Study of Education, 1955).

20. Adult Education Association, *Seeking Common Ground in Adult Education* (Chicago: Adult Education Association of the United States, 1959).

21. E. L. Thorndike, *Animal Intelligence* (New York: The Macmillan Company, 1911). By permission of the publisher.

22. John Locke, *Essay on the Human Understanding* (London: 1775).

23. E. L. Thorndike, *The Fundamentals of Learning* (New York: Teachers College, Columbia University, 1932).

24. R. S. Woodworth, *Psychology* (New York: Henry Holt and Company, Incorporated, 1929).

25. E. L. Thorndike, *The Fundamentals of Learning* (New York: Teachers College, Columbia University, 1932).

26. E. R. Guthrie, *The Psychology of Learning* (New York: Harper & Brothers, 1935).

27. *Ibid.*

28. *Ibid.*

29. C. L. Hull, *Principles of Behavior* (New York: Appleton-Century-Crofts, Incorporated, 1943).

30. W. Kohler, *Gestalt Psychology* (New York: Liveright Publishing Corporation, 1947).

31. E. C. Tolman, *Purposive Behavior in Animals and Men* (New York: Appleton-Century-Crofts, Incorporated, 1932).

32. Kurt Lewin, *Resolving Social Conflicts* (New York: Harper & Brothers, 1948).

33. Marshall McLuhan, *Explorations 8* (Toronto: University of Toronto Press, 1948). University of Toronto, copyright owners.

34. Kurt Lewin, *op. cit.*

35. Ronald Lippitt and R. K. White, "An Experimental Study of Leadership and Group Life," *Readings in Social Psychology* (New York: Henry Holt and Company, Incorporated, 1947).

36. Dorothy Stock and Herbert Thelen, *Emotional Dynamics and Group Culture* (New York: New York University Press, for National Training Laboratories, 1958).

37. Carl R. Rogers, *Client-Centered Therapy* (New York: Harper & Brothers, 1951).

38. R. S. Woodworth, *Contemporary Schools of Philosophy* (New York: Ronald Press Company, 1931).

39. W. K. Estes, *Modern Learning Theory* (New York: Appleton-Century-Crofts, Incorporated, 1948).

40. E. R. Hilgard, *Theories of Learning* (New York: Appleton-Century-Crofts, Incorporated, 1948).

41. Milton M. Schwartz and Irvine L. Harrison, *The Learning Process* (New Brunswick, N. J.: Institute of Management and Labor Relations, Rutgers University, 1956).

42. Peter Siegle, "The Adult Learner," *Adult Leadership* (Chicago: AEA), Vol. 3, No. 9.

43. Gale Jensen, *Adult Education* (Chicago: AEA), Vol. 8, No. 3.

44. Leland P. Bradford, *Adult Education* (Chicago: AEA), Vol. 8, No. 3.

45. Nathaniel Cantor, *The Teaching-Learning Process* (New York: Dryden Press, 1953).

Suggested Reading

ALLEN, FRANCIS R., and OTHERS, *Technology and Social Change* (New York: Appleton-Century-Crofts, Inc., 1957).

BENNE, KENNETH, BRADFORD, L. P., and OTHERS, "Essays on Philosophy," *Adult Education* (Chicago: AEA), Vol. 8, No. 2.

BLAKELY, ROBERT J., *Adult Education in a Free Society* (Toronto: Guardian Bird Publications, 1958).

BRUBACHER, JOHN S., "Consensus Among Philosophies of Education," *Modern Philosophies of Education* (New York: McGraw-Hill Book Company, Inc., 1950).

GETZELS, J. W. *Learning Theory and Classroom Practice in Adult Education* (Syracuse: University of Syracuse, 1959).

HALLENBACK, WILBUR C., "A Sociologist Looks at Adult Education," *Adult Education* (Chicago: AEA), Vol. 7, No. 3.

HENRY, NELSON B., ed., "The Psychology of Learning," *41st Yearbook of the National Society for the Study of Education* (Chicago: University of Chicago Press, 1942).

HUTCHINSON, ROBERT M., *Great Books—The Foundation of a Liberal Education* (New York: Simon and Schuster, Inc., 1954).

JENSEN, GALE, "Principles and Content for Developing a Theory of Learning," *Adult Education* (Chicago: AEA), Vol. 8, No. 3.

LEE, I., *Customs and Crises in Communication* (New York: Harper & Brothers, 1954).

LEWIN, KURT, "Field Theory and Learning," *41st Yearbook of the National Society for the Study of Education* (Chicago: University of Chicago Press, 1942).

OSBORN, A. F., *Applied Imagination* (New York: Charles Scribner's Sons, 1953).

POFFENBERGER, A. J., ed., *Modern Learning Theory* (New York: Appleton-Century-Crofts, Inc., 1954).

ROSENBERG, BERNARD, and WHITE, DAVID M., *Mass Culture: The Popular Arts in America* (Glencoe, Ill.: The Free Press, 1957).

UNESCO, *Adult Education Groups and Audio-Visual Techniques* (Paris: No. 25, "Reports and Papers in Mass Communications," 1958).

WELFORD, A. T., "Psychological Aspects of Learning," *Modern Trends in Gerontology* (London: Butterworth, 1956).

WATSON, JEANNE, and LIPPITT, RONALD, *Learning Across Cultures* (Ann Arbor: University of Michigan, 1955).

Chapter 8

SOME FIELDS OF PRACTICE

So far we have come a long way on our quest. We have looked searchingly at the learner and have seen how radically he changes, yet remains essentially the same, as he goes through life. We have examined the mainspring of his actions—interests and motives—how attitudes are developed and how they change. And we have had an all-too-brief look at some theories of learning, and considered how one can bring theory into some consistent pattern for oneself.

It does not seem possible to give a simple satisfying answer to the question "How do adults learn?" but we have observed many forms of learning in practice, and in consequence the very word "learning" is beginning to take on additional layers of meaning.

We have not found it possible to fashion a single comprehensive theory of learning. Indeed, such a goal seems further away than ever. This is true in part because we now understand more clearly the rigorous detailed preparation that may have to go into such a formulation. More important, we are now better aware that the things that we call by the one word "learning" are not all of the same kind and may not easily be comprehended in any single formula.

But that is no new problem. It isn't easy, for example, to include all the principles and ideas that we usually associate with the notion *democracy* in one single system either. And yet enough agreement on principles and practices which, for all the limitations and ambiguities, serves fairly well, has been attained. This is what has been needed for learning. A review of the theories, over which some men have quarreled and argued fiercely, reveals more similarities and complementary relationships than it does of irreconcilable conflicts.

Now we are going to turn from these general observations

and begin to review briefly (again risking the danger of over-simplification) what is being found out about learning in some practical fields of training, experimentation, and research.

This undertaking is important for a number of reasons.

First of all, disciplines other than philosophy or psychology are employed in these fields. In our century psychologists have not only dominated learning theory, they have made it almost a corner of their special garden. And yet the other social sciences have something to say about learning. Some of this we shall now review although it is not possible to do so in any systematic way.

Second, what has been called the "creative frontier," the growing edge, is just as often to be found in some practical field of work as it is in the laboratory. Ideas about learning are just as likely to come from an amateur scientist, like Galton, or one engaged in some pursuit other than that of learning, like Freud, than from those observing animals or men struggling with a problem box or problem. Whitman once talked about democracy itself as a great school:

> Political democracy, as it exists and practically works in America, with all of its threatening evils, supplies a training school for making first class men. It is life's gymnasium, not of good only, but of all.

Third, it is just as often in practice as elsewhere that occur the "creative intersections," which Robert Oppenheimer talks about. In a television interview, Edward Murrow asked Oppenheimer how ordinary people can ever keep in touch with the scientist who is forging ever farther ahead in his discoveries. Oppenheimer acknowledged that this is a perplexing matter. And he added, the difficulty is not one for the "layman" alone; it may be burdensome for the scientist, who, while he continues to cultivate his own "tiny patch of truth," may be equally ignorant as other men, of all other fields of inquiry. It is in the places where the paths of such scientists intersect or cross; it is at the intersections of two fields of work or inquiry that the greatest amount of growth may be expected, he pointed out. We shall note some examples of these "creative inter-sections" in this chapter.

No consistent plan of presentation has been followed here. The writer has selected, from the hundreds that might have been reported, a number of fields of work which, in his opin-ion, have contributed to our understanding of learning or hold particular promise of doing so in the future. Another observer might have produced a different list. The selected experiences are examined briefly, not so much in terms of their intended purpose as for what they infer about learning. This is a sug-gestive, not a comprehensive, record of some of the fields of activity that anyone interested in learning should keep in sight. Of course it is no easy task to keep up. It's like "Wonderland." "Here," said the Queen, "it takes all the running you can do to keep in the same place. If you want to get somewhere else, you must run at least twice as fast as that."

Large-Scale Training Programs

Harold Clark[1] has recently been reminding us that there are really two systems of higher education. In addition to the universities there are the training programs organized and run by great corporations. In number of "students," in size of teaching staff, in competence of staff, in library and research facilities, the *higher* education offered by business organiza-tions is of considerable magnitude.

Training today is a very large enterprise. It is carried on under a great many and a great variety of auspices. We shall deal particularly with three fields of training because of the mass of the operations and because of the impact that these programs are having, and will have, on theory and practice of learning:

- in agriculture
- in industry
- in the armed forces.

In each of these fields there is a substantial number of full-time teacher-trainers. For example, there are approximately ten thousand men and women engaged full time in some form of agricultural extension. In aggregate, the "student body" in these three fields must reach many millions every year. The training programs have budgets that usually exceed or at least compare favorably with that provided in schools and universities. Most of these programs can draw upon at least a small research staff which helps to plan and appraise the educational activities. Many of these agencies have had some opportunity for publishing and there have been voluminous reports, studies, pamphlets, and booklets dealing with some phases of the work. In sheer volume this is immense. It is difficult to judge quality, because there have been few attempts to apply rigorous evaluation. Nor will it be our task to do so, except in a very general way. We shall assume that a worker in any particular field is familiar with the writing in his field. Our purpose will be to derive general observations and principles from the three fields, and point to additional sources of information so that a teacher in one institution has a brief introduction to other related fields.

We shall make no attempt to deal with the origins or evolution of these training programs although this is a very large and fascinating topic of social history and one deserving much more serious attention by historians. In most fields training began with certain marked characteristics. Invariably it started in some form of apprenticeship, in which one man taught one man, usually in the manner of "Do like this." Later the skilled man was obliged to undertake the training of several. The *students* were obliged to copy the behavior of the *master*, with a heavy emphasis upon drill. Belief in the efficacy of repetition, and the efficacy of punishment, marked many training schemes, which also had to labor under the kind of assumption, current in the British Navy, but found in many forms elsewhere, that "what was good enough for Lord Nelson is good enough for you." Not all the training was poor; much of it may have been quite good. But it varied according to the insights and skills of individual trainers, there was no extensive body of knowledge about training to be passed on, and much of what was advocated was exceedingly limited or downright harmful.

The earliest fields for extensive application of what the psychologists were finding out about learning were large-scale training projects. The beginnings go back at least to the first decade of this century and the process was accelerated during World War I. In the twenties and thirties came an expanded program in agriculture and an increase in the number of "industrial psychologists" that were hired by industries. But the most rapid developments have occurred during and since World War II.

AGRICULTURAL EXTENSION

Agricultural extension used to be regarded as "aiming to make two blades of grass grow where one grew before." It is now conceived as something very much broader:

> To assist people engaged in farming and homemaking to utilize more fully their own resources, and those available to them, in solving current problems and in meeting changing economic and social needs.[2]

The content may encompass the entire range of agriculture and home economics, yet centering on the interest or need of the individual. The goals are broad and various. They may include:

- development of an awareness of the problem
- stimulation of a group to organize for co-operative action
- training of individuals in the skills of farming and home-making
- obtaining the acceptance of the findings of scientific research in the production, marketing, and consumption of agricultural products.

The chief methods used by extension agents have been (1) individual contacts which include farm and home visits, office calls, telephone calls, result demonstration and personal letter; (2) group contacts such as demonstration meetings, leadership training meetings, lectures, tours; and (3) mass contacts such as bulletins, news stories, radio and television, mass meetings. Those responsible for this widely ranging program have put considerable emphasis upon appraising results. The techniques employed may have lacked somewhat in depth or subtlety, but they are rigorous in at least one sense. The usual procedure is to count the number of times there is an actual *change in practice*. It is not possible to deal with all learning on this basis but it has added something to our understanding about learning when its effects are tabulated in this concrete way. By choosing a unit such as a change in practice, one is then able to compare and contrast the kinds of factors which may have produced that change. We say *may have,* for although this research rests upon an assumption that the change is *caused* by a method, or a combination of methods, and the assumption may be valid, no final proof is possible because of the number of modifying influences.

There seem to be five stages to this process of adaptation as described in a special report entitled *The Diffusion Process:*

1. Awareness or learning about the idea or practice
2. Interest, being concerned enough to seek further information
3. Evaluation, weighing the merits of the idea or practice
4. Trial, seeing how it works in practice
5. Adoption.[3]

Recent studies[4] have been conducted covering almost 50,000 separate changes in practice in over 15,000 farm families in 27 states. One of the most interesting findings is that changes in farm practice happen *indirectly* at least two times out of five. That is, farm people often learn from, or copy their neighbor. For men, the figure is even higher; the neighbor is a source of the changed practice at least 25 per cent of the time. For women, about half of the practices came as a result of a meeting in which some new method was demonstrated. Covering both men and women, changes occur about 25 per cent of the time from individual contacts with the extension agent, about 33 per cent of the time by various kinds of meetings and group contacts, and about 23 per cent of the time through the mass media.

There are other ways to look at these results. In addition to checking the kind of influence which seems to have produced the change, it has been possible to estimate what was the cost of the change. It was found, for example, that about 20 per cent of the total budget of extension workers was used for demonstrations of methods and leadership training which in turn produced about 20 per cent of the changes in practice. Farm and home visits cost about 14 per cent of the budget but brought nearly 16 per cent of the results. On the other hand, result demonstrations which took about 17 per cent of the budget produced 8 per cent of the result, or only one-half of what might be expected. The effectiveness of exhibits seems to have been less than one-fifth as much as the funds spent on it would warrant. News stories and radio, however, with one-twentieth of the budget, produced three times the result that might be anticipated.

The studies revealed other interesting facts. Efforts have been made to find out factors about the personality and the experience of the learner which seemed to be linked most closely to readiness for change. There is considerable evidence to show, for example, that some farmers can learn from almost any kind of stimulus—from neighbors, the agricultural agent, pamphlets, or radio talks. But others, usually those who have enjoyed much less formal schooling, are not able, or are not willing, to learn from reading or listening to the radio. They seem to require personal help; they can learn directly from the agent through demonstrations but seldom or ever from a pamphlet. In general, people with the least academic experience require the most personal attention. But the studies also revealed that many extension agents spend most of their personal time with the most able farmers (the farmers that could learn in all the other ways) and spend least time with those who do not learn easily except by direct contact. This seems also to be the experience of a number of other field services, operated by governments, universities, business corporations, and churches.

A factor which may result in resistance to change is the strength of the ethnic, religious, or social groups to which a farmer belongs. Duncan and Kreitlow[5] found that farmers who belong to groups or organizations that are cohesive adopt new practices less frequently and less readily than do other farmers of equal ability and experience, but for whom neighborhood or kinship ties are not so binding. We note elsewhere, that the strength of the bonds within the major groups to which one belongs will modify appreciably the perception of ideas or messages to which one is exposed. It is well established that new ideas are much more readily accepted (that is, learned) if they are or can be associated with existing values.

Considerable attention has also been given to the message itself, in print, radio, or picture—how readable, or how easily communicated, it is. Some of these findings will be summarized later under "communication research."

Some subject matters *seem* to be more readily taught in one way than another. Evidence *so far* shows that when it comes to changes in regard to tree fruits, for example, they occur most readily through a visit by the agent, whereas changes in alfalfa cultivation have occurred most often as the result of a meeting or distribution of leaflets. Though it is too early to generalize from such data, it is clear that there is no hierarchy of approved educational methods, with some always being best. Attention needs always to be paid to the relevancy of a specific method to a particular kind of subject matter or learning objective.

INDUSTRY

Most of the "training" for agriculture takes place in special colleges or in large-scale agricultural extension programs. Many variations can be found, from place to place, but it is all one system. There are a growing number of extension services operated by such private organizations as seed or farm implement companies, and there are also individual farm consultants. But nowhere in agriculture is there the variety of method and technique that is found in industry where the direction of training is largely in the hands of private companies.

A growing number of people are engaged in full-time industrial training. Many of them now belong to societies of trainers and may thus be enabled to share in common exploration of philosophy and method of training. For some people "training" is beginning to be a profession, with an increasingly well-organized body of knowledge and skills. One now hears much more often the phrase "training the trainers," and this implies that there is a body of theory and practice which is becoming established and which is being taught or communicated.

The industrial trainers have several factors in their situation that are favorable for further advances in learning theory and practice. Theirs is a comparatively new calling from which one can expect some freshness and flexibility of viewpoint—necessary alike for exploration and for integration of theories. Their task is important and is recognized as such; they commonly have funds at their disposal that are more ample than most educationalists have ever had and which can be applied to research. Moreover, variety in "students" and in learning objectives is sufficiently broad to allow for flexibility. Some of the "students" may be top executives, others may be research scientists. Corporations in the United States now employ nearly half a million research scientists, and such men may be obliged to go "back to school" regularly to keep up with radical advances in their own or allied fields.

At present training in industry covers many fields:

- apprenticeship of various kinds
- skills taught and supervised by foremen in informal, on-the-job situations
- classes, training departments or schools organized in the company or by an industry-wide trade association for employees or management
- classes outside the plant organized in some plan of relationship with an educational authority, such as college or school board, for employees or management.

Human Relations. The "Hawthorne experiments" carried on in the Western Electric Company, at the Hawthorne plant, were so dramatic in immediate results and so far-reaching in developing new hypotheses that they have become celebrated both in scientific writing and in folklore. The researchers and the company began, in a modest way, to investigate factors which influenced industrial efficiency. Most of the results were presented in terms of output of production because this could be expressed in quantitative terms and could be measured. But since the studies had to do with such matters as the aspirations of workers, and the way workers regarded, or frustrated, or supported each other, the results have had implications far beyond industrial production.

Executives of Western Electric had arranged for a relatively simple research project, namely how an improvement in illumination affects the rate of output. Their next series of experiments were to have much wider significance. It all began in a little room in the plant, with six girls as subjects.

In April 1927, six girls were selected from a large shop department of the Hawthorne works. They were chosen as average workers, neither inexperienced or expert, and their work consisted of the assembling of telephone relays. . . . This particular operation was chosen for the experiment because the relays were being assembled often enough so that even slight changes in output rate would show themselves at once on the output record. When arrangements had been made for the test room, the operators who had been chosen to take part were called in for an interview. "The nature of the test was carefully explained to these girls and they readily consented to take part in it, although they were very shy at the first conference. An invitation to six shop girls to come up to a superintendent's office was naturally rather startling. They were assured that the object of the test was to determine the effect of certain changes in working conditions, such as rest periods, mid-morning lunches, and shorter working hours. They were expressly cautioned to work at a comfortable pace, and under no circumstances to try to make a race out of the test." This conference was only the first of many. Whenever any experimental change was planned, the girls were called in, the purpose of the change was explained to them, and their comments were requested. Certain suggested changes which did not meet with their approval were abandoned. They were repeatedly asked, as they were asked in the first interview, not to strain but to work "as they felt."[6]

Before the investigation began, careful records had been kept and what each girl had produced over several months was already known, as well as a large body of information about production rates of all employees. The experiment was to study the output curve of the girls in the test for a long enough time and under various changes in working conditions, so that which conditions were most satisfactory in their effect might be determined.

At the beginning of the experiment the girls were kept for five weeks working under conditions very much as before, so that any changes in output brought about by the transfer would already be accounted for.

Over several months a series of changes were introduced, one at a time:

- increase in pay for piecework
- two rest pauses
- lengthening of rest pauses
- lunch provided in morning and afternoon
- shortening of work day
- shortening of work week.

With *all* these changes the output improved. Moreover, when an attempt was made to return to previous conditions, output did not drop, it continued high and showed some improvement. No matter what was done, it seemed, the girls produced more. How could this be accounted for?

The explanations were provided most readily through talking with the girls themselves. The girls said they liked to work in the test room; "it was fun." Second, though they were under the constant surveillance of the experimenters, the absence of the customary supervisory control made it possible for them to work freely without anxiety. Conversation was allowed. It had formerly been restricted in principle and barely tolerated in practice; now it was allowed natural expression. Third, the girls realized that they were taking part in what was considered an important experiment, their work was expected to produce results which would lead to the improvement of working conditions for their fellow employees. Fourth, there was development within the group itself. Parties and social occasions were arranged, and the girls became attached to each other, and to the group. When one girl would have a good reason for feeling tired the others would "carry" her, working especially fast to make up for her lower output. Within the group itself leadership developed.

At about the same time a group of men were being tested in a "bank wiring" operation, under *social* conditions which tended to produce opposite results. The work routines established for the men seemed to deny all that gave work its value, the men were afraid of supervision and acted in the most ingenious ways to nullify it. Production, and worker satisfaction, were equally low.

These facts and these explanations are not so surprising to us now as they seemed thirty years ago. Their result was a substantial shift in the direction of the concern of the industrial psychologists. From measuring the effect of physical and environmental factors upon behavior, the psychologist now gave greater attention to the factors within a person, and his personal relations with others. It was this direction and this work which is still going on, and which continues to be so fruitful, not just for production but also for learning.

Circular Effect of Morale and Efficiency. During World War II ample opportunities were afforded to study the importance of similar factors. One such study,[7] for example, had to do with "morale" and efficiency in the shipbuilding industry. Two shipyards owned by the same company, were located in the same city, but were operated under different management. The workers shared unsatisfactory housing conditions, a severe climate, and inadequate recreation for themselves and their families. One might therefore have expected similar output records. Yet in one yard a ship was turned out every 76 days, in the other it took 207 days or nearly three times as long. The community environment and the physical working conditions were similar, and so was the work experience of the men, but some marked differences were found in other factors. The earning situation (overtime and back pay) as well as the basic wage was much better at one plant. Poor morale in the other seems also to have been aggravated by broken promises. As one man put it, "If only they didn't keep promising these things! If they'd only keep the promises they make or didn't make any, maybe they'd get better work."

There was also dissatisfaction with promotional policy, the fact that some newcomers received higher pay than old employees, and rancor because of misuse of manpower. One of them complained, "*Putting in my time* would be more like it. ... I'm squawking because I haven't got enough to keep busy." Only 20 per cent of the men showed confidence in the management of the yard with low production; in the other the percentage was nearly 70.

Two general observations come out of this study that have a bearing upon learning theory as much as upon industrial production:

First, like other social processes, there is a *circular causal relation* between morale and production. Good production gives men a feeling of accomplishment and leads to increased effort. Low production reduces motivation which in turn leads to reduced productivity. Instead of a one-way causal relation, most social processes show this circular interaction.

Second, worker morale is directly related to its immediate physical and psychological context. The factors associated with the job itself are of primary importance in keeping the worker well or poorly motivated at his work. If production is going well, if his superiors treat him fairly, if promotional opportunities are good, if earnings are satisfactory, if the health and safety conditions in the factory are superior, then job satisfaction will be high. Moreover, under such circumstances most individuals can absorb considerable deprivation on the outside and still keep up their work morale. The inference should not be drawn, of course, that management has no stake in good living conditions for workers in the community. Rather the implication of these findings is that management should put its first emphasis upon making the job itself remunerative and psychologically rewarding.

Leadership. Another realm in which significant study has been made is in industrial "leadership." Many observers have noted that there are some basic similarities among three relationships—parent-child, teacher-student, and superior-subordinate. In all three cases the relationship is complex and subtle. Unfortunately the subtlety is not always recognized and the wrong inferences are drawn. For example, the fact of a very real and manifest dependence of the subordinate upon his superior is somewhat obscured by another emphasis, in film, and story, and advertising, upon the subordinate achieving full satisfaction of his needs *entirely* through his own efforts. An overemphasis upon individualism may actually get in the way of our understanding the vast potentialities of the individual, or equally, of our understanding the significance of certain groups like trade unions or trade associations through which the individual may seek to satisfy his individual wants and needs. It may also prevent us from seeing clearly that in the industrial setting or educational setting, there must be an adequate and balanced provision of the two components—security in the dependent relationship as well as the assertion of independence.

Security in the plant depends upon a number of factors:

• *Atmosphere of approval*—This is revealed not so much by what the superior does but how he does it and by his attitude to his employees. Without an atmosphere of approval employees can have no assurance that their needs will be satisfied, regardless of what they do—they then will feel threatened, fearful, insecure.

• *Knowledge*—The employee must know what is expected of him. This includes knowledge of company policy, rules, and procedures, an exact knowledge of the requirements on his own job, and his place in the organization, as well as advance information about any major changes in the work. It may also include some knowledge of the superior's personal attitudes to the work and the workers.

• *A discipline that is consistent.* In child rearing, in education, as in industry, the kind or form of discipline seems to be less important than to be able *to count on it*. The employee needs to know that he can rely on the support of his superiors for "doing what is right" and equally firm pressure to prevent his doing "what is wrong." But in addition to consistency, the discipline must be maintained in an atmosphere of approval. If a healthy state of security does exist, the conditions for healthy independence have also been realized and the drive for self-assertion and self-realization will take constructive forms. Otherwise there may be the familiar reactions of apathy, blind rebellion, sullen submission, conscious or unconscious attempts to sabotage.

Active independence also hinges upon a number of circumstances:

• *Genuine participation.* The employer needs an opportunity for expressing his ideas and making suggestions. This happens often in the higher ranges of management but not always in the lower reaches. An example that can be repeated endlessly concerns the owner of a small plant turning out gymnasium and playground equipment. This was a family-owned industry; the owner knew every workman by his first name, and often worked beside them at the bench. But when, in period of financial difficulty, he called on the help of a management-consultant firm, the experts were able to tell him nothing that he did not know. Nevertheless the inquiry led to results that raised his production and sales in a substantial manner. The consultants talked with *all* the workmen seeking their advice and suggestions. Six of their recommendations were followed up, and these brought about the critical improvement in the situation. Naturally such an operation cannot proceed in identical fashion in vast industries, but the efficacy of active participation in bringing results of higher quality does not require further demonstration.

• *Responsibility.* When subordinates have achieved security they are able to assume responsibility gradually and they accept it with pleasure and pride.

• *The right of appeal.* The growth of self-assurance and self-expression can be safeguarded only if a person feels that he can win approval for an idea and an action, if it is sound, regardless of views of an immediate superior.

In their book *New Understandings of Leadership*[8] Ross and Hendry discuss a number of other facets of "leadership" that affect learning. Perhaps the most important of these is *empathy* or social sensitivity—that is, the accuracy with which one person is able to perceive another. How well the "leader" understands the "follower" as the latter sees himself has a marked effect on the leader's behavior and consequently, upon the response that the follower makes to that behavior.

One approach to management training has been developed around this idea of *sensitivity*. In describing its application, Robert Tannenbaum observed that it may be a new and startling notion for business:

> My impression is that in business and industry we have for some time been primarily focussing on the other person. If we have difficulty in dealing effectively with Joe, it is Joe's fault; there is something wrong with him. And we don't very often ask ourselves the question, "What is it I do that makes it difficult for me to deal effectively with Joe? Do I know what it is that I do in relation to Joe that makes him respond the way he does?" You see, this is a rather new orientation to this matter. Perhaps we should start asking ourselves: "What is it in me that needs change?" This, in fact, is the basic starting point for the training that I want to describe.[9]

Tannenbaum states three specific objectives for "sensitivity training":

- a greater understanding of one's self
- an awareness of one's impact upon other people
- a deeper appreciation of what goes on between people when they interact in a social situation.[10]

An attempt is made to help the managers become better skilled at helping individuals in communicating more effectively, in counseling, and in dealing with situations involving tension and conflict.

In these studies all the factors mentioned are operating when the task is learning just as when the task is production.

We shall deal with other factors that also affect both learning and production in industry, under such heads as group development and research in communications.

THE ARMED FORCES

The staggering task of training millions of men and women, in and out of uniform, during World War I and again in World War II, provided new opportunities as well as new problems. We have seen how the use of psychological tests advanced tremendously during and after World War I, based in part on the fame of the army *Alpha* and *Beta* test scales. Until then, most observations of adults had been of very small samples, usually isolated in institutions. Now there were large numbers of men to test from every kind of background and experience.

Research in regard to training and education has been going on continuously during World War II and since. There is, for example, an entire project devoted to the study of audio-visual training aids and the conditions under which learning with such aids is effective. There is a vast comprehensive program of research conducted under the office of Naval Research, with some counterparts in other services. To the surprise of some, the aims and scope of this research are exceedingly broad. Admiral Stolberg, Chief of Naval Research, once stated:

> Almost 90 per cent of the ONR contracts are in basic research with no "applied" strings attached, for the Navy is fully aware that a sound basic research policy is the foundation of later developments on the applied side.[11]

Most of this work is carried out in universities by individual investigators, or in teams. There has been a certain amount of criticism of the approach and much laughter directed at "research by committee," and "the fetish of interdisciplinary projects." Yet this is one of the first large-scale attempts by men from different disciplines to work together on basic problems. The problems of such collaboration are many, and nothing is easier than to poke fun. But we have noted before that many human problems cannot be tackled solely from the point of view of a single discipline. Learning itself is one of the best illustrations of this point. Because it is *multidisciplinary*, the research associated with the armed services has much to contribute to general theory and practice.

The program of the Office of Naval Research has five main goals:

- *Comparative study of different cultures*—economic, political, cultural, psychological, and sociological structure of national groupings
- *Structure and function of groups*—the productivity, structure, and development of groups in relation to their assigned tasks
- *Problems of communications of ideas, policies, and values*
- *Leadership*
- *Growth and development of the individual.*

Findings During World War II. During World War II there were many examples of new applications of learning theory as well as activities which deepened our understanding of learning. Much attention was given to such basic questions as these: How could men be trained for their forthcoming ordeal? What facts, skills, or attitudes were most important? These major inquiries were usually preceded by field studies conducted by social scientists, *in the battle situation.* Then training goals were formulated, and methods and materials devised. For fast and effective learning the *real* situation was reproduced for training, through maneuvers and exercises. Combat problems were presented, in film and in actual test. The use of equipment was taught with the *actual* equipment, or in mockups, or with films.

Of course, information and skills are not everything. There is also morale. Could morale be taught? Perhaps not; at least not directly. But some factors in morale could be studied. A Canadian professor of philosophy[12] had been making a thorough study of young men who were idlers and drifters during the depression years, apathetic, morose, angry, and sullen. Three years later some of these men, and others like them, were the heroes of the Battle of Britain. Their squadrons were considered to epitomize morale. What were the differences? There seemed to be many, but three in particular:

- The airmen were well-trained and knew they were well-trained—their equipment was the best obtainable.
- The job they had to do was of the utmost importance and was so recognized.
- They belonged to a small select group and each man felt himself responsible to the others as well as to and for himself.

Later studies have given support to these findings. A flyer *valued* first his own crew, then the squadron, next the group, the wing and finally the air force itself. Ideas he might have about justice or democracy were not without significance in his behavior, but the key factor was his belief in himself and his associates. Other studies were carried out to discover what kinds of traits or experience were most closely associated with certain tasks. Measures were devised by which it was possible to predict, with reasonable accuracy, which of them might learn one kind of task, which another. There has been some application of this knowledge since, in selecting men for universities, and men for training for special industrial tasks.

Considerable study was devoted to learning procedures. How are men helped to achieve the most in class or demonstration?

One way is through providing careful explanation of both the immediate steps and the larger goal. In a study of thirty-three army companies more than half of the soldiers who rated their own company's battle teamwork as effective also reported that their leader had explained the combat mission to them, and had been careful not only to outline their particular objectives but their place in the whole battle plan. This principle seemed to apply in combat and in all the learning experiences associated with army life. Men learned well when, in addition to presentation of material, and opportunities for practice, they were also given some understanding of the principles involved. For example, a group of inductees at base camp who were given some theory in machine operation scored 18 per cent better than men of similar ability who were not.

Most of the evidence from these findings supports the notion that good learning comes best where a variety of methods and techniques are employed. Research from observation of the use of audio-visual aids has also borne this out. Informal methods were usually favored by men in the forces over more conventional class methods.

The adult who is made to feel responsible for his own education tends to achieve the best record. Instructional materials were most successful when they were based on the actual experiences and needs of the men and women for whom they were prepared. Army men learned fundamental skills of reading, writing, and arithmetic with far greater efficiency when the subjects covered in the exercise books were about army life and adult experiences; much less well when the instructional materials were about childish things.

Special Devices Center. One of the special research divisions has been concerned with the way learning is brought about with audio-visual devices and materials.[13] The following are typical of some of the studies made:

- comparison of teaching of factual and conceptual material by sound motion pictures and by teacher-classroom procedures
- effect of attention-gaining devices upon learning with films
- effect of increasing the "density" or amount of factual material in a film upon the amount learned
- the effect of color upon learning.

This is not the place to analyze the data, and we shall simply illustrate it with a selection of observations from these studies.

Some kinds of factual and conceptual material can be "taught" with sound pictures as readily and as well to a thousand men as to the class of twenty, if *learning the facts* is the measure of achievement.

Verbal introductions of films, when well planned and presented, may add as much as fifty per cent more information learned and may result in its retention for two to three times as long. However, "packing" a film with concentrated information will add only slightly to the total amount learned and there is some likelihood that not only will the separate parts not be learned adequately but the relationship of the parts to the whole may not be comprehended.

For effective learning the pace must be slowed down. Some tests indicated that much of the material in early training films was presented at least 30 per cent too fast and this was a particular handicap to older students.

Some Implications of "Army Education." Millions of men and women had studied in the classrooms of the armed forces. What was learned from these projects of training in use of equipment, tactics, literacy, language, international affairs, mathematics, and skill processes? This question was given intensive study by C. O. Houle and others. They report a number of findings:

- Interest in education among adults is very widespread.
- Far more people than ever before were exposed to education as part of their adult experience and are motivated to continue learning if suitable opportunities are provided.
- Educational experiences for adults should be introduced into the activities to which adults *choose* to belong.
- The more education people have the more they are likely to want.
- Participation in education will be increased if the activities are provided geographically close to the students.
- Programs of adult education must be directed toward the achievements of goals which the students feel to be real and significant.
- The success of an educational activity for adults is enhanced if it starts at the level of the students and then proceeds to more abstract things.
- The motivations for adult learning grow in part out of the social setting in which the learner lives.
- Almost all adults who lack the basic tools of learning can achieve them if the subjects are well taught.[14]

Other "Schools of Danger." Learning no less dramatic and no less crucial than in the army was occurring elsewhere dur-

ing the war. One key place was in camps for internees, such
as the Relocation Camps for the Japanese in North America.
Here there was a struggle between those who wanted to use
stern "discipline" as a tried and true method, and those who
felt that more rational measures were possible.

In one of the camps, sociologists and anthropologists were
brought into the staff. Soon an occasion arose for a test of
rational principles. An ugly strike developed, brought about
almost by group hysteria. For a while it seemed that nothing
could be effective but brutal "shoot-'em-down" measures.
However, some of the administrators were prepared to risk a
good deal for their principles. In the face of mob violence an
Emergency Council was created. Both the real difficulties and
those conjured up in hysteria were faced by the council and
proposals of how tensions could be reduced and human dignity restored were studied. No one pretended to know all the
answers, but camp inmates and staff agreed to try, *and try
together*. Order was soon restored. As a by-product some
hypotheses had been established for use in the tension problems to be faced in the future. As Alexander Leighton described
it: "I am certain that in the Relocation Camp experience, my
hands, groping blindly below the surface, touched here and
there on a real body of constants and laws in human living."[15]

In places under the horror of bomb raids, there were other
learnings of a grim and necessary kind. How did you help
people prepare themselves for an attack? Not by talk, or by
study about war; the anxieties created before the event often
seemed harder to bear; seemed to be more crippling than the
blow itself. Not by taking children away from parents; family
groups tended to stand firm against the dangers if family
members were able to give support to each other in mastering
the lessons of survival in the midst of terror. Not by taking
people from one environment or culture and thrusting them
into another. City people forced to leave their homes and
snatched up into comparative safety of the country often
seemed to crumple and break down when taken from the life
that they knew. It was found that the best chance for city
people to learn how to cope was to seek shelter in a compara-

tively safe part of the city, the environment in which they feel "at home." Above all, people must not be fed on lies and promises. In times of peril "truth seems to serve best," as Alfred Noyes once wrote:

> It might be
> The final test of man, the narrow way,
> That he should face this darkness and this death
> Worthily, and renounce all easy hope,
> All consolation, all but the wintry smile
> Upon the face of truth.

These are tragic lessons and one can hope that they will not need further application in similar settings. But they have validity for the way in which men will strive with any disaster, whether man-contrived or not. And in the process something has been learned about man, his nature, and how he learns.

Other Fields

So far we have been considering fields of practice that are part of, or associated with, large-scale training projects. We shall now turn to selected experiences from other fields.

GROUP DEVELOPMENT

Future historians may ultimately refer to the second quarter of the twentieth century as the era, not of depression and war, but of *the group*. It was in these years that interest in group life and what happens to individuals in groups, broadened and deepened. As more and more attention was showered on the group, particularly the small group, there was the usual and almost inevitable reaction. Some people who were specializing in studying group processes, or were working with groups, made claims and statements that could hardly be supported, and as a reaction to this there were those who felt or charged that interests and values associated with the individual were being slighted or endangered.

Flurries of this sort accompany most social changes and they need not occasion too much alarm. What ought to happen is a thoughtful examination of the new development to see if application can be made of it.

It would be incorrect and rather silly to say that there was no interest in groups in relation to learning before 1925. Nevertheless, the major developments have all happened since. Some of them were first associated with Mary Follett and propositions which she advanced in the late "twenties" in such books as *Dynamic Administration*.[16] In the thirties a few social workers in such agencies as YMCA's and community centers began to talk of their special field as "group work," and in 1934 Busch published a book using the phrase "Group Work"[17] in his title. Also in the thirties and early war years, efforts were made to apply group processes to certain kinds of therapeutic situations. Psychiatrists and psychologists in their treatment of bewildered boys, or adults who were emotionally injured by some wartime experience, used the life in a group as one experience for cure and relearning. This was also the time when Sherif, Asch, and others were studying experimentally the difference in performance of an individual, alone and in a group.[18]

From these several fields of inquiry some broad generalizations were established:

- Groups have certain characteristics, an existence and dynamics of their own, that make them more than a sum of the individuals who take part.
- Group characteristics such as size, atmosphere, flexibility, homogeneity, cohesiveness, leadership exist in an equilibrium so that changes in some characteristics may result in changes in others.
- Groups may therefore change and undergo processes through time.

The period in which the terms *group dynamics* or *group development* were generally employed began with those like Kurt Lewin and the group experiments and training situations which, in part, derived from these ideas. To one of these experiments we have already given some attention. That is the means by which women were taught facts about nutrition and how changes were brought about in the *practice* and *habits* of some of the women. We have also referred to another experiment, developed under Lewin's direction, on the effect of certain kinds of leadership or "social climate" upon learning and behavior. Late in Lewin's lifetime a Center for Group Dynamics was set up at the Massachusetts Institute of Technology and subsequently transferred to the University of Michigan with the name Research Center for Group Dynamics. In 1947 a National Training Laboratory in Group Development began to hold training sessions each summer at Gould Academy at Bethel, Maine. This Laboratory was established for the purposes:

- to develop a body of people prepared to carry on human relations training throughout a wide range of social institutions and activities
- to accomplish through research a gradual improvement in the theory and procedures of human relations training
- to work toward the general improvement of group problem-solving and member skills in society.[19]

The object of the laboratory training, research, and consultation have led to a wide range of activities. Among its major activities are an annual training and research seminar at Bethel, a year-round consultation program for interested individuals and organizations, a series of research projects on human relations training, a number of regional and local "laboratories" and workshops, and the production of various training aids such as films, articles, and training manuals.

Accordingly, most of the activities that may be included under the term *group development* are now associated directly or indirectly with the National Training Laboratory.

The National Training Laboratory. The specific objectives of the Laboratory have been stated as follows:

- to increase one's own sensitivity to the factors in intra-group and inter-group relations
- to increase ability to *diagnose* the significant factors in human relations situations
- to develop *insight* into the effects of one's own behavior upon another's
- to provide an evaluation of human relations training through the use of *research evidence*

- to provide opportunities to exercise group *problem* solving methods in human relations
- to provide opportunity to practice some *leadership skills*
- to relate the learnings of the laboratory to *back-home* situations.[20]

Three educational decisions were made when the Laboratory was established. First, it was decided that *changed behavior as well as knowledge* was a primary objective. Accordingly methods had to be devised where members would become more deeply involved in the project. Second, there was a concern that the changes would hold true when the member left the Laboratory and returned home. Third, it was agreed that training *and* research must both be present and be mutually re-enforcing.

In the Laboratory, then, the concern is for learning that results in change and in developing an understanding and skill in dealing with the forces that tend to promote or inhibit change. Procedures have been developed which display a number of novel features.

The Laboratory attempts to create, for purposes of analysis and practice, group situations where are present the kind of factors operating in other groups. The learner participates in a group and continues to study what happens to him, to the other members, and to the "culture" of that group. He hears lectures on theory, he studies and reads, but first of all he takes part in and studies his own group in action. He is aided to use rigorous methods of observation and analysis in respect to his group. Every attempt is made to create an atmosphere in which he feels free and able to examine his own and others' behavior and to accept help and criticism from others. Opportunity is provided for him to become better aware of problems of insecurity and resistance to change as well as to practice some of the group skills he has learned.

The Laboratory employs many training forms and devices:

- *The T group* or training group for achieving a greater sensitivity to what happens in the group and a better understanding of self in relation to groups. The T group may tackle such problems as style of leadership, overcoming group or individual apathy, and how to reach group decisions.

- *The S group* for practicing such skills as how to make decisions in a group. These skills are practiced, as far as possible, in actual reality situations.
- *Theory sessions* in which a background of information and theory is provided so that a member may relate his experiences in an organized way.
- Sessions on such practical problems as what methods to use in large meetings.
- *The C or community group* in which a member meets with others in a small intimate circle in which he can freely discuss his experiences under no pressure to make decisions.
- Counseling with staff members.
- "Back home" sessions for the study of what the learner will be doing upon return and the application of his training to his regular tasks.

Implications for Learning Theory and Practice. The National Training Laboratory and similar centers have made a number of contributions to learning theory and practice.

- There is a substantial body of research data about what constitutes training.
- There have been many and varied uses of *reality situations* in learning. (We mean by reality situation the establishment of a setting which has factors similar enough to those actually faced by the learner so that he can observe, and analyze, and actually test out his theory and method. We noted earlier that training in the armed services has increasingly been in "reality" situations—training maneuvers carried out under live bombardments, use of actual weapons, or carefully simulated conditions.)
- The attempt to combine training and research, though not uniformly successful, points the direction in which most satisfactory teaching must move.
- The concern not only with the learning of content but

with changes in behavior that carry over into practice has resulted in much more thorough exploration of how change is brought about.

- Many practical devices useful in other learning situations have been demonstrated and refined, such as observation techniques and role playing.

Research about small groups is going on in other institutions as well, and some of it in countries other than the United States. It may deal with a comparison of individuals and groups, or the internal dynamics of groups, or the way groups relate to one another and to the environment. We shall later discuss how the small group may affect the communication process.

One of the most interesting fields of research is that in which the productivity of the group is compared with that of the individual. For many tasks people achieve considerably more in groups. But for some others, particularly in intellectual tasks, they may do better alone. Lorge and Brenner[21] have reported the somewhat contradictory evidence that has accumulated from these studies. Though not yet conclusive in result, these studies should provide much guidance in the future for adult education.

There are also a number of studies which deal with the impact, the pressure of the group upon the individual's judgment. Both Asch and Sherif[22] report that individuals are influenced significantly by their associates, even in giving incorrect estimates of distance, or weight or volume. In early attempts to develop useful devices for film evaluation, it was discovered that it was essential to record the reaction to the film of the appraisers, *as individuals*, before any consideration within the group. Discussion was useful in bringing out subtleties, but it invariably resulted in some merging or polarizing of opinion, whereas both the individual impressions and whatever consensus was achieved were useful. If the group effort preceded individual appraisal fewer of the individual differences were displayed. The impact of groups upon "conformity" is of significance for educational practice; it is also a matter of great ethical importance.

Though the concept of leadership also has implications far beyond small groups, some of the functions we describe as leadership may be functions of the group. Much that has been learned about leadership and about groups has occurred as these two phenomena have been studied together; it is difficult, and may be pointless, to study either separately.

THEORIES AND RESEARCH ABOUT LEADERSHIP

We have already noted that some studies have been conducted about leadership in military situations. Gouldner and others have reported how leadership is expressed in such fields as industry, in a social institution, in athletics, in a committee, and in technical assistance projects abroad.

In their book *New Understandings of Leadership*[23] Ross and Hendry have brought together many of the findings from a multitude of separate studies. Leadership is seen in three aspects:

- as traits within the individual leader
- as a function of a group
- as a function of a situation.

It is quite clear from the studies reported that certain factors that had been assumed to be intrinsic to leadership are found only in some situations, and not at all in others. Of the multitudes of lists of traits (appearance, intelligence, and so on) that observers claim are associated with leadership, no two lists have much that is common.

However, some factors seem to be present in most examples of leadership. One of these, we noted earlier, is *empathy*. It seems probable that the leader, to an exceptional degree, is able to identify with, and to respond to, the emotional needs of the members of a group. He seems to have an enlarged sensitivity to their needs for recognition, affection, adventure; or he is perceived by the group members as being sensitive to such needs. Another factor is to be, or to appear to be, *practically concerned* with doing something about these needs. In one industrial plant men in high-producing sections felt that their foremen took a more personal interest in them than did men in low-producing sections. Likewise more men in the high-producing sections reported that their foremen were helpful in training them for better jobs than those in low-producing sections reported. Another factor, sometimes called *surgency*, has to do with liveliness, cheerfulness, and enthusiasm. The leader seems to display more self-assurance and internal strength, notably at times of crisis, than do other men. He seems, also, to *want* genuinely to be a leader. It may be becoming for a leader to hesitate until he is asked or drafted, but most leaders seem to be men who draft rather easily!

Ability to communicate, at a level deeper than just talk, also seems to be an essential. It seems equally important that the leader facilitates communication among the members, and is able to bring some color and excitement, some meaning and importance, to the activity.

As far as these findings are true, it becomes apparent that leadership is something much more complicated than the few skills that are often the content of courses termed *leadership training*. Such training may include skills like group organization, or mastering certain kinds of subject matter—but none of these learning experiences, useful though they may be, are of themselves essential or guarantees of acceptance as a leader. The *qualities* of the leader do evolve and change but not in any simple way.

It appears that the way in which a person grows and changes and develops *as a leader* has many parallels with other kinds of learning. Accordingly, close attention to leadership theory may be expected to be rewarding for teachers and other practitioners.

COMMUNICATIONS PRACTICE AND RESEARCH

Few words are used more often and more loosely today than *communication*. The possible exceptions are the words *democracy* and *leadership*. In a single day the author heard the following:

"They robbed our communications"—a boy of thirteen was complaining that the rival baseball team had become aware of the signals his team was using.

"We ain't communicatin' right"—a youth of seventeen was deploring the rift in relationships between himself and a young lady.

"There has been a serious breakdown in communications with the Capitol"—a radio news analyst was explaining that he had not been able to get certain information from Congress.

"That strike is a direct result of lousy communications by the general manager"—a labor leader was blaming management for causing an industrial impasse.

How men express themselves, how they talk with each other, how ideas are exchanged, how feelings are aired and shared, these are crucial matters for learning.

One of the reasons that the word communication, though long and clumsy, is heard from every lip, is that communicating is now possible through so many new and exciting forms, by the mass media of communication. Just having the means of communication is hardly enough, as Thoreau wryly pointed out a century ago:

> We are in great haste to construct a magnetic telegraph from Maine to Texas; but Maine and Texas, it may be, have nothing important to communicate. . . . We are eager to tunnel under the Atlantic and bring the Old World some weeks nearer to the New; but perchance the first news that will come through into the broad, flapping American ear will be that the Princess Adelaide has the whooping cough.[24]

But such means of communicating as television are so visible, and so omnipresent, that they cannot be ignored. Another reason is the growing interest in the *practice* of communicating, of using these new and remarkable tools by business men, advertisers, pressure groups, and government. Study about how ideas or slogans are transmitted, and what effect they may have, is going on constantly. Anyone today who wants to be aware of all the ways in which people learn cannot fail to keep in touch with various forms of communications research.

There was no such thing as organized communications research before 1930. A mail vote of the sort that the former *Literary Digest* magazine used to send out was considered an ample means of assessing public opinion. In the years since there have been studies of many kinds:

- *Control*—who owns the instruments of opinion and who determines what shall be said.
- *Audience*—what kind of people buy books, read newspapers, listen to radio or watch television? What are the predispositions of the audience?
- *The communications message*—Readability: do people understand what they read? Do they "get the point" of the radio or television message?
- *Social effect*—What is the response and the result of the message in changes in behavior?
- *Responsibility*—Freedom and responsibility of the editor, critic, broadcaster, teacher?
- *Political consequences*—how the *form* of communication, and its control, provides the opportunity for or modifies the results of different forms of government as a democratic or totalitarian power.

At another level, the effect of the form of communication upon personality and upon society, there has been surprisingly little attention so far. This *is* surprising because a moment's reflection will lead to the obvious understanding that how we talk, how we hear, how we see, mark our character and our life. In the first play in the *Ways of Mankind* series the commentator says, "We talk as we think; we end up by thinking as we talk."

Changes in the form of communication, such as the invention of the press or of television, have results that can be described only as revolutionary. Aristotle was sharply rebuked by Alexander for putting down words in a manuscript, it might result in rulers' being obliged to share power. Plato was equally concerned about the spread of written communications:

This discovery will create forgetfulness in the learners' souls, because they will not use their memories; they will trust to the external written characters and not remember of themselves. The specific which you have discovered is an aid not to memory, but to reminiscence, and you give your disciples not truth but the semblance of truth; they will be hearers of many things and have learned nothing; they will be tiresome company, having the show of wisdom without the reality.[25]

When the press became a true mass medium with the spread of inexpensive books and pamphlets, men like Newman were alarmed. But the fact that the form of communication has been instrumental in political control and the evolution of political power, has been only dimly perceived, right to the present day when the speculations of Harold Innis[26] and others have initiated a new approach to the study of its consequences. Innis has explored some of the effects of the printing press such as the breakdown of international communication, the impetus given to nationalism by the exploitation of all vernacular languages, the loss of contact between writer and audience, and the inhibiting and depressing effect of the press upon such other forms of communication as music, plastic arts, and architecture. Karl Deutsch[27] has recently carried this further in regard to developing nationalism, in his book *Nationalism and Social Communication.*

These consequences may, or may not, be desirable. They are of many kinds. Thus Marshall McLuhan has reminded us that a feature of the *book* is its "republicanism."

The page of print is not only a leveller of other forms of expression; it is a social leveller as well. Anyone who reads has at least the illusion of association on equal terms with anyone who has written. And that fact gave the printed word a privileged place in American society and politics. The Duke of Gloucester could say caustically to Edward Gibbon on the completion of his *History:* "Another damned fat square book. Scribble, scribble, scribble, eh, Mr. Gibbon!" But there were no fox-hunters in America to put the literary upstart in his place.[28]

The astonishing break with the past has come about comparatively recently. When writing was in manuscript, manuscripts were read aloud; and writer and learner were still in direct touch with each other. Manuscript readers memorized most of what they read because, in the nature of things, they still were obliged to carry their learning with them. Difficulty of access to the manuscripts made for different habits of mind and study. Most learning was oral and so was teaching. The spread of the inexpensive printed page helped to bring about solitary learning and private study. Today's emphasis upon the seminar and the group is not so much a break with the past as it is a return to it.

The effects of the mass media upon "freedom of speech" are far-reaching, more so than has been generally appreciated. As McLuhan has pointed out:

> . . . The instantaneity of communication makes free speech and thought difficult if not impossible and for many reasons. Radio extends the range of the casual speaking voice, but it forbids the many to speak. And when what is said has such a range of control it is forbidden to speak any but the most acceptable words and notions. Power and control are in all cases paid for by loss of freedom and flexibility.[29]

Learning from Mass Media. How well do people learn from the mass media? As a generalization, educational level is useful as a means of predicting the behavior of the recipient of a communication. At the time of the famous "Invasion from Mars" radio broadcast, when some panic-stricken listeners actually took to the highway to escape the invasion, it was found that the more highly educated tended to make a check on the broadcast before taking any such action. Other studies have confirmed a general tendency toward higher selectivity, more critical thinking, and "better taste" in the use of the mass media as the years of schooling rise. As is true of books, the individual tends to select mass media programs that are accessible to him, sometimes, in preference to what he says he is interested in, if the latter is harder to come by. People seem to learn more of what is concrete than what is abstract through radio and television. And as we have seen in another context, a variety of media seem to have a greater effect than a single method. Another way of saying this is that the greater number of sensory channels used in the learning process, the greater is the actual amount of learning. Studies have confirmed that learning is more rapid and efficient when the learner is a *participant* rather than simply a *spectator* and that learning *must be used* to be retained.

There have been many studies of learning by pictures, by moving pictures, by radio, by television. In the present chapter we have already noted some such studies in connection with training in the armed services. Schools and universities have also been at work, and the results have been frequently reported in such books as *Audio-Visual Methods in Teaching* by Edgar Dale.[30] With the arrival of television there came a flood of assertions about the probable effects upon learning.

pro   Television is the most important development for learning since the beginning of the recording of human experience—people learn magnificently well from television.

con   People may be entertained or propagandized by television, but they don't learn—television will destroy books, conversation, and most forms of effective learning.

Of course these are extremes and most people were more temperate in what they said. Experiments were devised to determine what or how much might be learned. One study can serve as an example of many. In one test conducted through the collaboration of the University of Toronto and the Canadian Broadcasting Corporation,[31] the subjects were undergraduates studying anthropology. A special lecture was prepared on the subject, "Thinking Through Language," chosen because it was assumed to be both difficult and stimulating. The students were divided into four groups, matched for performance on academic work, and each group was placed in a separate room. One group heard the lecture as delivered, a second by radio, a third over television, and a fourth studied it in the printed form. At the conclusion the students wrote a half-hour examination consisting mainly of multiple-choice questions of fact, plus one essay-type question. There was ample time, and so it was a test of power, not of speed. Those who received the message by television had the highest scores on the test.

The mean scores on the test were as follows:

Television	77.2
Radio	69.2
Reading	65.1
Lecture	64.9

In a retest, eight months later, it was found that there had been considerable loss, the means now being 61.5; 52.6; 47.5; and 56, respectively. Those receiving the communication by television and by radio had not only learned more but retained more than by the more "conventional" means.

Those responsible for the study were quick to point out some obvious limitations. The sample is small, the study was limited to university students (not to adults generally, or to children), and was limited to the presentation of a single subject. Moreover, the *increased motivation* that can be found in certain kinds of test situations and not under "normal" conditions, may have affected the results in the favor of television and radio. The authors make only one assertion about the result: "It is plain that under these conditions at least, certain of the mass media, and notably television, are very effective channels for conveying information."

This modest kind of claim can be justified amply from many other studies. As we have seen from the results of studies of the "Special Devices Center" it is possible to teach certain kinds of information and skills in very large groupings indeed.

It is quite obvious even from this scanty review that a system of communication whose *content* and whose *form* can so deeply influence human life must necessarily have many implications for learning. We shall deal with only three such implications, (1) the notion of *readability*, (2) the problem of *two-way* communication, and (3) studies dealing with the *effects* of communication.

Readability. How effective is a given sample of writing? Is

it readable? Two separate, yet connected ideas—*appeal* and
clarity—are involved in this question. Is the material of sufficient *interest* that people will want to read it? Is it *comprehensible* so that they will understand?

The problem is an important one. Governments, corporations, voluntary organizations all try to inform, instruct, warn,
and assist people through the use of printed material. In a
great many cases still, and this used to be true almost invariably, the printed message is in a form that people either
will not or can not use. In 1930, at a time when the adult
population had gone to school on an average only six or eight
years, most of the printed messages planned for their use were
prepared at about the grade-ten level or higher. The disparity
is not so great now, but the problem has not suddenly disappeared.

Readability is far from being a new problem. Writers in all
ages have been confronted by it. Many have been quick to
offer their favorite remedy, some useful, some not. There are
about as many quack cures for the disease of nonreadability
as for the common cold. Most of the attention has been focused
on words as if all the difficulty were found in them. "Write in
words of one syllable" is common, and very silly advice. We
are told to use *familiar* words, select the *concrete* rather than
the *abstract*, the *short* word not the long, and to employ the
word coming from a *Saxon* root rather than from one of the
romance languages. "Choose from the vocabulary which is
common to all your readers" is another bit of advice. Ingenious
ways of doing this have been devised. As long ago as 1875, a
Russian professor studied several thousand letters written by
farmers to learn what vocabulary and idiom he might safely
use in writing agricultural and educational bulletins.

Linguists have been forced to study other factors than word
difficulty. One of these is difficulty of concept. Much of the
writing in science and philosophy is hard to understand because the ideas as well as the vocabulary are remote from our
ordinary experience and everyday habits of thought. Nevertheless some rare beings have found it possible to write and
speak about difficult and complex subjects in a comprehensible

and interesting fashion. Is this a special gift, or can it be learned?

Some students of language assure us that anyone can learn to write most things in a way that can be understood.

In the last twenty-five years there have been several systematic studies of the factors going into readability. In 1930 Gray and Munroe published *The Reading Interests and Habits of Adults*, which was followed in 1935 by *What Makes a Book Readable?* by Gray and Leary. Work of this kind has been followed up more recently still in a series of publications from UNESCO.[32]

Meanwhile work had been going on in "reading laboratories," work of an analytical and experimental nature. Certain barriers to understanding were identified, such as the length of sentences, the number of propositional phrases, the number of difficult words. Those that seemed to be most significant were selected and worked into a formula for predicting reading difficulty by Irving Lorge.[33] Using his ingenious system, one can assess the grade level for most writing and thus estimate how difficult the reading may be for a class or group. One can also derive hints about how to write with greater chances of being understood.

Other studies and formulas have also been published. The best known is by Rudolph Flesch,[34] developed in a series of books such as *"The Art of Plain Talk"* and *"The Art of Readable Writing."* Flesch worked out his formula through a detailed study of popular magazines where he assumed he could find a key to reading comprehension. Flesch believes that in these media, and in ordinary conversation, we can find the best guide to comprehension. "The secret" he says, "is not difficult ideas expressed in easy language, it is rather abstractions imbedded in small talk. It is heavy stuff packed with excelsior." Gaining interest and attention is a large part of the answer. Flesch combined a somewhat different set of factors in his formula. He also uses sentence length, he adds as a new and positive factor personal references (names of people, pronouns, or other words which are "easy," which are interesting, and "which give a breather" in tackling the more difficult tasks). He also uses, in a negative way, the "gadgets" of language, the affixes which may shift the meaning back and forth—leading to errors as common as the use of *irregardless* meaning *regardless*. His formula gives a measure of difficulty ranging from *very easy* through to *very difficult*, or from the level of comic books up through standard (*Reader's Digest*) to scientific and philosophic journals.

These formulas do have a practical use in helping people learn and they provide some clues to learning. Used with judgment they can help to get rid of much that is dull and useless as well as provide some tips in the preparation of study material. It is possible to write simply and lucidly, without *writing down* or primerizing. The latter is a very real danger. The adult student who feels insulted by the childish level or substance of reading offered him will not be well motivated for further learning.

Two-Way Communication. For many older people the very term "mass media" raises the same mental image—a picture of Hitler or Goebbels screaming into a microphone—and forcing out a single set of ideas upon millions of listeners. This is one-direction communication, and we often talk about the mass media as if it always happens this way.

But let us look at another kind of communication system.

During the war, in London, certain men and women volunteered or were appointed to act as wardens. Their duties were to watch for fires and to rescue the injured. But as time went on, another role emerged. They began to be a means of transmitting news about how people on other streets were getting on, as well as reliable information from official sources to counteract the spread of rumor. Government now had an excellent means of distributing needed facts and maintaining morale. But this was not just *one-way* communication; much of its strength was in its *double* flow. The street warden reported back complaints, the fears that people had, their doubts and questions, as well as stories of achievement and heroism, and these were all used to modify policy. The officials now had an additional source of information, and a means of checking the effectiveness of policies, or—what may be of equal importance—how people perceived or felt about these policies.

We hear much adverse criticism directed about monolithic, propagandistic policies in the Soviet Union. If communication in Russia were all *one-way* it is conceivable that there might long ago have been a serious breakdown. Actually there is a highly effective oral-communication system in Russia,[35] mostly one-way in direction, but not entirely. Hundred of thousands of men and women hold an *official* position as a go-between from higher authority to cells or groups—the farm group, or block of neighbors, or a factory team, or a student class. It is their duty to bring information and to interpret decisions reached *above* to their group. But they are also charged with noting the questions and doubts that arise within their group and to estimate whether or not the group is prepared to act, or must be indoctrinated before the inception of a new policy. Russian political leaders accordingly receive an enormous amount of information *back* from local units, to guide them in policy making and the timing of certain actions, or, at the least, to know where to expect resistance.

These examples all deal with large numbers of people. What about two-way communication as applied to an individual learner?

Here there is also considerable evidence. In general, if material is presented with the opportunity for reaction and questions, the learning is more effective. You can talk *at* people, or talk *by* people, or talk *with* people. This can be tested by anyone through a simple experiment. Give paper and pencils to two classes or groups, who are separated. Now take a card on which there are half a dozen figures, triangles, squares or circles, of different sizes and in different positions. Have an *instructor*, yourself or a group member, describe verbally the figures on the card and their relationship to each other. Ask the members to draw the figures showing these relationships. Repeat the instructions as given until everyone has it approximately correct but do *not* allow the group members to ask questions or make comments. Now repeat the whole exercise with a second group. Only this time encourage questions and conversation about the test. You will find, almost invariably, the same kind of result. Many, though not all, of Group One will complete the assignment more quickly. But few of them, perhaps none of them, will understand the instructions perfectly the first time. Group Two will probably take longer to complete the assignment, but accuracy of all members will show considerable improvement over Group One. As a biproduct, they may also take a much greater interest in the test.

This and a dozen other experiments all indicate that the learner should have an opportunity to raise his doubts, air his misunderstandings, become *involved* by verbalizing, if learning is to be accurate and effective. This principle, often called by the ugly term "feed-back," is discussed further in Chapter 10.

So important is this fact in its many ramifications that some psychologists, and some poets, have said that all learning is a *dialogue*—between learner-author, or learner-teacher, or learner-fellow-learners. It is when the conditions for this dialogue are not present that we may fear the consequences.

Effect. However, human beings are not entirely powerless even in the face of one-directional communications. Recently a high school teacher was talking about a colleague who had argued that television would have little educational result because people could always turn it off. "I reminded him," said the teacher, "that I have a class of forty boys and girls all of whom were born with exceedingly precise instruments for turning *me* off at any time that suits them."

People are not just the innocent victims of anyone who controls the air waves. This is a problem that is serious enough, but not without its positive side.

In the past two decades there have been an increasing number of studies that have dealt not just with the message transmitted but with the effect of the message upon the recipient. In particular, attention has been directed to the blocks, or the modifiers, of the message.[36]

People respond to a message selectively, depending on their own experience. S. I. Hayakawa illustrated this point with the account of a recent episode:

The writer was driving a car at dusk along a western road. A globular mass about two feet in diameter appeared suddenly in the path of the car. My passenger in the front seat screamed and grasped the wheel attempting to steer the car around the object. I tightened my grip and drove right into it. In each case the behavior of the individual was determined by his own past and by his own phenomenal field. My passenger, an Easterner, saw the object in the highway as a boulder and fought desperately to steer the car around the object. I, native to the vicinity, saw it as tumbleweed and I devoted my effort to trying to keep the car on the road. But notice, at the moment of action, what the driver was trying to do made sense to the driver, but made no sense to the passenger.[37]

Not only does a man's experience condition his perception of a message, he "chooses" messages which he thinks will "reward" him, or that conform with his present attitudes. We have seen earlier that students with different biases learn and retain with varying success facts about communism, depending on whether they are favorably disposed or antagonistic.

One important factor in the communication process is how reliable the recipient feels the communicator is. If there is disbelief the audience may not respond. In one celebrated presentation *Is Anybody Listening?*[38] the author warned business men that millions of dollars spent in providing information to their employees would all be wasted unless the employees had some trust, otherwise the words would fade away unheard and unread.

Another factor is that of point of view. Is one or more points of view presented? In research in the use of army training films it was found that although giving *one* side produced positive change, giving both sides of an issue usually produced more change in the intended direction. A man was more likely to accept a new point of view, opposed to his initial opinion, if the film made what he considered a fair presentation of the grounds for that opinion. A film that "seemed one-sided" was immediately judged to be propaganda, and therefore discounted. It was also found, as was assumed, that the greater the critical ability of the subjects, the less likely they were to accept an unsound interpretation.

In 1955 appeared a book *Personal Influence*[39] which summarizes and relates much of the research about the effects of communication and advances some stimulating propositions. The book itself is an excellent example of what can happen when more than one stream of inquiry intersects. In this case, studies of the effect of mass media and studies of small groups were brought together.

In his introduction to the book Elmo Roper wrote:

> As a result of my own research into public attitudes I have come to the tentative conclusion that ideas often penetrate the public as a whole slowly and—even more important—very often by interaction of neighbor on neighbor without any apparent influence of the mass media. . . . Lazarsfeld . . . has here brought us a new supply of integrated data on the effect of communication *between* people as distinguished from the better known effect of mass media *on* people.[40]

In discussing this conclusion Roper refers to his own explanation of the way in which ideas are transmitted. He believes that the American public, in so far as the transmission of ideas is concerned, can be represented as six concentric circles:

- In the tiny inner core are the "great thinkers," a few in number in any age, and not necessarily widely known by their contemporaries, men like Plato or Marx whose ideas become distributed over continents and ages.
- A still tiny group of "great disciples" who are close to the source and become effective advocates. As examples, he lists Paul in religion and Abraham Lincoln in politics.
- The great disseminators—"as many as 1,000 or as few as 250 in American society today," the men and women who have a public for the ideas they talk about. Examples—Walter Lippmann, Henry Luce, or a "labor leader such as Walter Reuther."
- The "lesser disseminators"—editors, writers, broadcasters, organization officials—people who have a particular forum, but a limited one.
- The "participating citizens"—people who vote regularly,

work, and contribute to local and national campaigns and causes.

• The politically "inert" who are seldom active in their community.

Roper points out that these are loosely formed groups; that a "great disseminator" in one field may be "politically inert" in another. It is Roper's contention that the "politically inert" probably come to accept ideas more readily from their "participating citizen" neighbors than in any other way, and that these citizens are likely to be influenced in turn by the "lesser disseminators."

What conclusions are brought out by *Personal Influence?* First of all, there is an attempt to bring together research covering such fields as radio listening, effect of motion pictures, the impact of reading, particularly of magazines, and the influence of media upon political judgments. The book introduced new data from a study of the ways by which the people in a selected Illinois town decide to buy a new product, or vote, or choose their reading. The idea behind this survey is easily stated. People were asked who had influenced them in buying clothes or cosmetics, in selection of movies to attend, in reaching a decision about local public affairs, or in the choice of magazines.

One of the main conclusions came as a result of an earlier study of political opinions and how they are formed and altered, reported in the book *Voting*.[41] Successive interviews were held with the same families each week or month over an entire year. The subjects were asked each time whom they intended to vote for, and what had caused them to make this choice. In this way extreme shifts in political attitude (such as when a man who was planning to vote Republican decides to vote Democratic, or vice versa) were thus identified. In such a case the man or woman who has changed his opinion was asked the reasons for the change.

It was while studying what had affected these major changes that a situation was discovered which had not been expected:

- Practically no one did so because of the influence from a speech, reading newspapers, a radio talk, or a movie.
- *Almost everyone* who made such a shift did so because of belonging to, and exposure in, a small face-to-face group —for example, the family, the women gathering each morning for coffee, the men dropping in at a tavern together after work.

When a man has made a radical change of view, the mass media do seem to affect his views; that is, they tend to support his new position. He now reads and hears and sees selectively. Impressions reach him that tend to buttress his point of view. The mass media have considerable power in re-enforcing a decision already arrived at. With enough repetition they tend over a period of time to fix or weaken a choice. In a country like Nazi Germany, where there was little alternative to *official* messages, they would have a very strong effect. But the mass media are not so effective as *primary groups* as the source for *changing* opinions or attitudes. Their basic long-term effect seems to be a slow modification, or coloring, or infiltration upon the view of the world held by the individual, and therefore of the self. But it must be admitted that longitudinal studies of this influence are as yet few and incomplete.

Other kinds of studies have brought forth some additional evidence. In some subjects, like the study of international and public affairs, there is a greater tendency to accept "expert" opinion from people who have prestige. For such things as fashions, food, movies, even local public issues, attitudes are much more likely to be affected by the people in the primary groups to which one belongs.

In reporting on these and other studies, Lazarsfeld has made an important point about the people who exercise this influence:

> Some people seem to serve as personal transmitters for others. Without these relay individuals, messages originating from the mass media might not reach otherwise unexposed people.[42]

Thus certain people, and certain primary groups may transmit, may block, or may modify messages.

This function of transmitting messages (not necessarily origi-
nating them) has often been identified as an ingredient in
leadership. It is in this sense that Saul Alinsky in *Reveille for
Radicals* speaks of the leader as one "who knows the telephone number of the people."[43] Lewin speaks of a somewhat
similar function as that of *gatekeeper*, meaning a person who
can exercise control over the flow of information in regard to
an activity. For example, in the case of food the mother is
usually the "gatekeeper" and her attitudes and behavior tend
to influence the family, while in the case of baseball the father
might be the "gatekeeper."

These are only a few of the basic concepts dealt with in
communications theory and research. Enough has been found
to illuminate many learning principles and to convince practitioners of the necessity of trying to keep informed about this
rapidly developing field.

STILL OTHER FIELDS OF PRACTICE

We have reported, largely for illustrative purposes, a few
fields of practice from which much new evidence that bears
upon learning theory is being collected.

We shall now mention, in passing, a few additional fields
which also provide excellent possibilities.

Counseling. Personal counselors are now found in schools,
universities, corporations, trade unions, clinics, and social
agencies, and in private practice. The significant task of counseling is not giving information or advice. Many counselors
would say that it is never advice giving. The counselor's function is to bring about learning on the part of the client. The
client may have information and skills to learn but above all
else he must come to terms with himself, and accept not only
himself, his strengths, weaknesses, capacity for affection and
growth, but also begin to learn to be self-managing. This
process is closely related to most aspects of learning, as we
discussed in Chapter 2.

The parallels between therapy and education are so significant that some direct applications of theory and practice from
therapy has been made to the classroom. In this connection

we have several times referred to the word of Carl Rogers. Another field of work in which there can be employment of technique from therapy to education is the treatment of alcoholics.

The Teaching of Languages. It is now thoroughly understood that the way one uses one's own language has a marked effect upon one's personality. We can assume, therefore, that the learning of language may have important implications for general learning.

This point is well exemplified in the debate which still continues between those who favor the teaching of a second and third language in early years of childhood and those who say it should be postponed until the child has a thorough grasp of the mother tongue. Neurologists, such as Wilder Penfield, claim that the brain cells of the young child are much more receptive, and more capable of managing several patterns of language sounds than in the years after eight or ten:

> When a baby is born the speech areas of the cerebral cortex are like a clean blank slate, ready to be written upon. There is an optimum age within the first decade of life when these special areas are plastic and receptive. The method of teaching children their mother's own language has been the same in all lands and in all ages. It is extraordinarily efficient. It conforms to the changing capacities of the child's brain. . . . A child who learns three languages instead of one, early enough, learns the units of all three without added effort and without confusion. . . . During higher education it will always be desirable that some students take up new languages at a later period and there is a good deal of evidence that he who has learned more than one language as a little child has greater facility for the acquisition of additional languages in adult life.[44]

It is also true, of course, that the young child gets more satisfaction out of repetitive behavior and has less inhibitions about trying a new and difficult kind of behavior than does an older person.

Those who urge postponement often do so from a theoretical position. They claim that until a child has a firm grasp of his own language, an attempt to communicate in another tongue will confuse him and have an adverse effect, not only upon his ability to learn, but upon his entire personality development. This latter view is currently being challenged.

Early childhood seems to be the best time for the brain to store up sound patterns, but the cultural aspects of language, of course, are as possible for older people, as are other kinds of learning. There are examples of men and women well into their eighties learning to speak an additional language. However, as Penfield has pointed out, both interest and facility for this would have been increased by successful experience in the earliest years.

Learning a new language means to learn how to think, how to feel, and how to express oneself with the aid of new and different symbols. Students of language have been studying the ways in which this happens. All the major theories of learning are finding some application in the new language classes organized for men in the armed services, for people undertaking technical assistance assignments abroad, for immigrants, and for refugees. Moreover, in addition to learning theory, there have been valuable experiments concerning size and form of class organization. For maximum effect in learning in a language class, size should be small enough so that every student gets considerable individual practice, and just large enough so that there is some group support as well as an increase in interest and in motivation. Classes of five or six have been used with excellent effect. Results have also been obtained by subjecting a person to the sounds to which he must become familiar just as he is going to sleep and even while he is sleeping. This suggests interesting possibilities for other forms of learning, although it also opens up some new and difficult ethical problems, somewhat like those of subliminal advertising and other attempts to reach the individual beyond his conscious control.

Finally, the effort to teach languages is now a matter of considerable importance in most countries of the world. This is one field where advances that may be made in Israel, or Brazil, or elsewhere, may be of greater significance than any upon the American continent.

Cross-Cultural Education. Substantial numbers of people are traveling these days. Many of them are doing it for one main purpose—business or pleasure—but have as a subsidiary purpose learning about another culture.

It has usually been assumed that travel is broadening and if people will travel they will grow in understanding of other people. In general this may be true. But it happens in no direct or certain way. There is nothing inevitable about good human relations. It is well to remember, for example, that most, if not all, of the political leaders in Asia and Africa who are leagued against the West, have visited and lived in one or more of the countries of the West. What kind of exposure did they have to Western culture? What did they learn?

There are also the people who travel but seem to be touched not at all by their experience, or who may actually have had all their prejudices confirmed. A character in one of John J. Marquand's novels "traveled all around the world but never left Boston." How can people be helped to learn about another culture? And what will this tell us about learning itself?

Though there are few if any certain answers to these questions, fortunately they are now under careful study by social scientists and others collaborating through the channels of UNESCO.[45]

Technical Assistance in Underdeveloped Countries. There have always been men and women who went out to other lands, for religious, political, humanitarian, or commercial reasons, to take some part in the direction of new activities there. But the scale of such activities has shifted, the numbers involved are many times greater. "Experts" are being supplied not from a few countries only, but from all countries, and many of these "experts" work together as members of an *international team.* How they learn from each other, how they learn to get along as colleagues, and how they learn to deal with the new culture in which all are working, is a matter of great fascination, and full of implications for learning practice and theory.

In such situations learning new skills or knowledge does not happen easily unless attention is paid not only to individuals concerned but to the culture in which they live. Even if a new skill or resource results in better health or income, it will not be accepted if it runs counter to cultural values. This is just a special example of the more general case that the new learning must enhance the self, or it runs the risk of rejection or distortion. Examples are many.

In some foreign lands it is easy to conclude that the village markets do not provide an efficient or economic means of distribution of products. But the people will not be prepared to accept some other form of distribution if the social life, the opportunity for men and women to exchange news and gossip, is thereby eliminated. It may be more efficient to replace the work gangs who sing and labor together on each other's fields with some other form of work organization but the people may reject this change, even if it means some improvement in the economy, if it is gained at the cost of enjoyable social contact. Men or women who have perfected some skill, and gain prestige for that skill, will not easily give it up to learn other skills even though there may be some monetary gain. One's culture always modifies *what* one will learn and *how* one will learn.

This entire field is now under scrutiny in many parts of the world although it is not to be expected that much will be reported for some time to come. But it is quite likely that there may be many applications "back home." A united approach by different specialists in a clinic, or on a medical team, is not a new notion, in concept or in practice. Nor is the idea of tackling a problem of community education or community development, by a "team" of social scientists, new as far as theorizing goes. But there have been relatively few examples of it in practice on the North American continent.

Summary

This has been a chapter of exploration—both in outreach and in depth. We have not encountered many new principles but we have seen how these principles are capable of different forms and several dimensions of expression.

The exercise has been necessary for a number of reasons. It has been essential to observe, in practice, the main theories of learning which were stated earlier. Moreover, not only are these the fields in which present knowledge about learning is applied, but these fields also constitute the main laboratory in which theory is constantly being restated and reshaped. For adult learning, the "field" itself is the laboratory, not the conventional classroom. Unfortunately, though most practitioners may know their own work reasonably well, they have not found useful ways of keeping up with other related fields.

Three fields of practice almost rival the institutions of higher learning themselves in number of "students," in size and quality of "teaching staff," and in resources for research and teaching. They are agricultural extension, industry, and the armed forces. In agricultural extension application of considerable resources has been made over a period of almost half a century; many of the findings regarding selection of personnel, method, and techniques are applicable to other fields of learning. In industry have come some of the classic experiments affecting learning (for example, the Hawthorne experiments). The amount and complexity of training and education in industry is rapidly accelerating. It is interesting to note that some concepts of management training are identical with those employed in the training of teachers. Almost all the practices that make for morale and productivity in industry seem to apply equally well to productivity in learning —for example, maintaining an atmosphere of approval and a consistent discipline, as well as the encouragement of individual and group responsibility.

Wartime experiences, with the armed forces or civilians under stress, also provide evidence to re-enforce what is known about attitude change. People accepting new attitudes, or resisting physical attacks, are enabled to do so most successfully under *human* conditions, that is, where the individual has support from his family or group. In these cases where emotional tensions are heightened, one finds fullest corroboration for basic principles about the survival and modification of the self.

The chapter has reviewed some of the activities and research about "groups" and the place and role of the individual learner within a group. Group development is one of the most important fields for learning theory and practice during the past half century. Two other important fields also require investigation: research in "leadership" and in the use of the mass media in education. For all learning it is essential that *two-way communication* be achieved.

Fields like counseling, language instruction (where a man learns to think and express himself with new symbols), and education across cultures, are also yielding significant insights regarding learning. Because of involvement in technical assistance projects abroad we are beginning to appreciate how many of the principles of learning that we have assumed were "universal" are really a function of our particular culture.

We need a comprehensive view of learning theory applied to vast areas of human behavior and experience. But we also need to observe the application of these principles in the actual setting where the learning usually takes place. This will be the subject of the next chapter.

REFERENCES

1. Harold F. Clark and Harold S. Sloan, *Classrooms in the Factories* (New York: New York University Press, 1958).
2. L. D. Kelsey and C. C. Hearne, *Co-operative Extension Work* (Ithaca: Comstock Publishing Associates, 1949).
3. George M. Beal and J. M. Bohlen, *The Diffusion Process* (Ames, Iowa: Iowa State College, 1957), Special Report, No. 18.
4. M. C. Wilson and Gladys Gallup, *Extension Teaching Methods* (Washington, D.C.: U.S. Department of Agriculture, 1955), Extension Circular, 496.
5. James Duncan and Burton Kreitlow, "Selected Cultural Characteristics and the Acceptance of Educational Practices and Programs," *Rural Sociology*, December 1954.
6. Theodore M. Newcomb and Eugene L. Hartley, eds., *Readings in Social Psychology* (New York: Henry Holt and Company, Incorporated, 1947).

7. D. Katz and H. Hyman, "Morale in War Industry," *Readings in Social Psychology, op. cit.*

8. Murray G. Ross and Charles E. Hendry, *New Understandings of Leadership* (New York: Association Press, 1957).

9. Robert Tannenbaum, "Sensitivity Training for Supervisors." By permission of the author.

10. Robert Tannenbaum, *Ibid.*

11. Harold Guetzkow, ed., *Groups, Leadership and Men* (Pittsburgh: Carnegie University Press, 1951).

12. Gregory Vlastos, *Adult Education in Canada* (Toronto: Canadian Association for Adult Education, 1950).

13. Special Devices Center, "Instructional Film Research Program Reports," Pennsylvania State College, 1950.

14. Cyril O. Houle, Elbert W. Burr, Thomas H. Hamilton, and John R. Yale, *The Armed Services and Adult Education* (Washington, D.C.: American Council on Education, 1947).

15. Alexander Leighton, *The Governing of Men* (Princeton: Princeton University Press, 1945).

16. Mary P. Follett, *Dynamic Administration*, Metcalf and Urwick, eds. (New York: Harper & Brothers, 1942).

17. Henry Busch, *Leadership in Group Work* (New York: Association Press, 1934).

18. S. E. Asch, "Effects of Group Pressures upon the Modification and Distortion of Judgment," *Readings in Social Psychology* (New York: Henry Holt and Company, Incorporated, 1947).

19. Leland P. Bradford, ed., *Explorations in Human Relations Training* (Washington, D.C.: National Training Laboratory in Group Development, 1953).

20. *Ibid.*

21. I. Lorge and M. Brenner, *A Survey of Studies Contrasting the Quality of Group Performance and Individual Performance* (New York: Bureau of Applied Social Research, Columbia University, 1957), Technical Report No. 1.

22. M. Sherif, *An Outline of Social Psychology* (New York: Harper & Brothers, 1948).

23. Murray G. Ross, Charles E. Hendry, *op. cit.*

24. Henry David Thoreau, *Walden* (New York: New American Library, 1942).

25. Plato, *Phaedrus* (New York: Modern Library Edition, 1936).

26. Harold Innis, *Empire and Communications* (Oxford: Clarendon Press, 1950).

27. Karl Deutsch, *Nationalism and Social Communication* (New York: Dryden Press, 1956).

28. Marshall McLuhan, in *Explorations 4* (Toronto: University of Toronto Press, 1956). University of Toronto, copyright owners.

29. Marshall McLuhan, in *Explorations 8* (Toronto: University of Toronto Press, 1957). University of Toronto, copyright owners.

30. Edgar Dale, *Audio-Visual Methods in Teaching* (New York: Dryden Press, 1956).

31. Carl Williams, in *Explorations 4* (Toronto: University of Toronto Press, 1956).

32. W. S. Gray, *The Teaching of Reading and Writing* (Paris: UNESCO, 1956).

33. Irving Lorge, "Predicting Readability," *Teachers College Record,* March 1944.

34. Rudolph Flesch, *The Art of Plain Talk* and *The Art of Readable Writing* (New York: Harper & Brothers, 1946 and 1948, respectively).

35. Alex Inkeles, *Public Opinion in Soviet Russia* (Cambridge: Harvard University Press, 1950).

36. Wilbur Schramm, ed., *The Process and Effects of Mass Communication* (Urbana: University of Illinois Press, 1955).

37. S. I. Hayakawa, "Success and Failure in Communications," *Journal of the American Association of Training Directors,* Vol. 12, No. 7.

38. W. H. Whyte, *Is Anybody Listening?* (New York: Simon and Schuster, Inc., 1952).

39. Elihu Katz and Paul F. Lazarsfeld, *Personal Influence* (Glencoe, Ill.: The Free Press, 1955).

40. Elmer Roper, in Introduction to *Personal Influence, op. cit.*

41. B. Berelson, P. F. Lazarsfeld, W. F. McPhee, *Voting* (Chicago: University of Chicago Press, 1954).

42. Elihu Katz and Paul Lazarsfeld, *Personal Influence* (Glencoe, Ill.: The Free Press, 1955).

43. Saul Alinsky, *Reveille for Radicals* (Chicago: University of Chicago Press, 1946).

44. Wilder Penfield, "We're not giving our children a chance to learn a second language," *PR in Canada* (Toronto: Canadian Public Relations Society), Vol. 2, No. 1.

45. W. S. Gray, *op. cit.*

Suggested Reading

ADULT EDUCATION ASSOCIATION, "Workshop—Human Relations Training," *Adult Leadership* (Chicago: AEA), Vol. 4, No. 10.

——, "Workshop—Social Science in Action," *Adult Leadership* (Chicago: AEA), Vol. 2, No. 11.

ANDERSON, JOHN E., "Teaching and Learning," *Education for Later Maturity* (New York: William Morrow & Company, Inc., 1955).

BENNE, KENNETH D., and MUNTYAN, BOZIDAR, *Human Relations in Curriculum Change* (New York: Dryden Press, 1951).

BOND, BETTY W., *The Group Discussion-Decision Approach: an Appraisal of Its Use in Health Education* (Ph.D. dissertation, University of Minnesota, 1955).

GALLUP, GLADYS, and COWLEY, AMY, "America's Roadside Teachers," *Adult Leadership* (Chicago: AEA), Vol. 4, No. 10.

HARE, PAUL, BORGATTA, E. F., BALES, R. F., *Small Groups: Studies in Social Interaction* (New York: Alfred A. Knopf, Inc., 1955).

HOULE, C. O., and NELSON, C. A., *The University, the Citizen and World Affairs* (Washington, D.C.: American Council on Education, 1956).

HOWLAND, C., JANIS, I., and KELLEY, H. H., *Communication and Persuasion* (New Haven: Yale University Press, 1953).

LAMPARD, D., "Reading Abilities of Adults," *The Alberta Journal of Educational Research* (Edmonton: March 1955).

MEAD, MARGARET, ed., *Cultural Patterns and Technical Change* (Paris: UNESCO, 1953).

ROETHLISBERGER, F. J., *Training for Human Relations* (Cambridge: Harvard School of Business Administration, 1954).

UNESCO, "Cross-Cultural Education and Educational Training," *International Social Science Bulletin*, Vol. 8, No. 4, 1956.

Chapter 9

THE ENVIRONMENT
FOR LEARNING—
FORMS AND DEVICES

It is quite clear from the previous chapters that learning cannot and must not be confused with gimmicks, or devices, or organization. Unfortunately a good deal of discussion about content or curriculum suggests that these matters are separate and distinct from method but one cannot possibly consider method without reflecting about goals for learning. In the same way content and method, what is learned and how it is learned, are inextricably linked.

Of course the quality of learning is markedly influenced by environmental and organizational factors. Effective techniques and devices also have their place. In *Alice in Wonderland* the King said: "The horror of that moment I shall never, *never* forget!" "You will, though," said the Queen, "if you don't make a memorandum of it."

We shall now discuss, *in their relationship*, a number of factors that can facilitate or impede learning:

- environmental factors such as size and kind of facilities
- organizational and administrative factors such as forms of meetings, selection of participants
- devices and techniques.

But this is not a how-to-do-it chapter; it is not a manual on how to plan a forum or a group discussion. Our primary interest in these matters will be to analyze the kind and nature of learning that transpires. Nor have we attempted to be comprehensive; we have chosen forms and devices which seem to be best suited as examples. Many of the principles which have been discussed in previous chapters will be illustrated here, and the reader is asked to keep in mind these principles and consider how they may be planned for. He is also requested to remember throughout Emerson's observation: "Ends pre-exist in the means."

It should not be assumed, of course, that learning must always take place in a group of some kind. But it is often the case. Sir Richard Livingstone, who can scarcely be considered to bear the stigma of "groupism," once said:

> Even in education man remains a social animal. Consider how often education has burned most brightly at a common hearth, where men gathered together in company to warm their hands at its flame; in antiquity, Socrates in the marketplace and the gymnasiums, the great classical schools of the Academy, the Lyceum, the Stoa, the Museum of Alexandria; in the middle ages, the universities, culminating in the residential university, recognized, at least in the Anglo-Saxon world, as their ideal form. These examples may teach us something. No doubt the lamp of wisdom can burn in solitary shrines and even in dismal lecture halls, but for the many it will not burn, brightly, if at all, unless fanned by that social corporate life which both educates and makes education attractive.[1]

This chapter will deal mainly with group situations of various kinds.

Environment and Facilities

The facilities in which learning is carried on can vary tremendously in size, in character, and in relative comfort offered. Those who associate quality of learning with puritan virtues used always to recommend Spartan simplicity and even some physical hardship. But it is quite clear that learning is not aided by "mortifying the flesh." Luxury is not required, but comfort, excellent illumination without glare, absence from disturbing sounds or movements, provide a setting in which the chances for effective learning are increased. The atmosphere, whether fresh or stifling, may determine whether the person is an attentive participant, a slumberer, or a man whose energies are bent just to keep himself awake. "Emotional" atmosphere, whether full of threat or confidence, of indolence or of apathy, has an equal or greater effect upon the outcome.

The very size and shape of the facilities may have some impact. One of Winston Churchill's most eloquent speeches took place at the end of the war when the damaged House of Commons was to be redesigned. Churchill maintained that the physical form of the house would substantially modify decisions taken there for generations to come. Parkinson, in his book *Parkinson's Law* has some amusement with the same idea, but the laughter does not obscure the author's serious intentions!

. . . The House of Commons is so arranged that the individual Member is practically compelled to take one side or the other before he knows what the arguments are, or even (in some cases) before he knows the subject of the dispute. His training from birth has been to play for his side, and this saves him from any undue mental effort. Sliding into a seat toward the end of a speech, he knows exactly how to take up the argument from the point it has reached. If the speaker is on his own side of the House, he will say "Hear, hear!" If he is on the opposite side, he can safely say "Shame!" or merely "Oh!" At some later stage he may have time to ask his neighbour what the debate is supposed to be about. Strictly speaking, however, there is no need for him to do this. He knows enough in any case not to kick into his own goal. The men who sit opposite are entirely wrong and all their arguments are so much drivel. The men on his own side are statesmanlike, by contrast, and their speeches a singular blend of wisdom, eloquence, and moderation. Nor does it make the slightest difference whether he learned his politics at Harrow or in following the fortunes of Aston Villa. In either school he will have learned when to cheer and when to groan. But the British system depends entirely on its seating plan. If the benches did not face each other, no one could tell truth from falsehood, wisdom from folly, unless indeed by listening to it all. But to listen to it all would be ridiculous, for half the speeches must of necessity be nonsense.

In France the initial mistake was made of seating the representatives in a semicircle, all facing the chair. The resulting confusion could hardly be imagined if it were not notorious. No real opposing teams could be formed and no one could tell (without listening) which argument was the more cogent. There was the further handicap of all the proceedings being in French —an example the United States wisely refused to follow. But the French system is bad enough even when the linguistic difficulty does not arise. Instead of having two sides, one in the right and the other in the wrong—so that the issue is clear from the outset—the French form a multitude of teams facing in all directions. With the field in such confusion, the game cannot even begin. Basically their representatives are of the Right or of the Left, according to where they sit. This is a perfectly sound scheme. The French have not gone to the extreme of seating people in alphabetical order. But the semi-circular chamber allows of subtle distinctions between the various degrees of rightness and leftness. There is none of the clear-cut British distinction between rightness and wrongness. One deputy is described, politically, as to the left of Monsieur Untel but well to the right of Monsieur Quelquechose. What is anyone to make of that? What should we make of it even in English? What do they make of it themselves? The answer is, "Nothing."

All this is generally known. What is less generally recognized is that the paramount importance of the seating plan applies to other assemblies and meetings, international, national, and local. It applies, moreover, to meetings round a table such as occur at a Round Table Conference. A moment's thought will convince us that a Square Table Conference would be something totally different and a Long Table Conference would be different again.[2]

This is a subject for more than humor. Much is already known about the advantages of face-to-face communication that is possible in a circle or U shape arrangement of chairs. Much is also known about the inhibiting effect of the traditional screwed-down rows of seats or desks in a classroom or auditorium. Now that, at last, attempts are being made to design and plan *facilities specially for the learning of adults*[3] instead of having adults take over something planned for someone else, there may be considerable improvements in the environment provided for adult learning.

Forms and Devices

It has been to the advantage of adult education that such a variety of forms and devices for learning have been utilized.

The schools and universities have much more severely stand-ardized the ways in which learning is carried on. The most obvious example of this is in the building of classrooms. A visitor to the schools of North America might soon form the opinion that the Almighty has decreed, or a law has been passed, ordering that education must be carried out in a rectangular room and that learning only happens where there are forty students and one teacher. Of course we know that learning can happen in a variety of settings. We know, equally, that with well-planned use of audio-visual materials certain kinds of facts and information can be taught to 1,000 or 2,000 as readily as to 40, but that for the quick mastery of the "sound" of a new language, a class of five or six may be the maximum for best results. In planning for adult education the pressures of an administrative or historical kind to continue practices which are less than of maximum benefit are for-tunately not too strong.

However, views and prejudices about learning are held here as tenaciously as in any other field. It is interesting to note that the preferences or prejudices in favor of one prac-tice or another rarely have much to do with the relative effec-tiveness for learning by each form. There are teachers of adults who feel that it isn't learning unless it is by a lecture; there are others who feel that no souls are saved except in group discussion. Recently a group of adult students lam-pooned the idea that all learning must take place in a discus-sion group by producing a play in which new and inexperi-enced sailors are taking out a sailboat for the first time. Their procedure is to take turns reading aloud the manual of sailing instructions before agreeing to change course or "go-about." As a result of following a course of action that is excellent in another context, they were soon high and dry on a reef!

One can also note that there are "fads" and "styles" in adult education practice and even in the descriptive terms em-ployed. In many organizations the "panel" is used on almost every conceivable occasion. The term "workshop" was widely used for a number of years and applied to almost any activity, "where two or more people were gathered together." Some of the more common aspects of such workshops were described in an article entitled "The Folklore of Workshops."[4] The authors of the article have a number of amusing things to say; they also point out how harmful, how foolish, are some of the practices followed. Terms have been applied very loosely. It was amusing to note not so long ago, that when the word went round that a certain foundation was dissatisfied with the results of "seminars" for which it had provided grants, all the new applications were for "institutes" and "conferences." We are all familiar with the fact that certain terms cannot be used in certain places. In a branch of the armed forces in Canada one could include any topic or interest having to do with learning, from shooting a rifle to Shakespeare, under the head "training" but one must *never* employ the word "education."

But if learning of quality is to happen, the choice of form and technique is a matter of some consequence. Where the aim is excellence there is a need of careful selection. And the selection ought to be made with a full knowledge of possible opportunities and consequences. It ought not to be arbitrary, like that of one personnel manager years ago who used to hire dark-haired men on Monday and Tuesday, light-haired men on other days, and red-headed men on the 29th of February.

Nathaniel Cantor was once illustrating the error of mis-using what can be an effective educational method:

> The celebrated Mr. Dooley was visiting a progressive school in the days when the bonds of formalism were first beginning to be loosened from the classroom. Accompanied by a member of the school staff, he came upon a group of boys talking excitedly together. Voices rose, accusations resounded; there was a quick left to the jaw and one boy was down.
>
> "And what," asked Mr. Dooley, "are these boys learning?"
>
> His guide, abashed, was silent for a moment and then replied, "They are learning, I think, the futility of human endeavor."
>
> More accurately, they were learning the futility of trying to hold a discussion group when they did not know the conditions necessary for making a discussion group a profitable learning experience.[5]

We need some assessment of the possibilities of each form for learning and to be better informed about the ways in which learning does happen with respect to each form.

One of the most useful kinds of investigation in recent years, carried on at the Center for the Study of Liberal Education for Adults, and in several other places, has been a comparative study of "teaching styles."

In his paper, "Guide to Styles, Groups, Methods" Gyllenhaal provides both a summary and also a guide to the selection of forms and devices. The steps he lists are familiar:

What do we want to accomplish?
What sort of affair is called for?
What subgroupings should we have?
What presentation methods should we use?
How to get the audience more involved?

The material is organized according to type of meeting, kinds of groupings, and presentation methods.

EXAMPLES FROM "TYPE OF MEETING"

Purpose	Type	Features
To plan, get facts, solve organization and member problems.	Work conference.	• General sessions and face-to-face groups (15 or less).
		• Usually high participation.
		• Provides more flexible means for doing organization's work.
To share experience among "experts."	Seminar.	• Usually one face-to-face group.
		• Discussion leader also provides expert information.

EXAMPLES FROM "KINDS OF GROUPING"

Purpose	Type	Features
To take official action.	Plenary session.	• Includes voting members and takes care of only official business.

To work on specific problem.	Work groups.	• Mixed membership from total group.
		• May meet once or several times.
		• Report usually expected.

Purpose	*Type*	*Features*
To present information for several points of view.	Symposium.	• Two or more speakers.
		• Speakers help audience get understanding of specific subject.
		• Chairman summarizes and directs questions.
		• Audience usually does not participate verbally.
To help audience analyze individual or group action in "natural" setting.	Situation presentation.	• Members of group present role play, vignette or case study.
		• Commentator may call attention to specific points as situation progresses.
		• Audience gains a common experience for discussion afterwards.[6]

Some such schematic form in which the leading objectives are clearly stated and where organization and methods are specified with respect to objectives can be very useful.

We may also need to remember, however, that an activity may be chosen for reasons other than the possibilities of learning in it.

It has often been argued, for example, that the discussion group is a suitable form of adult education because it is inexpensive to provide. Such a claim needs to be examined critically; good education, like good anything else, rarely comes at a bargain counter. Similarly it has been argued that the discussion group, in addition to any learning that results, has a highly valued by-product, because the participants experience and practice some of the skills of democratic living. The discussion group and other forms have also been favored for other reasons, such as therapy. While there may be several purposes or achievements for a single activity, it is important to be clear about the primary goal. Not so long ago in one organization a dispute arose in connection with a film discussion project. Two different techniques were advocated. Staff members took sides, and the strife was such that it resulted in temporary paralysis in the organization. Then cooler heads prevailed, whereupon it was discovered that the two approaches were based on two different assumptions about what the project was to accomplish, one concerned primarily with decisions about social action and the other with therapy. Different goals in a single project may be maintained providing there is some precision and clarity about both goals and methods.

Another source of confusion, pointed out by Coolie Verner is in the use of terms, particularly between *methods* and *techniques*. Discussion is used to designate the method as in "discussion method" and to indicate the technique as in "group discussion." In addition, there are many instances in which the properties of a method or technique are ascribed to materials or devices that are actually adjuncts of a method or technique. Audio-visual aids, bulletins, and such are frequently referred to as methods when in reality they are devices. Verner himself defines both methods and techniques, and urges that the terms be used with more care and discrimination:

> Method, then, may be described as the relationship which exists between the learner, the knowledge, and the institution which has knowledge to diffuse in order to bring about changes in attitudes and behavior. . . . Once the method has been determined, a second stage in the diffusion process comes into play. . . . The agent may employ a wide variety of established

procedures or invent new ones that, in one circumstance or another, prove useful in furthering learning. These processes are the *techniques* of adult education.

Not all techniques can be used appropriately with all methods but some are useful with many methods. Thus a university conducting a program of correspondence study (the method) would not use role playing (a technique). However, an agency using discussion (a method) would use group discussion (the technique) or role playing and "buzz groups." Within the framework of the assembly or convention method, for example, the adult educator might utilize lecture, panel, forum or group discussion techniques.[7]

Some observers, who are concerned about the large number of adults that take no part in any educational activity, have noted that some forms of organization not only do not attract, but actually seem to intimidate adults who have had little academic experience. The university, even the library, may seem for some to belong to another social class. A "Great Books" program may appear remote and unprofitable. One important kind of research for the future concerns the forms and devices which people with little formal schooling will find attractive and in which they may undertake study that is satisfying to them. Experience with rural groups, workers, community development projects may all be useful toward this end.

Selection of Participants

The choice of the participants in any learning activity may have a major influence on the outcome. We noted earlier that there are three significant relationships in a learning situation: learner-teacher, learner-with-fellow-learners, and learner-subject-matter. Though all these are important, it is quite apparent that, in some cases at least, the second of these relationships affects all the others.

SIZE OF GROUP

We have already referred to the most elementary part of this, namely the size of the group. If the main purpose of activity is to have free and full interaction between the par-

ticipants, such as is the goal of group discussion, then the
limit in group size is the number of people one can easily
relate to. In practice this is about five to ten, depending upon
circumstances. But if the purpose is to produce an effect of
solidarity behind a single idea, or sentiment, the great mass
rallies of totalitarian nations, such as Hitler's demonstrations
at Nuremberg, may be the chosen form.

Group size is related not only to the extent and quality of
group relatedness but also to the means of communicating
chosen by the teacher or the leader. We shall note later that
ways have been devised in large groups for gaining some of
the same quality of attention and participation that characterizes small groups.

WHO CHOOSES WHOM?

But, size apart, who chooses the actual participants? What
relationship does this act of choice bear in regard to the way
that the participants relate and interact?

In recent years there has been a growing interest in *sociometry*, in the improvement of response or performance in
certain situations because the participants have chosen themselves and each other. Sociometry is a scientific variation of
the old parlor game "Whom would you like to have for a
companion if you were marooned on a desert island?" It has
been found in some situations, for example, when boys and
girls choose their own tent or cabin mates at camp, there is
more satisfactory participation by the campers in many phases
of camp life than if the choice is by chance, or made by the
director or even the counselor. The same principle was applied, during the war, to many dangerous combat missions,
so that men whose lives were dependent upon each other's
effort and responsibility were given the opportunity to select
their own mates. In certain work situations the self-selected
group has attained records of high productivity, always providing that other factors leading to good productivity are also
present. The same has been found true, experimentally, of
learning, particularly in seminars and workshops where member participation is of maximum importance. If the partici-

pants in a learning activity have a part in the choice of their fellows, at least one of the factors in good learning has been provided for.

But such results should never be applied without discrimination to every conceivable situation. There is a large place for individual effort, and a primary object of all education is the unfolding, the expansion of an individual, not his contraction or smothering in any kind of group or mass. "Each individual," said Whitehead, "is a more complex structure than any social system to which he belongs. . . . If a man is wholly subordinated to the common life, he is dwarfed."

Earlier we quoted such diverse scholars as Murphy and Livingstone, who both pointed out that the life in a group may be an excellent place for the individual personality to flourish. But the group also has within it the possibility of the stunting and the shrinking of human personality, and we need to be clear-eyed about this.

Moreover, as we have noted, learning and all kinds of growth arise in part through the excitement and stimulation of difference and tension, not just from a condition of well-being. For some purposes, for example, a workteam studying the effects of radiation, the participants would all need to be possessed of experience and skill to a high degree. Here a measure of homogeneity in interest, capacity, and experience is essential. For other purposes learning is most likely to happen if there is considerable divergence in background and experience. Here, heterogeneity is desirable. A discussion group in which every member knows every other member so well that he can predict the views and position that every other member will take on any new question may provide little zest, and a large part of the possibility for learning is also lost.

Some Forms of Organization for Education

LECTURE-TYPE ACTIVITIES

Despite the present popularity of the discussion group more use is still made of the talk, lecture, speech, address, and similar forms than of anything else. By similar forms we refer to the symposium, the forum, the panel and, to some extent, the debate. We also would include most classes and most large meetings although both of these are mixed forms.

These forms can be listed in order of increasing participation. (We should say *apparent* participation for, as we shall see later, it is not easy to be completely sure about the amount or quality of participation.)

- *The lecture*—one voice speaking to an audience.
- *The symposium*—two or more speakers giving prepared statements which are on the same or on related subjects. (Many so-called "panels" are really symposia.)
- *The forum*—one or more speakers, sometimes with some interaction between forum participants and almost certainly some interaction with members of the audience, usually by questions, but sometimes with observations and comment from the floor.
- *The panel*—in its original usage the term panel was applied to a small intimate, face-to-face group that conducted a "conversation" about a subject with the audience eavesdropping or listening in.

The advantages of these forms, particularly the first three, are that people with special knowledge or competence are able to organize facts and ideas and present them in an orderly way with a minimum of time and effort.

If the primary purpose is simply the learning of facts, it matters not at all that only one or at the most a few persons are being heard, providing that the facts are accurate. But, if opinions or values are being considered, the number of speakers, the point of view that they hold, and whether or not there is provision for rejoinder is important. If the topic is the number of pupils in elementary schools in the United States and their average gain in height and weight each year, no one will care particularly who presents the data. But if the subject is the integration of elementary schools in the Southern states the hearers will take a different attitude both to the number and the credentials of the speakers. However, our main interest here is *how much is learned how well*.

We have noted in several places that a lecturer directly, or by radio, or on film, can present material which can be learned, particularly if the substance is information or facts. We have also seen that it is rare for attitudes to be substantially altered in this way and that most skills or processes can better be learned by demonstration and practice than by having someone talk about them. It is possible to teach a woman how to bake a cherry pie, or a man to build a canoe, simply by talk, but there are easier and more effective ways to accomplish this objective. The talk or lecture is primarily for the presentation of information or ideas where their order and relationship are important.

But if learning from the lecture is to be effective, several factors are of primary importance, such as motivation of the learner, relevance to the learner, attainment of satisfaction by the learner and the extent to which the activity is a two-way process.

We have already asserted many times that without motivation the likelihood for learning is minimal. This is especially true where we depend upon a talk as the main stimulus for learning. Most adults have been exposed countless times to talk; sometimes they have been uplifted; but too often they have been bored. They have become adept at *tuning out* any speaker. Accordingly, it is imperative if any learning is to happen that their attention be engaged. There are many ways to do this. One of the most common is the introduction of the speaker. *Most introducers* seem to be oblivious of their particular role in the learning process. Frequently they seem to feel their task is to weave pleasant platitudes around some real or assumed virtues of the speaker, or proceed to demonstrate that at least, they have read his *curriculum vitae*. However, their real purpose is easily understood, and can be readily stated:

- to win attention for the speaker
- to show briefly how what he brings is related to, and consonant with, the goals of the members of the audience.

This raises immediately the subject of relevance. Children may attend to and learn many things that they are asked to do; adults need to believe that the new is relevant. This is true about learning where no deep feelings are present but even more so when emotion is strong. Some people believe that little or no learning happens as a result of speeches at a service club, because the subjects are so varied, and attention is desultory. But in a recent study in selected communities about the growth in understanding of international affairs, the surveyors found that considerable learning had taken place as a result of service club meetings. The writers had assumed that local business men would not consider that foreign affairs would mean much to them. Yet some business men are beginning to think about the implication of what Clarence Randall, a well-known industrialist recently stated: "The business man must now bring to the consideration of world problems the same hard sense of social responsibility which he is beginning to learn and to practice in his own community."[8] In any event club members had been persuaded that the study of world affairs was really a responsibility of their club and of themselves. When this was done, the result in learning and changed behavior was substantial.

But what about satisfaction? How can this be the result of a speech? Perhaps through achieving an increased ability to grasp, and talk about, the subject, perhaps through the efforts to see a new relationship, perhaps even by understanding that the subject is more difficult, and therefore more challenging, than had been considered. However, there is little satisfaction if the speech increases confusion, or brings a sense of defeat, or if the task seems too easy to be worth any effort.

Is the talk or lecture an example of one-way or two-way communication? Are the conditions of a *learning dialogue* established, where the mind of the learner is engaged with the words and ideas of the lecturer? This sometimes happens without any outward sign although such participation may be exhibited by gestures and facial expressions. It is much more likely to be present if opportunities are provided for the learners to respond, to ask questions for clarification, to react to the speaker's point of view, to express disagreement. Only in this way is there much surety that learning is actually happening. Moreover, only in this way can there be release of feeling which might inhibit learning, feelings which may have resulted from a misunderstanding of what the speaker meant. Without such an opportunity the lecturer cannot know he is making effective contact.

Much has been made of the necessity for winning attention. This is seen to be a more important consideration than ever before because there are so many competing claims to attention. The approaches used are many: humor, flattery, cajolery, even threat and shock. A minister one hot Sabbath morning sensed that his congregation was dozing. Raising his voice, he shouted, "Well, I'll be God damned!" There was a moment's stunned silence, but all eyes were now upon him. "That's what I heard a man say yesterday," said the minister, and proceeded to give a talk about the evils of profanity. But shock is seldom a useful tactic, and must be used with care if the result is to be as intended.

A number of devices have been developed for increasing the level of attention, particularly in large meetings. One is the device now known as 66. After a speech the audience is quickly arranged in groups of six, by having three persons sitting in each alternate row turn around and face the three people behind, thus forming a face-to-face unit of six. The six people then introduce themselves to each other. Already a subtle change has occurred. Individual members of the audience who had no previous relationship (and therefore no obligations other than to themselves) are now "members" of a loose-knit group. They are now given a task, usually that of selecting a question to be put to the speaker. (Notice that the task given must be one that can be managed in a short time and by a group that has very little cohesion. A complicated task, such as summarizing what the speaker has said, would almost certainly lead to failure and to dissatisfaction.) The six people in choosing a question tend to act in a responsible way, tend to weed out questions that seem irrelevant or of limited significance, or are poorly phrased, or those which are asked simply to exhibit one individual's "hobby" or prejudice. Through this sifting process there has been an improvement in the quality of many of the questions. Moreover, each group of six, armed with their question, are better prepared to take part in the question period. Most significant of all, the individuals are attending in a very different manner than might have been anticipated. They are interested to find out if other groups are asking the same question, if the questions of other groups are as pointed, as significant, as subtle as theirs. They tend to listen to each other and to the speaker's replies in a fresh way.

This procedure is useful after the speech and just preceding the question period. It can also be used effectively, just as the meeting starts, in order to inform the speaker about the kinds of issues with which his audience want him to come to grips. "Buzz groups" (small informal groups meeting for a limited time and with a carefully defined task) can be employed in the same fashion.

Another device for enriching the quality of attention is to assign a task of attention to members of the audience. The traditional auditorium has three sections of seats, left, center and right. The chairman can invite the audience to form three "listening teams." Those in the left section may be asked to pay particular attention to the points or arguments in the speech where further amplification, or clarification, or illustration is needed. Those in the center section may be asked to attend to the key arguments or observations of the speaker, the points which need emphasis. People on the right may be asked to note the points where they disagree with the speaker. When a listener has assumed some obligation in connection with a talk, his attention has been won.

GROUP DISCUSSION

We have selected "small group discussion" for special attention because the form is used for so many purposes and in so many ways. We shall consider only the application of certain learning principles and not attempt detailed description or analysis.

A great deal has been written about group discussion. Some of it is singularly misleading, because little or no attempt has been made to distinguish between the purposes intended which in turn determine the special technique or practice to be followed.

Earlier we stated an obvious but sometimes neglected point, that "small group discussion" is not a form that is satisfactory for every kind of learning. However, the range of use is very wide. Consider some examples:

- Business men studying industrial administration through the discussion of a typical case
- Mothers meeting together because of their concern about safe play areas for their children
- Union members trying to work out a plan of seniority that is as fair as possible for all concerned
- Neighbors gathered to listen to the radio and talk about community issues
- Farmers dealing with problems affecting all of them such as marketing and soil conservation
- People with marital difficulties seeking help in a "marriage clinic."

What goes on in these discussion groups can hardly be classified under the same category, yet many discussion manuals talk about the activity, and many discussion groups are organized, as if one set of rules or practices must always be followed. The first danger to be avoided, therefore, is from a "bed of Procrustes" approach. It is not a law of God or man that all discussion groups must be of an identical size and follow the same pattern. A related danger, to which reference has also been made, is that people who have found a particular practice suitable for achieving their particular goal will try to have that practice adopted by everyone else.

One could plot most of the uses of the discussion group along a continuum. At one end would be the activities which are largely intellectual in purpose and at the other end activities which are largely for the purpose of releasing and understanding feelings. At the one end the group would attempt rational exploration of facts, opinions, and experiences, hoping for the achievement of knowledge, the understanding of a particular subject matter, perhaps the making of decisions. At the other end there would be a free expression of feelings leading toward self-understanding, although subject matter might also be involved. In one case the members of a discussion group might agree to be rigorous in limiting what was said to the particular issue chosen for discussion, applying self-discipline, or asking the chairman to rule out anything that seemed irrelevant. In the other case it might be essential to have every member feel that any ideas, opinions, or feeling that he may bring to the group will be welcomed and respected.

Nevertheless, while considerable flexibility in practice is required, depending upon the objective of the discussion, there are also many common elements.

The "subject matter" of a discussion group is brought in through the members' sharing of their experiences, ideas, and feelings, or provided for in some planned way. A discussion group cannot be carried on effectively without any subject matter; it is not "pooled ignorance." If facts are essential, and they are lacking, they must be provided in some way. If the task is mainly an intellectual one, and if most of the facts or theories for vigorous discussion are not within the experience of the group, some other form of learning will usually be more successful.

The usual focus of any discussion group is on an issue, something about which people have different opinions or feelings or values. An *issue* is not a *fact*. One can argue about a fact but one cannot really discuss it. A fact is *so,* or it *isn't*; and this can be verified. For example, you may argue heatedly about whether there are more Republicans than Democrats in the state of New York, but this is waste talk; you would be better employed finding out how many voted for these two parties in the last several elections. Such a matter is barren ground for group discussion. However, if one asks, "Should everyone in New York state be obliged to vote by law?" (as the Australians do) one has an issue which can be discussed with considerable profit and around which one may learn a great deal about theory and practice in a democratic country. About such an issue people do have different feelings and opinions and they realize it is a matter of some importance. At this point the facts about how many people actually vote, take on some significance. The participants will also need to know or learn many other facts if the discussion is to move very far and be productive.

Some topics are far more productive of discussion and learning than are others. A rough test for choosing a topic is this:

- Can you state it as a question?
- Do people differ in their attitudes in response to the question?
- Are people likely to feel that the questions are worth some effort to answer?

Naturally enough, a question that leads to a "yes" or "no" answer does not get us very far.

Questions that can be used by most adult groups are those that deal with subjects that the members know something about from their own experience.

"Should a married woman go out to work?"
"How can we prevent highway accidents?"
"How can we make rural life more attractive to young people?"
"What are the conditions of a happy marriage?"

There are many other questions, often of equal interest, that demand considerable information before they can be discussed. Here it will be necessary to provide literature, show a film, arrange for a broadcast, or have someone present who has the necessary information. Examples:

"Do our prisons need to be reformed?"
"Are we facing inevitable catastrophe through overpopulation?"
"How well are technical assistance projects working out?"
"Are we making progress in the treatment of minority groups?"

Some questions are what might be called neutral in their tone, others are highly charged with emotion. Among certain groups a discussion of integration in the schools can be conducted rationally and objectively; in others it might be difficult to maintain any kind of control. Discussion of neutral or controversial questions may be equally productive, but if there is to be any learning in a situation of excessive emotion, special attention would have to be given to ways of lessening the tension. As we have seen before, people are not likely to change their attitudes under conditions of threat or fear, real or imagined.

If the objective of the discussion group is learning a particular subject matter, if a decision is to be taken or a problem is to be solved, it may be necessary to follow a plan or pattern which may go somewhat like the following:

Stage 1. Ensuring that the problem is recognized.

Stage 2. Having the problem defined in terms that have the same or a similar meaning for each member of the group.

Stage 3. Discovering the nature and causes of the problem and agreeing on a standard by which possible solutions can be judged.

Stage 4. Surveying possible solutions.

Stage 5. Choosing what seems to be the "best" solution.

Stage 6. Checking the solution against the problems as originally defined.

Many of the principles involved in good learning are present in such a plan, assuming that efforts have also been applied in motivating the members and securing attention. However, a good many discussions are carried on with considerably less form than this. And as noted earlier, the process followed when the object is more "therapeutic" than intellectual, will follow a different model.

Many and ingenious means have been devised for getting attention and increasing the strength of motivation. The following examples show the range of possibilities:

a. *Subject* What is meant by sportsmanship?
Participants—Nightschool students.
Before discussion, a "true or false" questionnaire of ten questions (example: Leo Durocher, former manager of the New York Giants, once said, "Nice guys always come last,") was filled out by all participants. No attempt was made to check on the answers, but as soon as everyone was finished the chairman asked which questions they would like to talk about.

b. *Subject* Collective bargaining.
Participants—Seminar for shop stewards of a union.
Four of the members enacted a five-minute play where members of the union approached the general manager with three proposals they wanted in a new contract.

c. *Subject* What is justice?
Participants—Neighbors meeting in a living room for an organized "Great Books" Group.
Members of the group in joining, *had agreed* to prepare themselves in advance by reading selected prescribed texts.

d. *Subject* What is democracy?
Participants—Farm men and women in a residential short-term course.
A film on the subject was available. Participants were asked before seeing the film to meet in small groups for about forty minutes and talk about what they would put in a film if they were to make one on the subject of democracy. They reconvened, each group reported on what it would plan. The film was now screened, and the group began to discuss the factors introduced, in the light of their background as well as their own preliminary exploration of the subject.

Satisfaction and reward in discussion always depend upon the purpose. A man and a wife may come to a group in a marriage clinic, each of them distressed at the lack of harmony in their home and additionally anxious because of feelings of guilt. Without stating it, each may feel that there is something different, perhaps something a little strange, about himself. At first in the discussion very little may happen except some faltering exchange of experience. But eventually there may appear the dawning realization on the part of each individual that other people have difficulties too, and that one need not accept defeat or the feeling that one is different or queer. At this stage it may be that some changes or improvements are possible.

Satisfaction, and what is learned from such a discussion, of course, is somewhat different from that obtained by a group of business executives who have talked together about an industrial case, how they might have handled it, and how they might face similar problems. In the latter, the satisfaction gained might be through achieving a fuller understanding of some problems, seeing new relationships, facing new ideas or approaches to a problem, seeing fellow participants in a new light, or even coming to some decisions about a problem.

Many observers have reported that group discussion is successful to the degree that the leadership is effective. Some organizations insist on the employment of specially trained leaders: others do not. Anderson[9] studied the use of discussion in eight agencies in Wisconsin. He reports that although five of the agencies used discussion as their main technique, leaders were sometimes selected for their local prestige rather than for competence in discussion leadership. Some leaders tended to use their position as a means of disseminating information or opinions rather than providing a free exploration of issues. Often the less well-trained leader did not allow sufficient time for issues that arose to be explored or, where desired, for agreement to be reached.

In another study, Kaplan[10] was interested in the response of group members to the behavior of the leader. Many of those with less than average education seemed to want strong directive leadership in their group. But the better-educated resented a leader who dominated the group.

There is usually room for controversy in discussion. But mere displays of pugnacity result in very little learning. The primary purpose of the discussion group is the sharing of experience and the search for truth, not defeating opponents, rooting out heretics, or converting the heathen. These may be worthy objectives on other occasions, but there is no place for them in discussion groups.

SKILL AND PROCESS LEARNING

Are there any practices to be followed in the learning of such different skills or processes as first aid, figure skating, a game like tennis, using a micrometer, or how to drive a car?

It is clear that there are.

First of all, it is well established that any skill can be learned with greater facility if the learner is given some understanding of the reasons that it is being learned. He needs to know the place or importance of that skill in his life, and also what he may expect to happen as he proceeds to learn. If there is to be difficulty or danger this information may actually lessen his anxiety. Most important, he has some framework upon which to build as he makes his first few efforts. This is akin to the principle of relevancy. The explanation, which need only deal with the essentials, can precede practice, or may come soon after the beginning of practice.

Second, in connection with most skills, there is also a body of information to be mastered and this of course must be clearly presented, preferably in a sequence related to his mastery of the skill. In *first aid* one ought to be learning the facts about how bones "set" at the same time as one is practicing how to care for fractures, not when one is practicing artificial respiration.

Third, it has been well-established that learning a skill happens with greatest effect if the practice of that skill is carried out under *actual* conditions and in the *actual* setting. The place to practice the use of the micrometer is in a machine shop; the place to practice the forehand drive is on a tennis court.

For speedy mastery of the skill or process an overview of that skill or process should be provided. An overview of a sport such as tennis should provide an introduction to the entire game, its strategy, its ebb and flow, and the relationship of the new skills to those which the learner may have acquired previously. Once the learner has some grasp of the *whole* problem, the strength of his motivation has been re-enforced. It is now time to demonstrate, analyze, and practice particular aspects of strokes of the game. Errors in performance should be corrected, followed by further demonstration and practice. Only when there has been some mastery of one particular skill should one go on to the next. The procedure is always similar; identify the skill, demonstrate the technique, follow by practice by the learner.

As we have seen earlier, good practice in the case of very complicated physical skills, like a "full twisting" dive, may require that the body is put through the required action, under conditions of comparative safety, until the pattern of response has been traced out and "learned" by the nerves and muscles.

Demonstration. Many skills and processes are taught by demonstration. This has long been the favored practice followed by agricultural extension workers, home economists, trainers in industry, and in the armed services.

The demonstration may be perceived through several senses and, if well planned, gives each individual learner a chance to practice each of the successive steps.

As one would anticipate, learning happens most readily when both the purpose and the practice are clearly understood. Again, this is provided in advance, as well as at each step in the demonstration, relating the separate factors to the whole. The demonstrator needs to organize his material in a step-by-step form, and needs himself to be adept at the skills so that he can demonstrate them clearly, with an air of confidence, in an orderly sequence. A gingerly, apprehensive approach to the demonstration creates added difficulty for the learner.

It is very important in the demonstration to plan time for questions, so that all points of difficulty are cleared up, along with ample time for practice by the learner.

Simulating the Real

Some psychologists studying learning have done so in the classroom or under contrived conditions in the laboratory. Others have drawn inferences from learning behavior wherever they have been able to observe it. But all agree that learning is most effective if carried on under conditions similar to where the knowledge, skill, or attitude will be practiced. By *effective* we simply mean a tendency that what is learned will be utilized and applied.

Our literature is filled with such aphorisms as that life itself, or experience, is the best teacher. This is true, but only up to a point. Learning from life, or from nature, requires at least two conditions. The learner needs some conceptual frame by which to understand and relate what one learns. Lacking this, the evidence of the senses may lead one to error. Without a theory of roundness men perceived the earth incorrectly for thousands of years. Or life can be too massive, too complex, or too tiny, for us to comprehend unless there is some selecting, simplifying, unifying principle. You cannot "take in" a city; it is much too complicated and baffling. You must see a map, know about its economic organization, its power structure, the kind of people in it, where they live, and what they do, before you can begin to understand or make any sense out of a city. Real experience is the best teacher only if it has been given some organization.

In earlier societies many of the most important principles and practices of living were embodied in dances, rituals, drama, and taught in this form. Many societies today also exhibit this tendency, but it is most readily observed in a relatively uncomplicated society. Thus in Jamaica, farm and village people still play singing games in which many of the skills and attitudes of living are displayed and practiced and young people growing up learn actual skills along with a body of beliefs and attitudes common to those communities. In the "new education" going on at present in China, plays and dramatic sketches are the chief means of teaching.

Our own learning methods are beginning to follow similar practices. Increasingly, we are devising means of learning in which the conditions of real life are simulated. Examples of this are various kinds of role playing, the mock battles of the armed services, and use of audio-visual materials and "mock-ups" or actual machines in training. An example at a more abstract level is the "case study."

In military training the reality practice may be as elementary as learning about the mechanism of a bomb through handling a specially simulated bomb, ranging to the most elaborate maneuvers in which whole armies engage in planned tactical combats, and for certain purposes, using live ammunition.

ROLE PLAYING

The use of various forms of drama in learning is as old as man, but the body of practices which go under the name "role playing" has been developed in recent years, dating from the publication of the books and the demonstration by J. L. Moreno. Moreno's book *Who Shall Survive?* was published first in 1933.[11]

Moreno used the psychodrama for both study and therapy in regard to certain kinds of personality disorder. Before long, other applications began to be made, particularly in training.

In role playing, members of the group act out a problem situation, usually without a script. The scene is customarily followed by discussion and may be replayed with variations of personnel or circumstances. The purpose is to provide an experience close to reality for personal understanding and insight. It is assumed that to the extent that the student is able to identify and involve himself with what is being en-acted, he may be able to appraise his own actions or under-stand the relationship in which he is involved.

In discussing the merits of role playing for learning, Alan Klein writes:

It introduces the actors as well as the observers to the situation with dramatic impact. It draws the group from a purely intel-lectual exercise into an emotional experience. The entire meeting is pulled into the stream of events which the members can feel as well as hear about. . . . When the meeting is focused on a problem or incident to this extent, discussion follows easily and can have depth. We do not need then to be concerned with how to cope with apathetic members and uninteresting meetings.

Such an exercise is a practice in human relations. One might liken this to scrimmage practice of the football team in its training session. The team play is perfected, mistakes are observed and corrected and the players learn how to cope with the problems of the game. Role playing is useful to learn how to work with other people, how to handle ourselves, and to observe and correct our human relations mistakes as we practice coping with the problems of group life.[12]

Klein then goes on to say that the main uses of role playing are (1) training in leadership and human relations skills, (2) training in sensitivity to people and situations, (3) the stimulation of discussion, (4) training in more effective problem solving by the group. Role playing is frequently used to practice such skills as negotiating a contract, or meeting in a committee to deal with a social problem like juvenile delinquency. It provides an excellent opportunity for people to learn what it may feel like to face a situation in which deep hostility may be expected. One can thus study the issue, without some of the threats that one finds in a genuine conflict.

Mistakes can be made in such practice which might be crippling in a real situation. The assumption is that one will be able to deal more calmly, more objectively and more understandingly with real conflicts through practice in simulated conflict situations where real feelings are released. In discussing a problem involving a minority group, members of the majority group can be asked to take the reverse role. Or if there are two or more sides to a dispute, representatives may be asked to take opposing sides and state that point of view to their opponent's satisfaction. Members of an "action-minded" local committee, impatient with delay, may be asked to act out a meeting of city council faced with all the conflicts involved in providing better transportation or better recreation.

THE EXERCISE

Sometimes role playing is organized as a major exercise lasting for some period of time. This has been arranged where a major campaign is being planned for a community, or if a national organization is training its field staff.

One exercise is to plan a major community activity such as bringing about the incorporation of several towns, villages, or townships into a metropolitan area. Data on the situation are supplied in detail, and the major groups and interests that may have a part to play in the interaction are identified. Members in the training seminar are assigned roles. A number of activities such as planning meetings, propaganda and advertising campaigns, protest meetings by those who oppose the move, metropolitan council meetings where conflicting groups are represented, are all held, and the interplay and channeling of interest and pressure are practiced in detail. In this way it is possible to study not only the stresses and changes *within* groups, but *between* groups and interests.

CASE METHOD

There is nothing particularly new about learning through the study of an event, but the careful refinement of using selected examples of experience for teaching has come about rather recently. The "case method" is usually identified with the Harvard Graduate School of Business Administration and it has usually, though not always, been applied to learning which has to do with business. One definition of a case is this:

> a record of a business issue, which actually has been faced by business executives, together with surrounding facts, opinions and prejudices upon which executive decisions had to depend. These real and particularized cases are presented to students for considered analysis, open discussion and final decision as to the type of action which should be taken.[13]

What makes a particular case useful is its reality, its relevance to problems faced by others, the completeness of available data, and the significance of the issues or values at stake.

It has sometimes been alleged that the "case method" is used only to teach the application of certain practices, that its main purpose is propagandistic. There is no such inherent weakness. The main purpose of the study of a case is analysis, identifying fact and opinion, weighing and testing alternatives, considering values. It is an approach of equal merit for studying ethics and philosophy, as in examining the soundness of certain market practices.

The explicit purpose of the case method is application in the actual world. It is not just the memorization, or even the understanding of principles but the deliberate effort to interpret these principles in a real situation. The problem of such learning has been illustrated in a limerick:

> A student of business with tact
> Absorbed many answers he lacked.
> But acquiring a job,
> He said with a sob,
> How does one fit answer to fact?

The case method has application particularly to fields where there are few or no final answers, and where judgment is the essential quality. Many of the characteristics of a small discussion group must be present if there is to be genuine learning. Its reality, and the effort to state principles in terms of good practice in real situations, makes it an approach of particular value to many adult groups.

"T" GROUP

As we have seen, the T (training) group was devised for training in human relations at the National Training Laboratory.

There are three essentials in the process of a T-group:

- Developing a group, rather than a collection of individuals, in which there may be found group cohesion, group standards, and growth in group maturity and productivity
- Developing an atmosphere of support and objectivity in which there are encouragement and support for individual growth and awareness about oneself

- Developing effective use by the group of methods of analysis and experimentation.[14]

The most significant fact, of course, is that learning in the T-group is learning through experience, through participation in a group activity and the examination of one's own behaviors and one's own feelings in this activity. The T-group has a number of objectives:

- Developing a mental attitude of observation about oneself and about others, developing sensitivity in regard to oneself and others
- Learning about control, and how it may be exercised under different conditions, particularly about how the group can learn to manage itself
- Becoming aware that communication can go on at different levels
- Gaining competence in problem solving in the group.

This is learning of different kinds, as well as degrees, and no single set of principles can be used to assess all the results. The work is still experimental, there is not yet full agreement by T-group leaders as to the most desirable conditions or procedures, but the method is one deserving careful study for possible implications for other kinds of training.

LIMITATIONS

In all these forms in which the real is simulated, one can anticipate an interest and keenness that may not be present in other forms of learning. It is no exaggeration to say that many of the most interesting advances in learning theory and practice in recent years have been of this kind.

But there are a number of limitations.

These forms and devices require considerable time to prepare and to use. An excellent plan is required, and considerable time must always be allotted for discussion and for identifying principles and practices. Learning in this fashion may have little consequence, even if the case, or play, or exercise is well presented, unless the essential task of analysis, understanding, and application is carried on systematically.

There is another obvious difficulty. There is considerable evidence to show that learning is increased if there is some variety in methods. But no one meeting should be crowded with too much content or too many shifts in method. Adults in particular need some time to adjust themselves to shifts in attention and pace.

Role playing, in particular, requires very careful planning and execution. If used in clumsy fashion people can feel threatened, or be embarrassed in the process, especially if they are asked to play themselves or if the particular situation allows any participant to "be put on the spot."

Recently a professor was asked to give a lecture to a minority group on the subject of racial prejudice. Without letting anyone know, he arranged for two of his students to enact a situation, just before he began to speak, in which prejudice was exhibited in a very direct form. The result was the galvanization of such hatred in the group that for the first hour of the meeting he was able to do little more than allow the group members to release their hostility. At that point he was able to interpret what had happened and have the group think together about hostility and prejudice in a constructive way. But had he not had enough skill to deal with the situation, the near-violence of which he had not anticipated, the result would have been negative learning of the least desirable kind. Role playing for *therapeutic* purposes is a matter only for people with special training. For other purposes it is a useful device but to be approached with the same thought and care that one would give to any important meeting.

Learning with Audio-Visual Aids

Both of the men, Edison and Lumière, who had most to do with the early development of motion pictures, believed that their inventions would find chief application in education. However, motion pictures were early associated with *entertainment*, and the use of these media for learning, with some notable exceptions, did not make much headway until shortly after 1930. This was the time when 16-millimeter sound motion

pictures began to be distributed. It was also marked by beginnings in production of the "documentary" film, in which all
the arts and skills of motion picture production were first employed in connection with subjects about man and how he
lives.

Radio has been utilized for learning for thirty years and
more. Wire and tape recorders, although the main principle
has been known since about 1905, did not come into common
use until near the end of World War II.

These media are now used for a wide number of purposes:

- providing information, facts or theories
- showing the proper execution of skills and processes
- raising questions and providing a background of experience for group discussion
- motivating study and action
- stimulating appreciation of the arts
- research in learning theory and practice.[15]

Techniques have been devised to gain the kind of attention
for the film that any learning experience requires. An example
of this was given earlier in regard to using a film for group
discussion.

All these media have particular as well as general uses. We
shall illustrate by reference to the sound motion picture.

Motion pictures have a number of special properties that
are of advantage to learning. People like to see them: they
rarely need encouragement or special motivation. This seems
to be true equally of men and women all over the world.
Films are concrete and real; are often closer to the experience
of some men and women than are more abstract printed
materials.

Films may combine all the arts—drama, music, photography,
graphic arts, dancing—in interesting and unusual combinations. They are thus able, not only to attract an audience, but
to hold attention. For the same reasons they appeal to, and
influence, the feelings. There is an emotional as well as intellectual response to films. It is not always known clearly why

this is so, or how to control it, but the fact that it exists is a matter of importance.

The motion picture is in some respects better suited to learning than is nature or actual experience. Telescopic photography can "bring up" distant objects for close study; microscopic photography can allow direct observation of objects otherwise too small; time-lapse and slow motion photography make possible the study of growth or motion which one otherwise could speculate about, but never observe. Artistry in film making can provide insights just as does any other art —insights not possible through rational processes.

The use of motion pictures in learning requires good planning and effective presentation. A number of books are available which give detailed suggestions of use. One essential fact about motion pictures is that although people will view a film with some eagerness, they may also approach it with some of the same attitudes they bring to any other entertainment. That is, they expect to be interested, distracted or amused, and may take no responsibility for putting themselves out, to understand, or do anything about the new experience.

In using films in place of a talk or lecture, one needs to remember that there are certain requirements. Just as it is important that a speaker is introduced, it is imperative that a film should be. There is evidence to show that an effective introduction, motivating the learner and securing his full attention, will double the amount that is learned from a film, and that what is learned will be retained longer. It is just as essential with a film as with a speaker to find out if the points of the film were established. If this did not happen, it is often useful to screen the film again. In using film or filmstrips for teaching some skill like tennis or learning a language, the particular sequence may need to be repeated several times. For this purpose the *film loops*, which allow a single portion of the film to be repeated and repeated, are most useful.

Films planned for skill instruction are used in a manner very similar to that described in the section on skill training.

Most films were not designed for group discussion. That is, their purpose is not to raise questions, but to assert, inform, instruct, preach, indoctrinate. If, however, there are significant questions implied in the film, discussion can develop. The film presentation does provide a background of common experience out of which consideration of the topic develops. But in the presentation of the film attention needs to be focused on the issues.

One of the most valuable uses of film is much like that of role playing. Some films present a social problem in dramatic form with which the participants can identify. The members can then consider together the implications or some related issues that may have been suggested by the film. This may provide a satisfying release of one's feelings, as well as a means of becoming more objective about one's own experience. In one such discussion a woman said: "I have known this (a particular practice in child care) all my life. If I had been given a written examination about it, I could have passed it any time. But I never fully understood it till tonight *when I heard myself* saying it."

Summary

This has been a chapter of *application*. No new principles have been advanced, but most of the major factors in learning have been reviewed, this time in a different context, and in the kind of setting in which a practitioner is most likely to confront them.

There is no hierarchy of values in learning; every factor can be of critical importance—on occasion fresh air may be as important as fresh ideas. Environment, the place, shape, and character of the facilities—all affect the amount and quality of learning.

An astonishing variety of forms, methods, techniques, and devices are available to the agent in adult learning. But ability in selection is required, and this is one of the chief skills of the teacher of adults. For example, it is possible to convey facts to very large groups of adults, but the sound patterns of languages are best learned in groups no larger than six. Where skills are being taught, ample opportunity and facilities must be provided for practice.

The choice of participants, those who have had similar or very different previous experience, markedly affects the educational outcome. For some tasks the best results are achieved when the participants are self-selected.

In every activity arrangements must be made for the expression of a number of factors—for example, anticipating and dealing with apprehension or resistance to learning, gaining and holding attention, providing for clear exposition, allowing for a two-way flow of communication, ensuring that there is testing, application and appraisal of the knowledge, skill, or attitude.

One of the most important developments in recent years has been many new applications of the "reality" principle—planning a learning experience that is concrete, vivid, and relevant. Examples of this are the use of actual machines, devices, or mock-ups in training, role playing, the "exercise" (or mass role playing) the case method, and the T-group.

Another noteworthy gain has been in the application and use of learning devices such as motion picture films. Devices do not replace the teacher, but they can be an effective and economical means to good learning.

The key to learning is engagement—a relationship between the learner, the task or subject matter, the environment, and the teacher. Some of the factors within this relationship are already established by the nature and experience of the learner, but many of the factors are not fixed in any way; they can be modified and improved with planning and practice.

With this chapter we complete the cycle of theory, practice, and application. We shall next review the entire teaching-learning transaction.

REFERENCES

1. Richard Livingstone, *On Education* (New York: The Macmillan Company, 1942).
2. C. N. Parkinson, *Parkinson's Law* (Boston: Houghton Mifflin Company, 1957). By permission of the publisher.
3. Commission on Architecture, *Architecture for Adult Education* (Chicago: Adult Education Association, 1956).

4. Dennis Trueblood and Franklin Roberts, "The Folklore of Workshops," *Adult Leadership* (Chicago: AEA), Vol. 7, No. 7.
5. Nathaniel Cantor, *Adult Leadership* (Chicago: AEA), Vol. 1, No. 10.
6. Hugh Gyllenhaal, "Guide to Styles, Groups, Methods," *Sales Meetings*, Jan. 4, 1957.
7. Coolie Verner, "Methods and Techniques," *An Overview of Adult Education Research* (Chicago: AEA, 1959).
8. Clarence Randall, *Toward the Liberally Educated Executive* (White Plains, N.Y.: Fund for Adult Education, 1957).
9. J. E. Anderson, "Teaching and Learning," *Education for Maturity* (New York: William Morrow & Company, Inc., 1955).
10. Abbott Kaplan, *A Study of Liberal Arts Discussion Programs for Adults in the Metropolitan Los Angeles Area* (White Plains, N.Y.: Fund for Adult Education, 1958).
11. J. L. Moreno, *Who Shall Survive?* (Boston: Beacon Press, Inc., rev. ed., 1953).
12. Alan Klein, *Role Playing* (New York: Association Press, 1956).
13. Kenneth D. Andrews, *The Case Method of Teaching Human Relations and Administration* (Cambridge: Harvard University Press, 1958).
14. National Training Laboratory, *Explorations in Human Relations Training* (Washington, D.C.: National Education Association, 1953).
15. Harry Strauss and J. R. Kidd, *Look, Listen and Learn* (New York: Association Press, 1947).

Suggested Reading

ADULT EDUCATION ASSOCIATION, "Workshop on Audio-Visuals," *Adult Leadership* (Chicago: AEA), Vol. 3, No. 4.
——, "Workshop—Rules of Freedom and Order," *Adult Leadership*, Vol. 5, No. 6.
——, "Using Resources," *Adult Leadership*, Vol. 1, No. 3.
——, "Improving Larger Meetings," *Adult Leadership*, Vol. 1, No. 7.
——, "Leading Discussion," *Adult Leadership*, Vol. 1, No. 9.
——, "Workshops and Institutes," *Adult Leadership*, Vol. 4, No. 7.
BENNE, KENNETH D., and MUNTYAN, BOZIDAR, *Human Relations in Curriculum Change* (New York: Dryden Press, 1951).

BURCH, GLEN, *Progress Report on Experimental Film Discussion Project* (White Plains, N.Y.: The Fund for Adult Education, 1952).

CRILE, LUCINDA, *Findings from Research on Meetings* (Washington, D.C.: U.S. Department of Agriculture, Extension Circular 507, 1956).

DALE, EDGAR, *Audio-Visual Methods in Teaching* (New York: Dryden Press, 1954).

GEIER, LEO, *Ten Years with Television at Johns Hopkins* (Baltimore: The Johns Hopkins University Press, 1958).

HOWLAND, C., JANIS, I. L., and KELLEY, H. H., *Communication and Persuasion* (New Haven: Yale University Press, 1953).

KELLEY, EARL C., "Human Relations in Workshop Teaching," *Adult Leadership* (Chicago: Adult Education Association), Vol. 3, No. 2.

KNOWLES, MALCOLM, *Informal Adult Education* (New York: Association Press, 1950).

LIVERIGHT, A. A., "A New Way to Look at Adult Education Programs," *Adult Leadership* (Chicago: Adult Education Association), Vol. 5, No. 5.

PIGORS, PAUL, and PIGORS, FAITH, "Case Method on the Spot," and "The Incident Process," *Adult Leadership* (Chicago: AEA), Vol. 3, Nos. 6 and 7, respectively.

PITKIN, ROYCE S., *The Residential School in American Adult Education* (Chicago: Center for the Study of Liberal Education for Adults, 1956).

SHEATS, PAUL, JAYNE, CLARENCE, and SPENCE, RALPH, *Adult Education* (New York: Dryden Press, 1953).

SIEGLE, PETER E., "The International Conference on Residential Adult Education," *Adult Education* (Chicago: AEA), Vol. 6, No. 2.

VERNON, M. D., "Presenting Information in Diagrams," *Audio-Visual Communications Review*, 1953.

ZELKO, HAROLD P., *Successful Conferences and Discussion Techniques* (New York: McGraw-Hill Book Company, Inc., 1957).

Chapter 10

THE TEACHING-LEARNING TRANSACTION

So far in our inquiry we have set out certain hypotheses about the self and about learning, examined many sources of information about the learner, considered how these factors have been woven into theoretical formulations, observed how they are working out in certain fields of practice, and examined the environmental and organizational circumstances affecting learning. Hypothesis, study, formulation, testing of theory, observation, have all gone on. Now we shall attempt some application of what we have found out, first setting out some of the main considerations in regard to the whole process of learning and then concentrating upon the *teacher* or *leader* or *practitioner* in the process.

John Dewey often wrote about learning as a transaction. He said that active perception, interpretation, or understanding comes as a result of a transaction in which are linked the interpreter and the interpreted, or between the observer and the observed. In the marketplace, unless both the buyer and the seller bring something of value, there is no transaction. So it is with learning. Many students of learning over many centuries have also used this term because they have been acutely aware of both process and *continuity*—continuity between the learner and his past, the learner and his environment, the learner and the content, the learner and his teacher.

The nature of these interrelated actions have occasionally been described. One example is in a book by Nathaniel Cantor with the significant title—*The Teaching-Learning Process.*[1]

We have already seen that learning involves change and growth, in the individual and in his behavior. "You don't change," said Eduard Lindeman, "until you do something.

You don't change by listening. You don't change by talking. You actually change when something happens to your muscles. When you step or move in a new way, then the change becomes really significant." Thus, while learning may include *cognitive* learning, *motor* learning, *emotional* learning, it is broader and deeper than any one of these.

We have also had a glimpse of the nature of the *self* and have seen how the self must become committed or involved if effective learning is to happen.

We have established that adults have the equipment and the capacity for learning, and even where there has been impairment, there are also means of overcoming most of the disabilities. The teaching-learning transaction has not just *two*, but *five* main elements:

- the learner
- the teacher
- the group (usually)
- the setting or situation
- the subject matter.

But the main protagonists in the transaction are the learner and the teacher.

At the risk of boredom induced by repetition, let us once more ask ourselves what the learner brings to the transaction.

What are his perceptions about the need for change? How deep is his uneasiness, his dissatisfaction with the present, or his desire for the new? What are the inhibitions to learning that he brings, his ambivalence, his resistance to change, his refuge in the present?

What does he know about his own capacity for learning? Does he perceive the content as abstract and irrelevant? Does he expect understanding and helpfulness from the teacher or some kind of threatening behavior? Does he feel a part of, or rejected by, the group?

Learning may be adventure, but for the learner it may also pose unknown difficulties, or raise images of past failures, or boredom. Does the learner perceive the situation as it is, or are his perceptions distorted? Is he likely to protect himself by verbalizing about the subject matter without internalizing or reorganizing it within himself. Whitehead has warned that passive learning of "inert ideas" may not be just wasteful but actually harmful, since the result is a decrease in satisfaction gained from learning and probably an increase in his resistance to further learning.

What does the teacher bring?

Like the learner, the teacher also brings a great deal to the transaction, much more than his mastery of a skill or his knowledge of subject matter. Does he have much awareness of the continuity, or the interaction that is involved? Does he look on it as an encounter with another self, or perceive himself simply as a transmission system for presenting certain material? Nothing is more deeply belittling than the self-image that some teachers have of themselves as being but the repositories of facts or ideas, ready to display them before others, but themselves taking little part except as transmitters. A tape recorder might do as well; a univac could do better; at least it reacts to the questions that it is asked.

How well is the teacher aware of the delicacy of his role, of the need that the learner has to be both dependent upon and independent of him? How well does he understand his own needs, his need to control people, or his need for affection, or his fear of hostility from the learner? How well is he able to accept the learner, not just as pupil, but as a person?

Within the group, its experience, its skill (or lack of it) in supporting the learner, its encouragement to him to stretch out, its capacity for obtaining assistance from the teacher, there are factors of considerable consequence. As we have seen, this is equally true of what might be called the environmental factors and the subject matter.

For the purposes of summary and application we shall now look at the teaching-learning transaction according to a somewhat different plan. To a considerable extent we shall be reviewing and recapitulating—but with illustrative examples and with some expansion of principles. We shall also follow a three-step time sequence that is usually present in any learning transaction—that is, planning the curriculum, establishing the learning situation, and evaluating. The same dominant notes and chords will be struck as in earlier chapters, but we shall now experience them in the kind of frame or setting most applicable to educational or training institutions.

We cannot escape some dangers here. No one statement can do justice to differing points of view that still exist about philosophy or method. Nor can it apply equally well to learning situations as different, for example, as teaching the use of the slide rule in a factory contrasted with the study of comparative religion; or the relatively free exploration of poetic forms as contrasted with the teaching of a catechism or the preparation of a nightschool class for an examination in mathematics. These situations are far from identical and any statement of practice, no matter how flexible, can be applied only with the exercise of considerable ingenuity. We believe, however, that what is suggested here does have application to most learning situations for adults.

Curriculum

The study of curriculum for elementary and secondary schools as well as universities has been going on for some time. Much less attention has been given to developing curricula for adults. However, some of the same principles are applicable, particularly those discussed in a syllabus by Ralph W. Tyler, entitled *Basic Principles of Curriculum and Instruction.*[2]

The essential difference, of course, is that the adult learner, far more than the child, may expect to take a much more active part in the consideration and selection of what he is to study. With children the amount of choice, and the degree of participation in the choice, of learning materials and experiences, will usually be limited. But with adults there can be a very wide range. Where examinations are set by some authority, or where the readings are already established (as in the case of a Great Books program) choice may be considerably restricted, but even in these cases there may be considerable opportunity for variety of illustrations or applications of principles. Whatever the limits, it is clear that where the learner does take part in the development of the curriculum, this act leads to a learning experience that is markedly different in quality. However, as we shall see in the next section, the learner may not have had any previous practice in choosing what to study. This may at first be a strange and perhaps even forbidding task for him, and he may need guidance in trying it.

A curriculum must start with educational objectives. Tyler identifies three general sources for these objectives:

- the learner himself
- contemporary life and society in which the learner lives
- the subject matters—for example, history, literature.

NEEDS OF THE LEARNER

We have dealt with the learner at some length. In Chapter 5 we identified two kinds of needs, both of which have some application in curriculum building:

- a need in the sense that the learner lacks some information or skill that it is assumed he should have, or that is enjoyed by most members in society
- a need in the sense of a tension or disequilibrium—for example, if the body lacks food, or if the person lacks affection, or lacks a philosophy of life.

A study of the needs and wants of the adult learner is one means of beginning the development of a curriculum. Needs are so many and so varied that one must have some way of bringing them into order. One rough classification is (1) health (2) family and friendship relations (3) socio-civic relations (4) consumer aspects of life (5) occupation (6) recreation (7) religion and philosophy.

Many ingenious ways have been used to identify both needs and interests, employing questionnaires, interviews, and similar devices.

Objections have sometimes been raised to the employment of such information in developing a curriculum. It is claimed, for example, that information about interests may give the *range* of interest but not the intensity. It is also possible that adult students may come with mixed, or twisted, or unworthy interests and goals.

A further objection is that placing too great a reliance on individual "interests" may result in the slighting of information gained from community surveys and the analysis of social patterns and social groupings which, in practice, have been the source of many useful ideas for educational activities for adults.

The most frequent criticism is that an interest-based curriculum will result in re-enforcing what may be a degraded level of taste. It is clear that some producers of the mass media in "giving the people what they want" are not only underestimating what people really want, but are themselves modifying wants and interests.

The errors here are threefold. The first is to assume that people have had enough experience to know all that will interest them. One way to help people discover an interest is to expose them to a range of experiences. When, over a period of time, listeners to radio were given the opportunity to hear concert music they began to demonstrate an interest in such music by buying more tickets for concerts than for baseball games.

William E. Hocking once said, "There is many a horse which does not know it is thirsty and which, when led to water, finds that it wants to drink." This is often true of the adult student whose horizons of experience have been restricted. How can he know how fascinating some of the "unknown countries" may be? The only way he can discover this is by exploration which sometimes may be difficult and unrewarding, but may also prove a great adventure.

A second error is putting undue reliance upon superficial interest-finders of the questionnaire type. Results of such measures usually are very limited. On the other hand, well-conducted interviews, or thorough investigations, have revealed a surprising range and depth of interest among adults. A recent study of radio listeners in England by Joseph Trenaman[3] reports that there are desires for learning among "ordinary people" of a kind that are seldom supplied in the daily run of broadcasting.

A third error can arise in the decision about a course of action based on what has been found out about his interests. Supposing one discovers that men in a certain work gang read nothing but comic books. One then has the choice between supplying them with even more comic books or continuing the search for an interest or need around which other forms of reading or study may take place. Of course it is possible always to capitulate and accede to any want that is expressed. A well-known American comic once claimed, "My audience is made up of high school kids. High school kids like to see me spit on people. So I spit on people." But it is also possible to use information about interests and needs in a responsible way. A study of comic books carried out for an institution, Frontier College, working in the bush camps of Canada, revealed a number of interests that became the basis for several courses of study.

The main reason, of course, for the concentration on interests as a source for educational objectives is the close relationship that this seems to bear with gaining the attention of people and having them participate in educational endeavors. Considerable study has been given to those adults in society who are infrequently or never found in educational activities. Despite recent growth in enrollment in adult education, the number of men and women who never take part in formal or informal activities must still be very large; particularly, it has been found, amongst those who have less than an eighth-grade education, are over 55 years of age, are laborers or service workers, and are close to a subsistence level of living. Many who have studied nonparticipation believe that if more adults are to be brought into educational activities, not only must the curriculum be modified but also many of the traditional forms of organization may have to be revised.

Concern about how to engage interest and to achieve a greater quality of participation has led some teachers of adults to use measures of participation, one of the best-known of which is the "Social Participation Scale" of F. Stuart Chapin.[4]

CONTEMPORARY LIFE

Those devising a curriculum may search contemporary life for clues to the selection of learning experiences. Here, just as much as in analyzing interests, the amount of material is so vast and complicated that some categories or other organizing devices are required.

Sources for this purpose are many. They include different kinds of data as supplied from the census, or from studies of society by social scientists, such as the "Yankee City" studies[5] or *Crestwood Heights*,[6] or from novels and plays.

Subjects may be suggested that have occupied the attention of men in all ages; or they may be about contemporary phenomena such as the impact upon people of industrialization and urbanization, particularly of the "great city" where many millions of men and women are now linked together in a gigantic aggregation of living and working.

Objections can be and are raised against a narrow restricted use of contemporary material. For example, if a study is undertaken about a single institution, or activity, or social problem, without seeing it in its wider setting, or lacking in any principles for wider application, the study may not be very rewarding. But the reverse of this would be equally barren. Few people believe any longer what used to be a common assumption, that a few basic principles are all that are needed; that these can be readily learned, and that when learned they can be applied to any new situation. It is now well established that learning happens with greatest efficiency where there is some similarity between the learning situation and the life situation. It is a caricature, of course, but still there is some force in the complaint of the young man who claimed: "I have an education that has equipped me in every respect to be a Roman emperor, but, alas, I am going to become a father!"

THE FIELDS OF STUDY OR SUBJECT MATTERS

An excellent source of learning objectives is in the established fields of study, such as mathematics and history. This has long been recognized in adult education, and not much comment is necessary. But there have been curious gaps. For example, although we live in an age that is often described as the "scientific era," the time allotted to science in the curriculum for adult education has been only a tiny fraction of the whole. Moreover, the use of subject matter has been for learning objectives that have been surprisingly narrow. Often it has included little more than the acquiring of information. To take the example of science again, it is claimed that there are at least four main educational objectives for any *ordinary citizen* studying science:

- to contribute to the health (both physical and emotional) of the learner through his changed behavior
- to contribute to the conservation of natural and other resources as well as the improvement of his occupational capacity
- to give the learner a more accurate, more satisfying picture of the world and his place in it, including the release of some of his fears through a better understanding of what may now appear strange
- to help him adopt more effective methods for studying and for solving problems.

By seeking the aid of the subject matter specialist in developing a curriculum, not only can important fields be covered but they can be opened up in the depth and breadth that they deserve.

In these three ways far more educational objectives will be identified than can possibly be followed up by any single educational agency. How can selection be made of those of greatest worth? Tyler[7] proposes two main "screens" for selection—one's educational philosophy and the understanding that one has of what learning is or can do.

EDUCATIONAL PHILOSOPHY

We have already listed a number of questions in educational philosophy. These need to be asked with respect to any educational objectives proposed. There are additional questions, for example, "Should the same kind of learning experience be provided for a man in a labor union as in a chamber of commerce?" The rigorous application of these questions to a proposed curriculum may make it possible to develop some priorities; those educational objectives in harmony with one's philosophy will be identified. However, in order to do this, it is essential that one's educational philosophy be stated lucidly and the main implications for educational objectives may have to be spelled out.

UNDERSTANDING ABOUT LEARNING

The second screen to be applied is made up of what we know about the educational process. There are some learning objectives that are potential only, there are some that are possible only with years of application, there are others that can be accomplished in a single course, or a single presentation. We know, for example, that it is possible in therapy for a considerable reorganization of the personality structure of an individual to be effected. But after the first two decades of life this is most likely to happen only over considerable periods of time. One ought not to expect revolutionary outcomes from a week-end course labeled "Personality 101."

From our knowledge of learning we can more readily organize material in time sequences. Some content may come first because it can be mastered more easily or because it provides necessary background, or a system for understanding what is to follow. It may seem an odd remark to make but another useful guide is our knowledge about "forgetting." A college student, for example, may forget as much as 50 per cent of what he learns in one year, or as much as 80 per cent in two years. But if he practices or uses the new he is not so inclined to lose it. It is desirable therefore, to choose learning sequences which the adult student is in a position to practice and apply. Moreover, things that are learned that are consistent with each other tend to re-enforce, and those that are inconsistent tend to interfere. This understanding can also guide us in selection of subject matter. We have seen that material which is inconsistent with the learner's view of the self is likely to be rejected or distorted. Where such material is a necessary part of the curriculum it ought to be introduced with some care and in ways by which the learner may be aided to face up to the implications squarely.

Some decisions may need to be made about the objectives that are "educational" and those that require some other form of behavior. For example, some of the problems faced by an unemployed laborer with five children may be dealt with through education; others may require action through welfare, therapy, or politics.

Two final actions are required in the development of the curriculum; a careful statement of objectives and selection of the actual learning experiences.

STATEMENT OF OBJECTIVES

In the ways already outlined a group of major educational objectives can be listed. If they are to be developed into actual learning experiences they must now be stated precisely.

On several occasions it has been noted that the important thing about learning has to do with changes in the learner; it is not behavior by the teacher, or kinds of subject matter. Accordingly educational objectives ought to be stated in a form which identifies the expected changes in the student. It is not enough to state that a learning objective is history or shopwork, or even in some generalized form such as "History develops an historical point-of-view." Two elements should be included in the statement—the kind of behavior change expected and the subject matter to be employed. Examples:

- To prepare a clear and well-organized newspaper article about the reorganization of city government
- To develop an appreciation of modern architecture
- To achieve familiarity with dependable sources of information about the teaching of mathematics.

In this way there is clarity about the selection of specific learning experiences. Moreover the objectives are stated in a form that is required if there is to be any satisfactory form of evaluation.

SELECTION OF LEARNING EXPERIENCES

The final step is the selection of the actual learning experiences. How this is done has already been suggested by what was said earlier about learning practice. If the objective has to do with a skill like reading or discussing, or using a tool, the experience must provide both the necessary content and the opportunity to practice that skill. The learning experience must be one in which the learner gains the kind of satisfaction set out in the objectives. We have all suffered occasions where this has not happened. If, in a course in musical appreciation, in the way that musical examples and musical form are analyzed, the learner comes to hate music, there has been a disastrous error both in selection of the learning experience and probably in the methods employed. The learning objective needs to be gauged as being within the possible range of accomplishment by the learner at his present level of experience. Discomfort will be produced if it is too elementary just as it will if there is too great difficulty.

To summarize: choosing a curriculum for adults means several things. It means understanding the needs and interests of the learner, understanding the situation in which he lives, and the kinds of content that may serve his needs. It means a careful statement of objectives in form that sets out the desired changes as well as the subject matter. It means selection of the precise learning experiences that may best accomplish these objectives. It assumes the fullest possible participation by the learner in curriculum building.

Moreover, it is now clear that devising suitable curricula for adults, though a fascinating enterprise, is somewhat complicated. If the learner is himself to play a large part in this, it is essential that more assistance be provided to him. Houle,[8] in his survey of adult education in the armed forces, proposed that counseling, both in the development of curriculum and in the choice of studies, ought to be provided in every educational situation for adults. He and others have maintained that since in adult education the possibilities of choice are usually greater than in most schools or colleges, it is even more essential for the adult student to be able to secure counsel in making an effective choice.

If all this happens, the learning transaction is well under way.

The Learning Situation

With the curriculum chosen we can look at the second phase or aspect of what is really a continuous process.

Whether the learning occurs through individual effort or in some kind of educational or training institution, the key concept is the same. As we have noted it is best expressed in the word *engage* (particularly in the French, *engager* from *gage* or pledge) meaning to bind oneself, to pledge oneself, to become engrossed, to become involved. Learning happens as the result of engagement, and the task of those guiding learning is to bring about engagement.

Naturally this does not happen by chance or by luck. It must be carefully planned. We say naturally, but it is not always deemed so. Since there is often considerable stress put upon informality in the learning of adults, and the term "informal education" is sometimes used as a synonym for adult education, it has been assumed by some that the learning transaction can proceed as an improvisation. But improvisation is possible, just as in music, only where there is a *mastery* of all the principles that must be brought into some harmonic arrangement. It requires planning and practice, even if it might appear artless.

There are a number of related aspects to this plan and practice:

- selection of forms and devices
- physical arrangements
- achieving helping characteristics within the group
- exploration of needs for, and resistance to, learning
- exploration of the subject matter
- testing and application.

These aspects have some parallels with the phases that Lippitt has identified as transpiring in any example of planned change (we must substitute the word *learner* for *client,* and *teacher* for *change-agent*):

Phase 1: The learner discovers the need for help, sometimes with stimulation by the teacher.

Phase 2: The helping relationship is established and defined.

Phase 3: The change problem is identified and clarified.

Phase 4: Alternative possibilities for change are examined: change goals or intentions are established.

Phase 5: Change efforts in the "reality situation" are attempted.

Phase 6: Change is generalized and stabilized.

Phase 7: The helping relationship ends, or a different type of continuing relationship is defined.[9]

Lippitt's phases and his more generalized concepts represent a careful extension of the traditional three-stage model —presentation, analysis, testing and application, which has been followed by many teachers for centuries. The three stages have never been more clearly stated than by the rural minister who was asked how he went about preparing his sermon, and replied: "First, I tells 'em what I'm going to tell 'em; then I tells 'em; finally, I tells 'em what I tole 'em."

We shall ourselves employ these three stages with some modifications, while reviewing some of the most important and most relevant considerations.

SELECTION OF SPECIFIC FORMS AND DEVICES

In any field where there is richness of opportunity the process of *selection* becomes more important and correspondingly more difficult. In the old one-room school, with no aids to learning but a slate and a tattered arithmetic book, the teacher had few problems of selection. But a teacher or leader of adults today best demonstrates his competence by his understanding and skill in the selection and use of an astonishing range of alternative resources and forms.

Naturally selection must be based on purpose. This is discussed and illustrated in the paper "Guide to Styles, Groups, Methods," by Hugh Gyllenhaal, reported in Chapter 9.

ARRANGEMENTS

The second aspect is making sure that all administrative arrangements are in accord with what we know about learning. This will include, at least, the following:

- Arranging for meeting places in line with the program objectives (keeping in mind the effect on learning of facilities and organization as discussed in Chapter 8)
- Having all equipment (chalk-boards, audio-visual equipment and the like) in excellent condition, set up for immediate use, or available for practice at the time when needed
- Applying the suggestions devised to help overcome some of the sight and hearing limitations of older people
- Arranging the learning sequences in time units that challenge but do not fatigue the adult learner (as discussed in Chapter 3)
- Taking care that the pace of presentation is not too rapid, particularly for the older adult (Chapter 3).

CHARACTERISTICS OF THE GROUP WHICH SUPPORTS LEARNING

We shall not attempt to repeat here the material about groups and learning that was presented in Chapters 8 and 9. Instead we shall simply note three characteristics that need to be present in the group if effective learning is to happen:

- *A realization by the members of the group* that genuine growth stems from the creative power within the individual, and that learning, finally, is an individual matter
- The acceptance as a *group standard* that each member has the right to be different and to disagree
- Establishment of a group atmosphere that is free from narrow judgments on the part of the teacher or group members.

EXPLORATION OF NEEDS FOR, OR RESISTANCES TO, LEARNING

If he is to become deeply engaged, the learner must perceiv his needs and the relationship that the subject matter has to them. It may be useful for him to have some verbal discussior of this. Some teachers make the exploration of needs, as seen by the learners, the central core of the opening session of a course. It may also be useful to have some open discussion of blocks and limitations to learning that may be expected. Sometimes it is useful to have some expression of anxieties, that one is too old, or "rusty," or has been unsuccessful in such kinds of situations before. Sometimes it may help if the teacher warns the members what to expect. For example, they may be told that the subject matter may be difficult until a certain stage is achieved, and that perseverance will be required.

It ought not to be expected that this exploration will take place without incident or some difficulty. People who have been used to governing their own learning will take part in such a preliminary as a matter of course. But what of the adult student whose previous experience has been of a very different kind? Perhaps in any previous educational situation he was *told* how and what to study. Now you are expecting him to assume some responsibility for his own learning. He may feel somewhat puzzled, or frustrated, or even threatened by a situation unlike anything experienced before.

When we ask an athlete to try out a forward somersault dive his muscular contortions may at first be violent.

When we ask a woman to try out a delicate embroidery operation the initial result may be clumsy.

When we ask any human being to behave in a way that is outside or runs counter to all his previous experience the immediate response will be uncertainty, at the very least.

In all cases the individual may need encouragement. This is not mollycoddling, or sugar-coating, or soft pedagogy. This is simply understanding and co-operating with the dynamic way in which a human being grows and changes.

The principle is simple enough to understand and even to

state as a generalization, but it is endlessly variable and fascinating in practice.

If the learner has never had the experience of sharing in the planning of his own study, if he has always been in a class or squad or gang where he was expected to listen, repeat certain kinds of instructions when ordered, or reproduce the thinking of his teacher, then the first occasion when he is confronted with the opportunity for greater participation is likely to be difficult. There may be the emergence of negative feelings, perhaps very strong ones. These may be slow to appear, because the tradition is that "the teacher is always right," but it may not be long before someone will blurt out that "time is being wasted," or that he "didn't come there to listen to some other students," or that "the teacher ought to take charge and get on with the teaching."

Naturally, unless these negative feelings can be expressed, there is little chance of the development of much understanding of what has produced them, or acceptance by the learner of a greater degree of responsibility. But if the learner finds that he can express feelings without being condemned, if he can take action or try out ideas that will not lead to his rejection by the teacher or by the class members, he has little need for a brittle defensiveness. If no one is attacking, blaming, or condemning him, he is freed to face his own ambivalent feelings. Not having to face hostility all about him, he can decide to face, or not to face, himself, in regard to the particular learning goals. It is not enough for the teacher to be patient with the learner. He must, himself, be prepared for the puzzlement, frustration, even the hostility that may be expressed. If such feelings catch him "off guard," his own protective responses such as returning hostility, ridicule, or censure, will serve to increase the tension and thus the learning difficulties.

One more point: the student not only needs to be prepared to handle his own difficulties but he may need the incentive of some forward view of the results. The superintendent of a park in the Rocky Mountains once reported: "We found that as soon as people could see the peak from every point on the road, many more completed the climb to the top."

EXPLORATION OF THE SUBJECT MATTER

We have seen that the presentation of the subject matter can take many forms, such as reading, lectures, observation and experiment, or practice of reality situations. If the attention of the learner is fully engaged he will want, in increasing measure, to experience the subject matter in all its fascination, or its difficulty, even its bewilderment. He may want or need the information or opinion of an "expert." Or he may be prepared for frank exchange of views. Some differences of opinion are healthy: the I-think-this-for-this-reason kind; rather than the you-are-wrong kind which we usually call an argument, and which usually is quite sterile as far as learning is concerned.

This exploration can and should go on, in depth. But there are also endless possibilities for breadth. With so much experience among the group members to start from, the possibilities of generalizing and of perceiving new relationships are many. This potential richness of generalizing is, for writers like Peter Siegle,[10] one of the chief marks and of the most absorbing aspects of adult education.

TESTING AND APPLICATION

In the case of a skill, or motor learning (like learning to play badminton) little result can be anticipated without opportunity for practice. Actually this principle is valid not only for motor learning, but it is not so well recognized in other fields. Along with the presentation, exploration, and relating of subject matter must go the practice of ideas and skills, the try-out and testing of assumptions and hypotheses, checking them against alternatives, and counterclaims, estimating their validity with respect to inner logic or in application in real life.

If the learning has to do with the acquiring of new skills and attitudes, an essential part of the learning process will be imaginative applications in the home setting. The learner may want and need help in diagnosing the forces that may be resistant to change, in measuring his own strengths and weaknesses, and in seeking to re-establish himself back in his own situation.

The learner may also need help in developing a "continuing system" of learning. If he has attained satisfaction in learning, already he has a "bent" for more. What he may also need is to improve his skill in learning, to use more scientific methods of observation and analysis, to become more sensitive and understanding of his own inhibitions to learning (and through understanding reduce these resistances), to become more self-accepting, and, through gaining more security and becoming less defensive, freer to perceive without distortion.

This entire learning transaction proceeds most effectively if it is guided by "feed-back" and evaluation.

Evaluation

We shall now turn to the third phase of the transaction—evaluation. We plan to deal with this subject in its proper place and simply on its merits. In recent years so much attention has been directed to it that the word itself has become invested with feelings and is something of a semantic battle ground.

The function of evaluation was stated succinctly by a national committee of the Adult Education Association:

- The purposes of education are growth and change—change in behavior of individuals and groups. People behave differently as a result of education.
- The primary purpose of evaluation in education is to find out how much change and growth have taken place as a result of educational experiences. One evaluates a total program or major parts of it to find out how much progress has been made toward program objectives.[11]

The American Library Association once stated what were termed as "four basic steps" respecting evaluation:

"those taken before the activity"
1. setting of goals—what specific outcome is expected?
2. establishing a base-line—what is true of this situation now?
"those taken after the activity"
1. noting and recording change—what happened?
2. considering the change in the light of circumstances—what does it mean and what should be done about it?[12]

This model may not suit all forms of education but it can be adapted to most.

Earlier we also asserted that evaluation should be carried out with respect to specific learning objectives. Indeed, one of the principal reasons for being sharp and clear in the statement of one's objectives is so that appraisal can be conducted in a meaningful way. If, to take an earlier example, the learning objective is "to develop familiarity with dependable sources of information about the teaching of mathematics" it is not too difficult to devise an interview or questionnaire, or task, by which that objective can be appraised.

We have also claimed that evaluation should be carried on as a *regular, ongoing* part of the total learning process.

Now if the objective of the learning program were merely the reproducing of information supplied by the teacher, or giving back the opinions of the teacher, evaluation might be expressed as some measure of facts or opinions committed to memory.

Usually, however, the objectives have to do with *changes* in observing, identifying, analyzing, understanding, organizing, applying, and testing information as well as the development of certain work habits, skills, and attitudes. Some way must therefore be found of measuring the changes, directly or by inference.

It is well to stress a variety of measures because it has often assumed that evaluation means the use of pencil-and-paper tests. Obviously written tests have a part in evaluation. So do tests of performance in certain skills (for example, typing, gymnastics, welding, dissecting, leading discussion). So also does appraisal of samples of performance, such as selections from a student's writing. So do oral examinations of many kinds.

Not only does evaluation mean the measurement of changes in behavior but it usually signifies more than one test, more than a final examination. If evaluation is to mean much there must also be pre-examination so that there is a base from which growth can be measured. There is also systematic ongoing evaluation which we shall discuss in a moment under the term "feed-back." There is testing at the conclusion of the program. And there is further assessment at some point in time afterwards, to note any application of the learning. In reporting on the research about the teaching of the facts of nutrition we have seen that at the end of the formal program of instruction the women all seemed to have acquired about the same amount of information about nutrition, but six months later, when tested concerning what they had done about the facts that they had learned, some of them showed considerably more gains than the others.

In his book *Informal Adult Education*[13] Malcolm Knowles reports that "to most adults the words 'test,' 'quiz' and 'examination' call forth such unpleasant memories that it is often difficult to use them in voluntary adult groups." This seems to be true, and thus far there have not been devised many satisfactory substitute methods. One difficulty we have dealt with already. If the learning objective is not defined in a precise way it is difficult or impossible to make any assessment of progress. However, various kinds of written "objective" tests have been adapted from schools and universities. These are of the sort in which the learner indicates whether he thinks the statement is true or false, or in which he makes a choice among several statements.

But little attention has yet been put on developing these for adult purposes. In English adult education, particularly in the classes of the Workers' Education Association, it is expected that every student will write a number of essays and much of the effort of the tutor in guiding the adult students comes in connection with this written work. Essays and projects are not unknown but are much less common in North America.

Some attempts have been made to use projective tests (notably the Rorschach "ink blot" test) in which the learner constructs an imaginary story or describes how he feels or what he sees when certain unstructured shapes are presented to him. Analysis by a trained psychologist of his responses can give a good deal of information about his attitudes, social adjustment, and personality structure. But such use is possible only in psychological clinics and institutions; it is not at all for general purposes unless highly trained professional staff are available.

Some teachers have made use of studies of attendance, and of "drop-outs," in evaluating their program. However, such statistics by themselves do not reveal very much unless it is possible to follow them up with interviews with a selected number of individuals. Studies of participation are becoming more common, as we have noted in another connection.

Each teacher can and does make some subjective assessment of the performance and growth of the learners. But that is rarely satisfactory to furnish data for any kind of comparisons. Recently Kropp and Verner[14] have developed an attitude-scale technique for evaluating the changes that occur in a single meeting or conference, which they feel will provide results that can be compared. The scale is based on the feelings and judgments that the learner has about the experience in which he has just participated.

The *agent* of evaluation may be very important. If the learning objective is simply reproducing what the teacher has taught, the result may just as well be measured by the teacher. But if a primary learning objective is for the learner to become increasingly autonomous, to begin to take over direction of his own learning, then it is highly important that he take a large share, if not the complete control, of the evaluation.

In many learning situations, the participation by the learner in the evaluation is difficult to manage. Where there is a standard program of teaching skills, such as lifesaving, there is usually a fixed examination system. A factory, a school or university may also have an established examination procedure which is required by law for licensing, or to receive the payments of grants, or because it is backed by some other sanction. What can be done in the face of such rigidities?

First of all, it should be repeated that the measuring of performance against certain objective standards is an excellent way to obtain knowledge about oneself if the learner is himself making these comparisons, and if the process is carried out without some form of punishment for poor performance. Films or tape recordings by which he can observe good work, and appraise his own performance against what is excellent, provides one means of doing this. It is also important for him to measure his performance against his *own* previous performance and against his learning objectives. Again, the use of tape recordings makes this possible in such fields as speech and music. Motion picture film is sometimes used for appraisal in sports like football.

In the classroom many teachers, obliged by the institution to give some test, have experimented with various means of testing that are also conducive to the development of self-appraisal. One practice is to have the class members themselves prepare the test form. Contrary to what might be anticipated, the resulting test is often more rigorous than that which would have been devised by the instructor. Another variation is where the students are asked to state a dozen or so major propositions in regard to their subject, bring them to class, and then be examined critically on their understanding and application of a selection of these propositions.

But where academic credit is not an issue, the number and variety of "examinations" used is surprising. Often the test is some form of application of the subjective matter and principles learned. For example, in one school for trade unionists who had been studying collective bargaining, the class members were asked to nominate five of their number to take part in a full-day "case," along with an equal number of business men, and guided by three industrial conciliators. During the proceedings a special "chair" was left open so that any class member who sat there would be recognized by the chairman and allowed to make an observation or ask a question. Two- or three-day exercises which feature the direct applications of principles have been devised in projects of in-service training for the staffs of national organizations. In a one-week-long intensive seminar on Shakespeare, the participants read, hear lectures, and attend performances of the plays. For their examination, the entire seminar group utilize the knowledge they have gained about the stage, the actors, design, costumes, and Elizabethan music and apply it in the design of a production of a different Shakespearian play. In this case, the seminar participants themselves decided upon the form of examination. They also identified the criteria to be used and methods to be followed in appraising their own performance.

The important factor of course, is not just interest in the activity, but how much engagement of the person can be attained in the process of measuring and understanding his own progress. Evaluation of the learner in more traditional ways has sometimes been criticized as resulting in a restricted curriculum. The complaint is made that the teacher prepares students "for the examination" rather than pursuing the subject. It is sometimes claimed that the "examination system" does violence to the learning transaction itself. Carl Rogers, from his experience has come to the conclusion that *anything but* self-appraisal may have harmful results:

> As we have struggled with this problem of grades and academic bookkeeping, and have contrasted it with those experiences in which students are free to evaluate themselves, we have reached a conclusion which to some will seem radical indeed. It is that personal growth is hindered and hampered, rather than enhanced, by external evaluation. Whether the evaluation is favorable or unfavorable, it does not seem to make the development of a more mature, responsible, or socialized self, but indeed tends to work in an opposite direction.[15]

And Donald Snygg has had similar comments to make about traditional measuring devices:

> It is very questionable if our traditional marking system is able to give the student the feeling that he is making progress. The marking standard is based on the class mean. The student who progresses at the same rate as the class does not improve his mark and the student who progresses more slowly sees his mark drop even though he is making progress. . . .
>
> Another defect is the fact that since the mark is one official symbol of success, the mark itself, rather than growth and progress, becomes the student's goal. . . . If students can get a mark without changing their opinions they will do so.
>
> We shall have to find better ways than marks to help students perceive and evaluate their progress. More appreciative comment on student papers, more attention and respect for student ideas

will help, and I should like to say that that implies serious discussion and constructive criticism. Perfunctory acceptance of all a student's ideas does not mean respect. It means indifference and sooner or later the student finds it out. But the best promise seems to lie in giving the student more opportunities to work on real problems which he recognizes as important and on which he can evaluate his progress by objective results.[16]

Whether one accepts these views or not, it is not difficult to note the different behavior of students when they are working toward and appraising learning objectives which are their own. Recently a group of school superintendents took part in a month-long workshop. At the beginning it was not known if formal credit for achievement in the workshop would be allowed or not. For the first two weeks the men worked assiduously, both individually and collectively, in the study and consideration of subjects and problems which they selected themselves. But at this stage the department of education announced that credit would be given for the work. Now class members who had worked with some help from the staff but with a certain assurance on matters *they knew* were of importance and concern began to ask what the *instructor thought* was important, and what the instructor said should be studied.

The professor directing the workshop claims that tensions increased and that satisfaction and deep application diminished in the second period.

FEED-BACK

One of the ugliest terms in common use is *feed-back*. But it is used to represent a very important idea.

We have seen in the reports on studies of communication that when a message is being communicated from one person to another, if there is an opportunity for the recipient to report back what he is receiving, a great deal of error is eliminated.

Feed-back is the process by which, in any communication, or any learning process, the recipient or learner is able to state what is his perception of the situation at any given time.

Examples of this are many. The members of a class, at the end of a lecture, may state what they understood from the lecture. Feelings they have about what has transpired may be identified as well as facts. Much of the value of the feed-back is to discover with what feelings the activity or content is being received, and this can be used to guide both teacher and learner. At the conclusion of the first day of a conference the members may indicate to what degree the sessions are meeting the objectives that had been established for the conference, as well as some of the personal objectives that each of them had. They may also state what is lacking; what issues or emphasis ought to be included, or what has been unclear. The use of such material in planning subsequent lectures or sessions is obvious.

There are other by-products. The practice of regular assessment of what is occurring leads to improved performance in self-appraisal. Moreover, being able to measure his own success is perhaps the strongest motivating force for an adult to continue or to put fresh energy into the chosen study.

Devices for obtaining "feed-back" sometimes used are simple meeting reaction forms filled out quickly by every participant, or detailed questionnaires, or interviews, brief or sometimes in depth.

Effect of Evaluation

It seems to be clear from all the evidence that adults, even more than children, are interested in the application of what they learn. Adults seem to be more interested in the directions in which their learning is taking them. The motivation of adults, since they engage in most activities from free choice and not by law, is dependent upon their being convinced that progress is being made toward some goal. For all these objects evaluation is essential.

Adults want to know in what ways they have been changed. Several years ago the late Eduard Lindeman reported that a class of trade union members, studying international affairs with him, wanted to know if their study had changed them in any of the following respects:

- Has it increased my usable fund of reliable information? (The principal feature of their concern appeared to be (a) the relationship between different bodies of facts and (b) ways of distinguishing the various grades of reliability of information.)
- Have I changed my vocabulary? Have I, in other words, learned how to make use of some *new concepts?*
- Have I acquired any new skills? (e.g. learning how to interpret statistical tables and graphs.)
- Have I learned how to make reliable generalizations?
- Have I learned how to sort out the moral ingredients in the various situations considered by this study group? Have I learned to think in terms of values?
- Have I altered any attitudes?[17]

It is quite clear from this list of questions that Dr. Lindeman was assisting his class to learn how to evaluate, as well as how to read and study. It is not enough to recognize the importance of self-appraisal for the adult learner: he will need guidance in how to go about it, starting, as we have seen, with the statement of learning objectives.

Recently some effort has been made to measure progress in the reading of adult students, not in terms of simple speed, recall, or comprehension tests, but in terms of the *mature reader* concept that was discussed in Chapter 2. As more and more becomes known about the mature adult learner, and the self-motivated learner, these concepts will add useful tools for evaluation.

One final word: we have seen that most adult learners have both educational and what might be called noneducational motives. For example, belonging to cohesive social groups may, as was reported earlier, affect the amount of growth or educational change. But many of the instruments presently used for evaluation take no account of factors such as this. Evaluation in its full sense is a more subtle complex process than is yet represented in the techniques that are usually employed. Accordingly, any results of these devices should be interpreted with some care.

REFERENCES

1. Nathaniel Cantor, *The Teaching-Learning Process* (New York: Dryden Press, 1953).
2. Ralph Tyler, *Basic Principles of Curriculum and Instruction* (Chicago: University of Chicago Press, 1950).
3. Joseph Trenaman, *Education in the Adult Population* (Oxford: Oxford University Press, 1959).
4. F. Stuart Chapin, "Social Participation and Social Intelligence," *American Sociological Review*, Vol. IV, April 1939.
5. Lloyd Warner, *The Social Life of a Modern Community* (New Haven: Yale University Press, 1941).
6. J. R. Seeley, R. A. Sim, and E. Loosely, *Crestwood Heights* (Toronto: University of Toronto Press, 1955).
7. Ralph Tyler, *op. cit.*
8. Cyril O. Houle and Others, *The Armed Services and Adult Education* (Washington, D.C.: American Council on Education, 1947).
9. Ronald Lippitt, Jeanne Watson, and Bruce Westley, *The Dynamics of Planned Change* (New York: Harcourt, Brace and Company, 1958).
10. Peter E. Siegle, "Mountains, Plateaus and Valleys in Adult Learning," *Adult Education* (Chicago: AEA), Vol. IV, No. 4.
11. Adult Education Association, *Program Evaluation in Adult Education* (Chicago: AEA, 1952).
12. American Library Association, *Guide to Activities* (Chicago: ALA, 1957).
13. Malcolm Knowles, *Informal Adult Education* (New York: Association Press, 1954).
14. Russell P. Kropp and Coolie Verner, "An Attitude Scale Technique for Evaluating Meetings," *Adult Education*, (Chicago: AEA), Vol. 7, No. 4.
15. Carl R. Rogers, *Client-Centered Therapy* (Boston: Houghton Mifflin Company, 1951).
16. Donald Snygg, *Some Motivational Aspects of College Training* (Syracuse: University College of Syracuse University, 1956).
17. Eduard C. Lindeman, "Adults Evaluate Themselves," *How to Teach Adults* (Chicago: AEA, 1956).

Suggested Reading

ADULT EDUCATION ASSOCIATION, "Evaluating Program and Performance," *Adult Education* (Chicago: AEA), Vol. 1, No. 11.

BRADFORD, LELAND P., "The Teaching-Learning Transaction," *Adult Education* (Chicago: AEA), Vol. 8, No. 3.

BRIM, ORVILLE G., "Evaluating the Effect of Parent Education," *Social Science and Parent Education* (New York: Russell Sage Foundation, 1956).

CANTOR, NATHANIEL, *The Learning Process for Managers* (New York: Harper & Brothers, 1958).

KLINEBERG, OTTO, "Introduction: the Problem of Evaluation," *International Special Science Bulletin* (Paris: UNESCO, 1955), Vol. III, No. 3.

POWELL, JOHN WALKER, *Learning Comes of Age* (New York: Association Press, 1956).

Chapter 11

THE TEACHER IN THE
LEARNING TRANSACTION

In Chapter 1 we stated that this book was planned primarily for practitioners who have some part in adult learning—teachers, librarians, training directors, coaches, foremen, perhaps educational administrators.

It is interesting to note that in English we do not have any term that describes quite what is needed here. We use the word teacher for want of something else. What is needed is a noun that means he-who-assists-learning-to-happen. In the book *The Dynamics of Planned Change*[1] the authors use the term "change agent" to express this idea and it might serve if it were not so clumsy, and if it had no misleading connotations.

Nearly everything that has been written about learning refers to what happens to someone else. It is usually about *them*, the students. But this chapter is about *us*, those of us who take some part in bringing about learning. Our inquiry started with us, it has now gone full circle. What do we do? What are we like? What do we need to remember? What growth should we try to bring about in ourselves?

Many Different Acts and Roles

By now it must be sufficiently clear that in learning there are many different roles. The traditional, somewhat romanticized picture of a teacher, a *Mr. Chips*, who inspires, cajoles, exhorts, stimulates his students to vigorous intellectual effort, covers only one part of this. Commonly we think of a person who is lecturing, or giving a talk, as being the chief actor in the drama of learning. Yet, from our own experience, we may remember that the one whose contribution was critical in achieving learning may have been the janitor who saw to it that there was enough fresh air so that nobody became inattentive or fell asleep. Or the members of the committee who welcomed the newcomers at the door and somehow were able to convey that the occasion was one of significance, requiring unusual effort. It could be an anonymous photographer or film editor who may have supplied the main content for the evening, or it may have been Plato with whose ideas the members grappled so that their understanding enlarged.

In attempting to gain some appreciation of the significance of roles in teaching there is much that is relevant in what has been written about leadership. As we have seen in Chapter 7, some writers have described leadership as consisting of a number of actions which one designated person, the leader, or several of the participants, may carry out. Similarly there are many possible actions in regard to teaching, such as the following:

- presenting information or demonstrating processes
- raising relevant questions
- clarifying difficulties or obscurities
- drawing parallels or finding relationships
- reflecting feelings
- expressing agreement and support.

But just as one needs to remember that any task that leads to an educational result is worthy of respect, it is equally important to remember that there is no learning situation so minute, so self-contained, or so well-defined that other learnings are not implicated. No teacher can claim, for example, that because his task is elementary or modest, because what he teaches is limited to a routine skill, such as instructing in the operation of a simple machine, he doesn't need to know or to care much about other kinds of learning. On the contrary, whenever a human being is the learner, no matter how rudimentary may be the specific subject of instruction, a whole complex personality is engaged. It should not be necessary here to repeat any clichés such as that "the whole person is involved in any learning transaction." Still, this truism, like most, represents an idea of great importance.

All the roles and acts respecting teaching have their place and importance: all may be utilized at one time or another. Most of them are based upon or require a particular kind of skill or understanding. The successful practitioner not only values any role that does contribute to effective learning but attempts to become competent, at least, in many or all of the required skills.

No Blueprints

Several hundred volumes of how-to-do-it books have been published with a sale of millions of copies. So far there is none that describes adequately how to be a teacher. Of course, one might quail if such a book were offered. Still, it is somewhat surprising how few books or descriptions there are about the teacher. If you talk with teachers themselves, the only book which many will refer to is *The Art of Teaching*[2] by Gilbert Highet. In English adult education, the *tutor* has a recognized kind of role and responsibility, and there are a number of books dealing with the training and responsibilities of tutors.[3]

No one yet has attempted to deal in a single volume with all the capacities and characteristics of the teacher, or learning agent, in the way that we are thinking of him in this chapter.

There are a number of promising leads, however. The Center for the Study of Liberal Education for Adults is investigating what some have referred to as "teaching styles."[4] A number of such styles have been identified and the requirements, effectiveness, and limitations of each are being studied. Just as there are many acts and roles, there may be several kinds of teaching styles, each of which may have particular advantages for certain learning situations.

Successful teachers have always developed their own styles, based on their own experience and to some extent through the observation of others. For most of us, the opportunity for observing good teachers has not been too frequent, but, potentially at least, we now have sizable stocks of materials for studying effective teaching. Many hundred tapes and several hundred films now exist in which are recorded teachers on hundreds of subjects, following varied teaching styles in scores of different learning situations. With a little bit of ingenuity and organization these tapes, films, and kinescopes can provide excellent examples for observing and analyzing at least some of the qualities needed in the learning process.

There are excellent precepts for this. Years ago, through the work of Thomas Fansler[5] and others, many adult leaders improved their skill in group discussion by studying transcripts of discussion. Students in social work listen to tapes and study records of interviews and group meetings. Excellent results of a similar kind have been achieved in the study of nondirective counseling under Carl Rogers.[6] Nathaniel Cantor[7] is another teacher who has supplied transcripts of class meetings that are useful for analysis.

Some of the most useful, and readable, pages in Highet's book contain his remarks about teaching style. He tells us, for example, that in Scottish universities there is a direct form of two-way communication between audience and lecturer:

> When they admire a phrase or an idea, the students applaud by stamping, none too gently; and when they miss something they shuffle their feet until the sentence is repeated. It may sound odd, but it is extremely helpful to the lecturer, and also ensures that the Scots get full value for their fees.[8]

Highet also, by quoting Conan Doyle, tells of the kind of speaker that is still to be found in our midst, even when public address systems are in general use, and in more countries than England:

> Professor Brown will, I am sure, excuse me if I say that he has the common fault of most Englishmen of being inaudible. Why on earth people who have something to say which is worth hearing should not take the slight trouble to learn how to make it heard is one of the strange mysteries of modern life. Their

methods are as reasonable as to try to pour some precious stuff from the spring to the reservoir through a nonconducting pipe, which could by the least effort be opened. Professor Brown made several profound remarks to his white-tie and to the carafe upon the table, with a humorous, twinkling aside to the silver candlestick upon his right.

No text or blueprint exists which sets out in any definite way all the arts or skills needed by the teacher, but many of the tools for his practice and study are available, if he will organize and use them.

"A Learner Himself"

When asked what was the most important attribute of the teacher, Harry Overstreet once replied, "He must be a learner himself. If he has lost his capacity for learning he is not good enough to be in the company of those who have preserved theirs." Dr. M. M. Coady, former director of the Antigonish Movement, once put it even more bluntly. "The man who has ceased to learn," he said, "ought not to be allowed to wander around loose in these dangerous days."

From our examination of attributes and motivation it is quite apparent why a teacher must be a learner, must himself possess strong motives and an attitude toward learning. For, as we have seen, it is this attitude which itself communicates most forcibly, not his words. Nothing is as transparent as the attitude of another to learning. And no one sets up such a block for others as he for whom learning seems so unimportant that he is not bothering with it himself, even though he claims it might be useful for others.

This is clear enough. We must have long since concluded that learning is such a complicated affair that one never fully *masters* it; one needs to be constantly alert for new manifestations. Keeping up to date in regard to learning is only comparable with keeping up to date in regard to medical practice. Every good doctor assumes such a responsibility as part of his job; any good practitioner in education has a similar obligation.

One question is often asked. What about training for adult education?

There is no complete agreement on this. Some favor a broad general education in the humanities and social sciences, as being the main requirement. Others feel that some form of apprenticeship is essential, regardless of the general level of education.

Full-time preparation of people who will specialize in adult learning is now offered in a few universities in Canada and England and Western Europe. Many universities in the United States now offer courses in adult education, and some American universities have graduate programs, covering philosophy, psychology, methods, curriculum, and administration. Scores of universities and other organizations offer programs of shorter duration in the evening, in summer school, or in intensive short-term residential seminars.

An important part of the continuing education of the teacher is the development of skills. We have already noted that each role or each style may require a special kind of skill, and a few of these are easily acquired. Skills such as presentation, developing curricula, evaluation, and administration can be practiced and learned but this happens most readily when one has most need of them. These are not skills to be mastered early at college and always kept burnished and complete: they must be worked over and maintained by use.

As is true of some other fields, the agent in learning is not only an artist, but a craftsman as well and needs to take over some of the attitudes, such as the concern about skill, the devotion to self-improvement, the slow maturation of skill that is the hallmark of the genuine craftsman.

Leland Bradford, and others, believe that what is most important for the teacher is to learn about himself:

> In learning about ourselves, we need to understand, as well as we can, our own motivations. Obviously none of us can understand all our motivations, but the clearer we are about why we are doing what we are doing, the more capable we are of directing our behavior and understanding ourselves and others.

We need, second, to recognize the consequences of our behavior on others. . . .

We need, third, to understand the consequences of others' behavior on us. Frequently we don't have adequate insight into how other people really affect us or how we react in human situations. . . .

Fourth, most of us have not developed the ability to listen. We think we listen but we only hear a small portion of what's trying to be said. We hear on only a surface level, and we don't really understand the other. . . .

Finally, we have many resistances to accepting suggestions and reactions. We resist cues telling us something about our behavior and how we are relating to others. We thus lack the basic ability to continue learning through experience.[9]

It will be noted that there is a very close similarity between what is here advocated, that a teacher should learn about himself, and "sensitivity training" for industrial managers described by Tannenbaum in Chapter 8.

Dr. Overstreet has stressed the importance of a different kind of learning competence by the teacher: "The adult educator cannot be simply a person of good will and generous impulses—and large ignorance. He must know something well."[10]

If the teacher is himself a learner this will mean periodic change in his beliefs, theories, and practices. Ordway Tead once remarked that the good teacher should "recognize the priceless asset of intellectual integrity and rational candor; let him eschew also the constant driving for agreement with his own doctrine."

Developing a particular field is one defense against an affliction which may attack anyone in adult education. As we shall note later, most practitioners are generalists and part of their usefulness grows out of that fact. But they live "in an age of specialists" when most people have a function in life which is well defined and at least partially understood. If a man is asked what he does, and he is able to reply that he is a lawyer or salesman or carpenter, the inquirer may not know precisely what he does but he is satisfied that this is a proper function in life. If his answer is *adult educationist,* or something like that, the next question can easily be predicted—"What's that?" People who are generalists, or are performing a kind of service which most people don't yet understand, sometimes feel ill at ease or become defensive about this. The generalist may fear he is nothing more than "a jack of all trades." The development of some competency, even if it may not always be understood or appreciated, assists in bringing and maintaining the self-respect and self-assurance upon which good performance depends.

This is particularly true for the many whose main tasks in regard to learning are in organization and administration. It is scarcely a revelation to say that sound learning principles must permeate all parts of the organization responsible for the learning situation. Administrative practices must be consonant with the best thinking about learning.

Some administrators and organizers are assailed occasionally by feelings that their role is insignificant or, even if very important, that it has little to do with the central objective, namely, learning. But there need not be any chasm between the learning situation and administration if the same general principles govern both. Administration, of course, can be an intensely creative job.

There is a corollary to all this. The administrator who has the taste and skill for it, and who manages to find the time for teaching in at least one activity, has a much better opportunity for keeping in touch with the whole learning enterprise and also keeping alive intellectually.

Overstreet believes that a teacher or administrator needs at least four qualities:

He must himself want to go on learning; he must have some expertness that gives, as it were, a vertebrate character to what he says and does; he must have a sense of relationships broad enough to redeem him from narrow specialization; and he must have a sense of community—a power to think and act in terms of the real problems and resources of real places where real people live.[11]

Research

A great deal is said and written about the necessity for teaching and research to go "hand in hand." Much of this is myth or wishful thinking: few enough teachers in universities, and many fewer outside, have the resources or are in a position to carry out much that can properly be called research. It would be ridiculous to expect that those guiding the learning of adults would be able to make many fundamental contributions of this kind.

But there are some favoring circumstances. Not the least is that there is so much that has not been done. The "law of diminishing returns" does not yet apply to adult learning. As we have seen, systematic research in connection with adult learning has been infrequent and incomplete. One need not fear the fate of many workers in other fields, where study is not so much *to learn* but for the sake of learning a method, because the important questions have already been studied or are being studied with much more ample resources. In almost any field of adult learning, careful observation, careful recording, analytical thinking will by itself make a contribution, will add something to what is already known.

We noted in Chapter 7 that many of the additions to learning theory have come from practical fields of work where the experience was organized and gathered by a teacher or trainer. Any teacher of adults is on the "learning frontier."

Second, adult students can be enlisted in many inquiries. They may be just as able and just as resourceful in pursuing the inquiry as the teacher. There are actually many examples where the members of adult classes have participated in such an inquiry with considerable benefit in terms of what they themselves learn as well as adding somewhat to the store of knowledge about a particular subject. Much of what has been recorded about the folk arts in Trinidad, for example, has been observed, classified, identified, and discussed by "students" in university extension classes in that island. In this process of fact finding they have also seriously studied how people brought up under one culture are quickly taking over many of the attributes of a different culture, which is one of the most important practical problems in learning theory.

Enough has been said earlier to underline the probable effectiveness of an activity in which the participants are sharing fully in a project of research, when they are having a part in the plan and conduct of the project.

There may be a further by-product when a teacher and students engage in some form of research. Most of us have developed the ability to find praiseworthy reasons for *not* tackling some difficult problems. One of the preferred explanations for refusal to face hard facts, or hard actions, is to say "we don't know enough," "we must wait until there is more research." This device loses much of its efficacy with men and women who are themselves engaged in some form of organized research. In such a procedure they come to understand better ways of obtaining information necessary for sound action, and at the same time become more aware of the limitations of research.

It is true, unfortunately, that a number of studies that have been called research in adult education have not been very profitable for anyone. When the process becomes one of counting noses, lacking any useful hypothesis, or any rigorous analysis of the data collected, the effort may be more frustrating than rewarding. There are many problems of adult learning in which the greatest achievement might come from no activity so much as from hard thinking. It may not have the vogue enjoyed by certain techniques devised by the social scientists, but there is, of course, nothing at all unscientific about persistent, vigorous, and critical thought.

A number of conceptions of notions have been reported in Chapter 2 that seem worthy to guide and be tested by speculation. Observations of study in which there has been some shift in the methods of teaching, may also throw considerable light on learning. Examples of long-established fields in which the teaching-learning methods are being substantially revised are mathematics and languages.

But the chief part in research which most practitioners will play is to share in the research undertaken by colleagues in the social sciences. Otto Klineberg has pointed out that when attempts are made to appraise social action projects, the adult educationist is in the best position to supply statements about the goals of social change that are to be measured. But if he is to be an effective collaborator, Klineberg argues, he must develop the capacity for stating such goals with much greater clarity:

> If it is a project in fundamental education, for example, it is usually beyond the competence of the social science consultant to formulate the goals; without such formulation however, his aid may be greatly restricted, and may be worthless. Something can of course occasionally be done to study the effects of a program without too much concern with goals. If one has asked merely what has happened as a consequence of establishing a new school, or a change in diet, it may be possible to give a partial answer. We might refer to this as the natural history approach to evaluation. More frequently, however, the techniques of evaluation must be adapted to the goals. That means that practitioners must be prepared to supply to their social science consultants, in the clearest and most direct form, a statement of the general principles under which they are operating, as well as the specific purposes for which the project has been launched in the particular case. Such a clear formulation has not always been forthcoming.[12]

It is perhaps needless to say that if the practitioner is able to collaborate effectively in well-designed research, there will be useful results for his own teaching.

Other Traits or Skills

One hesitates to begin to list desirable traits for the agent in adult learning. There is considerable doubt about the practical value of any list of traits, either about reaching agreement on the items in the list, or learning from it. Such a list may reveal more about the list-maker than about the subject. However, certain traits have been selected for special attention in nearly all speeches and writings about adult education. These can be identified and quickly summarized.

It goes without saying that the teacher must be clear in speech and writing. Or can we assume this? These qualities are not common, one is not born with them; they come only with hard work. It used to be believed by some that certain kinds of obscurity were not only to be tolerated, but to be cultivated. Dicken's picture of schoolmaster Squeers is not a bit overdrawn:

> Philosophy's the chap for me. If a parent asks a question in the classical, commercial or mathematical line, says I gravely, "Why, Sir, in the first place, are you a philosopher?" "No, Mr. Squeers," he says, "I ain't." "Then, Sir," says I, "I am sorry for you, for I shan't be able to explain it." Naturally the parent goes away and wishes he was a philosopher, and equally naturally, thinks I'm one.

Everyone is in agreement that for a field of work that is relatively new, and where there are more unresolved problems than certainties, enthusiasm and a sense of humor are indispensable. Whitehead used to argue for the necessity of irreverence in education: "Laughter is our reminder that our theories are an attempt to make existence intelligible but necessarily only an attempt, and does not the irrational, the instinctive, burst in to keep the balance true by laughter?"

Most writers are equally in agreement that one engaged in adult learning must himself have a rich experience of living. Some individuals who throughout history have markedly affected the art or thought of the ages were men who held themselves somewhat aloof from their fellows. But most great teachers seem to have been men who have had more, not less, experience of living than anyone around them. The good teacher seems to be one who is at home with people, and they with him, because he has walked and talked with all kinds. In saying this, one does not deny for a moment the value of developing graduate courses in adult education. But it is to be hoped that those who will guide adult learning will, in addition, have spent some time in kitchens and workgangs as well as in colleges, on shipboard or even in taverns as well as in churches, libraries, or lecture halls.

Perhaps the most important trait is imagination. Or so Whitehead believed it:

> . . . so far as the mere imparting of information is concerned, no university has had any justification for existence since the popularization of printing in the fifteenth century. Yet the chief impetus to the foundations of universities came after that date, and in more recent times has even increased.
>
> The justification for a university is that it preserves the connection between knowledge and the zest of life, by uniting the young and old in the imaginative consideration of learning. The university imparts information but it imparts it imaginatively. At least this is the function which it should perform for society. A university which fails in this respect has no reason for existence. This atmosphere of excitement, arising from imaginative consideration, transforms knowledge. A fact is no longer a bare fact; it is invested with all its possibilities. It is no longer a burden on the memory; it is as energizing as the poet of our dreams, and as the architect of our purposes.[13]

Another trait that is on everyone's list is balance. Perhaps no two observers mean the same thing by balance. But one can guess what they intend. It usually has something to do with the old Greek virtue of moderation. It may mean the ability to benefit from different points of view without being lost in partisanship. We have noted, for example, that several of the "schools" of psychology and philosophy have provided insight and understanding useful in adult learning even though, temporarily, there seemed to be much conflict between them. A vigorous, questioning spirit directed at any proposal or theory is not out of place in a teacher who is also patient enough to wait until he thoroughly understands a proposition before endorsing it or assailing it.

One more trait, and we shall conclude. It is that those who are engaged in adult education need to learn how to deal effectively with controversy. A famous report on adult education has had a good deal to say about matters of controversy:

> The remedy for one-sidedness in education is, in short, more education. . . . We do not think that the controversial character of many of the subjects most commonly studied by adult men

and women prevents them from possessing a high educational value. If it makes it especially necessary to guard against one-sidedness of presentation, it also gives them the advantage of appealing to interests which are vivid and strongly felt. It seems to us a positive gain, indeed, that topics which are discussed with partisan heat on the platform or in the press should be sifted at leisure by groups of students with the aid of books and in an atmosphere of mutual criticism. The course of wisdom, we suggest, is not to attempt the impossible task of restricting education to subjects which are not contentious but to ensure that whatever the subject, those who desire to form a reasonable judgment may be aided to do so by seeing that facilities for study with regard to it are available. Provided that discussion is free, and that the teacher takes pains to call attention to aspects of the truth that are in danger of being overlooked, one point of view tends to supplement and correct another.[14]

All teachers face this directly. Members of the class will be curious to know what the teacher himself thinks about questions of public interest. In some programs, such as Great Books, where many and differing opinions are provided in the readings, the method is to try to understand, and to be able to state clearly, the differing points of view. In such a case, a vigorous airing of conflicting opinions is already provided for, and the leader is bound by the arrangement already understood. But in other cases he may properly be asked for his opinion, an opinion to be supported with what evidence is available and to be subjected to the same kind of questioning that would be directed to any other material or point of view dealt with in the course.

The teacher or agent cannot expect that he will always have an easy time of it. President Neilson of Smith College once wrote:

There are many teachers who through principle, or indolence, or lack of imagination, failed to connect their subjects with the living issues of the day; not only failed themselves, but bitterly attacked colleagues who labored in season and out to arouse their students to the dangers which everyone recognized at last.

Courage in dealing with controversy is required; it doesn't always lead to popularity either with one's colleagues or the public.

How to deal effectively with controversy is a subject of considerable importance on which there has been much thought. One issue of *Adult Leadership* publishes a series of papers on handling controversial issues, dealing with such matters as gaining perspective, timing, studying consequences, and the art of constructive compromise.[15]

Hayakawa has described how tensions between two individuals may be lessened where the conditions of *listening* and *communication* are maintained:

Mr. A. has listened to Mr. B. and instead of trying to shove things down his throat he is permitting the messages to come through. Nothing is so relaxing as being listened to, and Mr. B. begins to moderate the rigidity of his defenses. When this happens there is a direct linguistic reflection of this in the fact that Mr. B.'s statements from here on out become less dogmatic, less absolutistic, not only in tone of voice, but in their actual verbal content. . . .

All linguistic processes being processes of social interaction, the relaxation of B. means the relaxation of A., and the relaxation of A. becomes the relaxation of B. As you become less afraid of Mr. B. and less horrified by his position this reveals itself in your facial expression and the very posture of your body as you sit there listening to him. And this change in postural stance is subliminally sub-verbally picked up by the other fellow and in turn relaxes him and ultimately both of you may be making sense.

But there is a point at which (and this I think is the most important point) when, after receiving Mr. B.'s communications, Mr. A. is finally able to say, "I still don't agree with you, Mr. B., but I can see why you believe as you do. I can see why you feel as you do." I think this is the real turning point in communications and therefore in all human relations. "I don't agree with you, but I can see how you get to your present position." When you say this, you are, in a sense, admitting the other individual into the human race. Isn't that right? That is, you are admitting that this other person has rational processes, starting on different assumptions from mine, and therefore coming to different conclusions from mine, but nevertheless, traceable rational processes. And once this admission that you too have rational processes as well as me is made, then communication is possible.[16]

Responsibility

Anyone who is engaged deliberately in producing change—and as we have seen, all learning involves change—must sometime be confronted by uneasiness. In what ways and by what right is he helping to bring about changes in the thinking, behavior and attitudes of another human being? Is he manipulating another self?

This is not the place for any exhaustive discussion of the moral and ethical problems confronting anyone engaged in adult learning. But it is necessary to identify, at least, one or two aspects of it.

It has been the assumption throughout, both implicit and explicit, that the teacher or leader, in dealing with adults, will present the truth, as far as he knows the truth, and will subject all truth to the same kind of inquiry. He will also, as far as his self-knowledge goes, make known his own biases, so that they can be allowed for. He will not delude his class or group. But neither should he delude himself. Particularly should he not deceive himself that he can ever, in a class or in some form of community action, behave *simply as a catalyst*, unchanging. All actions, his own not excluded, have consequences. He can, of course, withdraw from any contact with others, in which case he will still have influence of a negative kind. He needs to understand *and accept* the fact that he has considerable influence.

The stresses faced by any agent of learning have been well described in *The Dynamics of Planned Change*:

> Sometimes the change agent himself will experience uneasiness about the justification for what he is trying to do. The causes of his uneasiness may be rational or irrational, and the uneasiness itself may assume any one of a number of forms. The change agent whose clients refuse his help may wonder, for instance, if he really has much to offer them. Or he may wonder about his own emotional involvement in his client's problems;

perhaps he cares too much or too little, or perhaps he is merely attributing to the client certain problems which are really his own. . . .

Often the uneasiness of the change agent may arise from his unconscious tensions and anxieties. Unresolved personal problems may inhibit his ability to respond to others in an appropriate and helpful way. . . . By no means, however, can all of the emotional stress experienced by change agents be attributed to unconscious personal difficulties. The task itself—trying to help other people—often creates special strains.[17]

The authors go on to point out that such uneasiness, where it exists, is readily communicated to the learner and may interfere with the learning objective. What the teacher requires to do, therefore, is to make a thorough self-examination.

He needs to think through for himself the reason why he wants to help others. Included in this question is the matter of what rewards he wants for himself—money, prestige, professional advancement, research data, emotional support, or simply satisfaction in seeing an important job done well.

These personal needs of the teacher, the authors say, must then be examined in terms of what the learner needs and is able to give. If it seems that the learner's needs can be fulfilled, "the work at hand can proceed." The teacher who accepts himself, with some understanding of his will to dominate, may continue with his task free from some of the internal stress that might otherwise be his lot, less likely to manipulate the learners "for their own good" or become the victim of the delusion that he has no responsibility for what is transpiring.

Conclusion

Does this task sound bleak and forbidding? Formidable it is, as is any high calling. In this the teacher is not unique. Last year the writer was in Jamaica, up in the hills in an old car, as high as an old car would go, and higher, talking with a farmer, who had spent all his life in the Blue Mountains, those hills that are, for Jamaica, the symbol and promise of freedom. The flank of the mountain was incredibly steep, yet he was planting yams there, in a terrace. Venturing to gaze over and far down to the sea, the writer asked him how he kept his balance and he replied very simply. He said: "If you get dizzy, you don't deserve the hills."

Most great teachers have associated learning with *light*. Illumination, opening up the dark patches, these were the constant themes for Bishop Gruntvig, founder of the Danish folk high schools. "I can always tell a good teacher," Dr. M. M. Coady once said. "All I have to do is to speak to him of some transforming idea and then watch him light up just as an electric bulb does when the current is connected."

"THE TRUE ENDS OF KNOWLEDGE"

But perhaps the most profound thing that can be said of the teacher is that he can't help it! Searching for and revealing truth, assisting in the way that others grow—these are the means by which he comes to grips with and expresses the life that is in him. Three centuries ago Francis Bacon said: "I would address one general admonition to all: that they consider what are the true ends of knowledge, and that they seek it not either for the pleasure of the mind, or for contention, or for superiority to others, or for profit, or fame, or power, or any of these inferior things; but for the benefit and use of life."[18] For the teacher the "use of life" is learning—for himself and for others.

REFERENCES

1. Ronald Lippitt, Jeanne Watson, and Bruce Westley, *The Dynamics of Planned Change* (New York: Harcourt, Brace and Company, 1958).
2. Gilbert Highet, *The Art of Teaching* (New York: Alfred A. Knopf, Incorporated, 1951, and Toronto: McClelland and Stewart, Ltd.).
3. British Institute of Adult Education, *The Tutor in Adult Education* (Carnegie: United Kingdom Trustees, 1928).
4. A. A. Liveright, *Annual Report* (Chicago: Center for the Study of Liberal Education for Adults, 1958).
5. Thomas Fansler, *Creative Power Through Discussion* (New York: Harper & Brothers, 1950).

6. Carl R. Rogers, *Counseling and Psychotherapy* (Boston: Houghton Mifflin Company, 1948).
7. Nathaniel Cantor, *The Teaching-Learning Process* (New York: Dryden Press, 1953).
8. Gilbert Highet, *op. cit.*
9. Leland P. Bradford, "A Look at Management Growth and Development," *Journal of the American Society of Training Directors*, Vol. 12, No. 7.
10. Harry Overstreet, *Leaders for Adult Education* (New York: American Association for Adult Education, 1941).
11. Harry Overstreet, *op. cit.*
12. Otto Klineberg, "Introduction—the Problem of Evaluation," *International Social Science Journal*, Vol. 7, No. 3. By permission of UNESCO.
13. A. N. Whitehead, *The Aims of Education* (New York: Mentor Books, 1949). By permission of The Macmillan Company, copyright owners.
14. *A Design for Democracy*, an abridgment of "The 1919 Report" by the Adult Education Committee of the British Ministry of Reconstruction (New York: Association Press, 1956).
15. Adult Education Association, "Workshop—Handling Controversial Issues," *Adult Leadership* (Chicago: AEA), Vol. 2, No. 6.
16. S. I. Hayakawa, "Success and Failure in Communication," *Journal of the American Society of Training Directors*, Vol. 12, No. 7.
17. Ronald Lippitt and Others, *op. cit.*
18. Francis Bacon, *The Great Instauration* (London: Spedding, Ellis and Heath, 1904).

Suggested Reading

ADULT EDUCATION ASSOCIATION, *How to Teach Adults* (Chicago: AEA, 1955).
——, "Workshop on Teaching Adults," *Adult Leadership* (Chicago: AEA), Vol. 3, No. 9.
BRAMELD, THEODORE, "The Ethics of Leadership," *Adult Education* (Chicago: AEA), Vol. 4, No. 2.
CLARK, B., *Adult Education in Transition* (Los Angeles: University of California Press, 1956).
COLE, LAWRENCE E., and BRUCE, WILLIAM F., *Educational Psychology* (New York: World Book Company, 1950).

EBY, KERMIT, "A Confession of Bias," *Adult Leadership* (Chicago: AEA), Vol. 7, No. 1.

EDUCATIONAL POLICIES COMMISSION, "The Changing Role of the Teacher," *Mass Communications and Education* (Washington, D.C.: National Education Association, 1958).

HOULE, C. O., "Professional Education for Educators of Adults," *Adult Education* (Chicago: AEA), Vol. 6, No. 3.

KAPLAN, ABBOTT, "The Lost Art of Controversy," *Adult Leadership* (Chicago: AEA), Vol. 3, No. 2.

LEE, I., *How to Talk with People* (New York: Harper & Brothers, 1952).

SCHWERTMAN, JOHN B., *I Want Many Lodestars* (Chicago: Center for the Study of Liberal Education for Adults, 1958).

INDEX